House Beautiful

If These Walls Could Talk

& MORE THOUGHTS OF HOME

EDITED BY

ELAINE GREENE

HEARST BOOKS
A DIVISION OF STERLING PUBLISHING CO., INC.
NEW YORK

Copyright © 2004 by Hearst Communications, Inc.

Library of Congress Cataloging-in-Publication Data

House beautiful if these walls could talk & more thoughts of home / edited by Elaine Greene.

   p. cm.

 Includes index.

 ISBN 1-58816-426-8

 1. Home. 2. Home--United States. I. Title: If these walls could talk & more thoughts of home. II. Greene, Elaine. III. House beautiful.

 HQ734.H8653 2004

 304.2'3--dc22

                                        2004003310

10   9   8   7   6   5   4   3   2   1

BOOK DESIGN BY DEBORAH KERNER/DANCING BEARS DESIGN

Published by Hearst Books

A Division of Sterling Publishing Co., Inc.

387 Park Avenue South, New York, NY 10016

House Beautiful is a trademark owned by Hearst Magazines Property, Inc., in USA, and Hearst Communications, Inc., in Canada. Hearst Books is a trademark owned by Hearst Communications, Inc.

www.housebeautiful.com

Distributed in Canada by Sterling Publishing

^c/o Canadian Manda Group, 165 Dufferin Street

Toronto, Ontario, Canada M6K 3H6

Distributed in Australia by Capricorn Link (Australia) Pty. Ltd.

P.O. Box 704, Windsor, NSW 2756 Australia

Printed in China

ISBN 1-58816-426-8

Contents

SECRETS AND MYSTERIES

CHILDREN AND ELDERS

CONTENTS

ONLY IN AMERICA

Preface

The great Russian author Maxim Gorky said provocatively, "Writing depends on who your grandmother is." We take him to mean that the child is parent to the artist, and several memoirs in this book bear him out literally: Hope Cooke, Teresa Wendel, and A. M. Homes had grandmothers who helped to form them. But memorable writing depends on many other crucial particulars of your home life, including where your house was, who shared it with you, and whether you stayed or fled.

For each of us, the meaning of home is as different as our faces, but one of the all-time profoundly true clichés, "home is where the heart is," gathers them in. In hundreds of essays since June 1991, *House Beautiful* has explored unique personal histories in our "Thoughts of Home" column. This new volume is our second anthology.

Three *House Beautiful* editors have been associated with the feature. The first was Louis Oliver Gropp, who originated the column when he took over the editorship in January 1991 and asked me to bring our publication "another dimension of home—something literary and emotionally compelling." He opened each issue with "Thoughts of Home" for 113 consecutive months—more than nine years. Countless readers subscribed just for the monthly essays, which were widely used as models by university professors in their writing classes. Some famous writers participated; some writers appeared for the first time in a national magazine. Literary careers were launched and previously unsold manuscripts were accepted after the publication of "Thoughts of Home" essays.

In her two-year tenure, Lou Gropp's successor Marian McEvoy dropped "Thoughts of Home" in favor of a shorter personal essay under the rubric "Changing Places." A few of these, including Sharon White's Norwegian saga, appear here.

When Mark Mayfield became *House Beautiful's* editor in chief in July 2002, his goal was to bring back and enhance the glories of the *House Beautiful* of the 1990s, including its original memoir column. This book would not exist without his vision and enthusiastic support.

ELAINE GREENE
New York, New York

A Passion for Place

The Blessed Paradox

EDNA O'BRIEN

IT STANDS STILL IN COUNTY CLARE, THE HOUSE I WAS BORN IN, surrounded by its own variety of trees, prey to wind, rain, and sun and, I think, haunted. The person who most haunts the house, is, and always will be, my mother; not simply because she toiled and strove to make it beautiful and because she covered ears of corn with tinfoil as decorations and because she got up on ladders and stuck rags into the corners to stop the leaking roofs, but because she was the presiding spirit of it. When she was absent, gone to the town or to the hospital to have her veins seen to, the house itself felt lonely and quenched. To a visitor it would not seem that luxurious, what with its cold tiled hallway and assortment of furniture bought at auctions over the years so that every period was represented—Georgian mirrors, Victorian sideboards, ornaments won at fairs and carnivals, rocking chairs, and proud solid dining-room chairs lined along the vast unused dining-room table. But to my mind it was an empire.

The gates are locked now, my brother, its owner, lives elsewhere, and up the long avenue there is an electric fence. I dream of this house every night. It takes on many disguises: a hotel, a church, a hospital, a theater, a place of beauty, and a place of carnage. A house is like a book, perhaps. James Joyce, when writing *Finnegans Wake*, was asked what it was about, and he said it was about birth and love and pain and death. So is a house.

When I was born, the doctor could not be got but a midwife came. In those days mothers were not given ether, and from overhearing of it I could and still do imagine my own birth—a dark blue room, a cold room, walnut furnishings, the crows in the chimneys, and so many holy pictures that all heaven's fraternity seems to preside. They were painted locally by emigrant Italians, representations of the sacred heart and our lady luridly colored to emphasize the sacrifice, the faces somewhat portly, not the rarefied Semite creatures painted by Giotto or Leonardo. Those holy pictures were meant to be a constant charge to one's conscience.

No one slept in that room; it was kept for birth and other grave occasions and I would not venture in there alone at night, none of us would. A lumber room nearby also seemed to contain certain secrets. In a brown trunk with a metal handle had been the letters, cards, diaries, and memorabilia from my mother's youth, which she must have put a bonfire to one day. She was not one to leave evidence of herself behind. Maybe that is why she hated literature, hated the written word, because she believed that in some way it inculcated sin and fornication. When I had gone home on holiday in my teens, she found Sean O'Casey's autobiography in my suitcase and took it away, and when she herself died I found, in a bolster, my first novel, *The Country Girls,* which I had inscribed to her, and which she gone through inking out in black any of the offending words. I sometimes think that my need to write, my obsession with writing, sprang from that taboo placed upon me by my mother. I never dared ask her why she dreaded literature so much, but it was as if she had read Molly Bloom's soliloquy in a previous incarnation and was still reeling from it.

The house was called Drewsboro and adjoining, though some distance away, was the ruin of a larger house where my great-grandparents and their tiddly servants had once lived. The empty old house was bigger than ours with endless passages, reception rooms, and even a ballroom. I was told there remained a set of gongs along the kitchen wall and tongues of rotted wallpaper, until it was burned in the troubles in the twenties, burned by the Irish themselves, burned by my own forebears to prevent the British soldiers using these large houses as barracks. Young men like my father went in with cans of petrol and matches to bid adieu to their heritage.

So the old house stood as a ghost and a model for the new house, built in the mid-twenties. It was of cut stone, that pale gold stone that changed texture in different lights, and there were two side windows of stained glass in a gable wall, and bay windows in the front, one round and one square. In the vestibule were old walking sticks and an umbrella with an amber handle, which my mother promised to leave me. Sometimes the two of us did a tour of the house, simply to look into the china cabinets at the ornaments and the cut glasses and the carnival glasses, and reading again the last letter of her brother who had been shot during the troubles and who wrote a rending letter to his mother as he expired.

The downstairs rooms may have been cluttered, but upstairs things were not quite so lavish. Our fate had been that fairly familiar Irish fate—we had been prodigal with money. I recall coming home from school once and seeing a strange man in a tweed suit, a bailiff, smoking a pipe, and watching my mother go from room to room, distraught; raised voices, tears, my mother returning to make the man some tea, his following her to the kitchen, my father and he going outside to try to come to some agreement and afterward the man giving me sixpence and my asking him if it could be taken off our bill and everyone laughing at the childishness of it.

I have no idea how the crisis was averted but we did not have to leave that house, not then. Evictions were very alive in the race memory, my mother's family having been evicted from the fat plains of Kildare and driven over to the stony west 60 or 70 years before. I think probably what happened when the bailiff came was that my father sold off a bit of land, a pattern that repeated itself down the years, so that strange farmers and strange herds were in the fields that we once thought of as our own. There was always a shortage of money and I remember having to go to the lodge where the old gatekeeper lived who used formerly to work for us and, in an acute state of mortification, asking for the loan of a penny for the dance class at school. To this day I cannot dance, and likewise I am rather profligate with money. Yes, this was our cherry orchard except that we had apple trees instead, apple blossoms strewn all over the grass in the month of May.

Winters and summers are quite different in the life of any house. In summer the hall door was propped open, windows were cleaned and re-cleaned, and the beauty and luxuriance of the landscape was such that nature itself came into the rooms: the smell of grass and chestnut blossoms, the smell of animals, the smell of hens, the smell of young nettles. Once, and I remember that my mother and I almost fainted, a man with an iron hand was standing in our hallway asking if we wanted our ticking, our pillows, and our mattresses repaired, and my mother being too afraid to speak, too afraid to stir. He caught our agitation and he must have been a nice man because he asked me what name spelled the same frontwise as backward. I couldn't speak either. The name was Hannah. My mother gave him a cup of milk and a slice of cake, which he ate in the garden.

To call it a garden is a euphemism. There were just a few wildflowers, some devil's pokers, which looked as if they had been lit, and in a swamp nearby wild irises, yellow-gold spears. I wanted to be a writer, to capture—I think that is the word—the beauty of nature, the changeability of nature, and the spirit life that seemed to be in every single thing.

The landscape was both friendly and threatening, the inside of the house composed of its own tensions. I longed to know the story, the several stories of my mother and father, the things that had happened to them before they met and the disenchantments that followed. Ours was not a harmonious upbringing. Whatever happiness there was, was mostly connected with food. My mother prided herself on being a good cook. Mrs. Beeton's cookery book on the kitchen windowsill was stained with egg yolk and egg white. Smell is my keenest sense, and to this day I smell and, in my mind, taste orange cakes, the crust slightly seared, the smell of orange juice and orange rind issuing out. I see my mother lift from the oven a rectangular dish with the Queen of Puddings and the meringue on top, slightly floating, which in my childish fancy I thought was like a cloud. I see scones and soda bread and shortbread and very seldom do I see savories because we did not have the money for roasts.

There was chicken on Sundays in summertime, and in the fishing season in the month of May, when mayflies hovered over the Shannon lake, my father went out to fish with the visitors who came from Dublin and England and abroad. He would come home with a big can of pink trout and my mother would cook them for the visitors and afterward the men would play cards and later still my father would sing and tell stories, often stories against the English themselves, which they seemed to take in very good part. When they came, we sat in the best room, which I thought of as heaven. It had many ornaments, the most precious being a pair of plaster ladies brought from America, gilt mirrors, a sideboard crammed with silver, and pride of place given to a tea strainer that had a colored picture of the pope on its handle. There was a marble mantelpiece black and crimson, but no fire was ever lit there. Instead the fireplace had a tapestry that my mother stitched, depicting the ancient Ireland of swans and round towers. I used to sit there with my dolls admiring each and every ornament but especially a cupola of artificial tea roses that had been painted in bright red and bright gold.

I wanted to set a story in each room. Across from the best room was the vacant room in which there was no furniture at all, just apples, so that the smell of ripening and rotting apples filled the house in autumn. To go in there meant having to kick a whole load of apples to one side. The wallpaper had been hung upside-down and visitors were often shown this peculiarity, not only for its own sake, but because the day it happened, long before, my mother had been in the city and had gone to a clairvoyant who had appraised her of this mishap.

Visitors were always brought on a tour of the downstairs rooms except that of our farm helper. His room was so full of clutter that the door would not fully open, and he being corpulent used to have to squeeze his way in. He was the person I was fondest of and resolved to marry. He had every conceivable object in there: bits of bicycles, old machinery, tattered clothes, jam jars, little stolen mementos, which he was supposed not to have, and occasionally between him and my mother a feud broke out about these mementos and the filthiness of his room. One day my mother told me he had decided to leave us. Standing outside the door I listened and could hear him packing. I believed it meant death for us all and barged into that tiny, foul-smelling place where he was piling things into sheets and sacks and went down on my knees to prevent him from stirring. I hope he forgave me for keeping him captive for years longer, because, in truth, he craved to go to England to earn a proper wage and find a wife.

We were a family of four children, and because I was youngest I felt in awe of my brother and sisters and was excluded from their domain, especially their bedrooms, which meant of course that I stole in whenever I could. My sisters had treasures that I coveted—hair slides, hair bands, handkerchiefs with greetings on them, and minute bottles of perfume. The perfume of the time was Evening in Paris, which came in an opaque blue bottle and looked as if it might contain poisons, certainly some elixir. I would remove the little rubber stopper and sniff it but never once risked putting a dab behind the ears because I might be found out. Under their pillows were letters and diaries, names of boys they had fallen for, slanders about each other, awful things. In my brother's room there was a particular treasure—a large tin of sliced peaches that had been given him as a prize by his music teacher. I could taste these peaches by simply looking at the tempting picture on the label. Hints were given by my mother, especially at Christmastime, that we might all enjoy them, but he kept them as a trophy.

Between my mother and myself was the understanding that one day she would give me the house, simply because I loved it as she did. Then came the breach. The house, the trees, the field, and some of our private histories was the material for my books. Although my mother allowed me to return on holidays, there was between us unspoken strain. During this time her son had brought her to the local solicitor and, true to Irish tradition, she had willed him the house and the remaining lands, but as she got closer to death she repented of it and asked me to take her from the hospital to see another solicitor so that she could at last leave me the house. I didn't. I cannot say that it was decency that stopped me although maybe it was, or maybe it was quite simply that I could not accept that she was about to die.

But she did die, and the house became my brother's. I decided to go back not long ago, to trespass, to walk about it, to look in windows, and I felt, as people do, how much smaller and more cramped the rooms were than they seemed to me as a child. Likewise the stained glass did not have the beauty or the complexity of say, a window in Chartres, which I always thought they had. It looked sad for want of my mother; it was a house in waiting. What struck me most though was the simple and blessed paradox that because I was not given the house it is mine in my imagination. Had I owned it I would be wondering now how much a new roof might cost or if the damp walls were crumbling and if its fate would be similar to the ruin of 100 yards away, whereas being banished from it I can go on filling it with stories for as long as I like.

The House I Mean to Haunt

ELAINE GREENE

WHEN WE WERE COURTING AFTER THE SECOND WORLD WAR, my future husband and I visited a small village named in *Moby Dick.* It was less than 100 miles from my apartment house in Queens, so we borrowed my father's car for a day's outing in early spring.

I still remember my first impression of the clean light and the tarry smell of the wharf. The onetime whaling port was quiet, beautiful, run down, and agreeably foreign to New York City natives, possessing the otherwordly quality of the period houses and rooms at the Brooklyn Museum, where I was taken every year in elementary school, becoming permanently addicted to old places.

Twelve years later, we lived there.

One of the hundred little dreams that made up our one big dream— a house in the country—was to grow our own herbs. The first summer we planted common thyme and it did so well there was enough to dry for winter. On an October morning I made up three nice bundles of thyme, tied them with butchers string, and went with a hammer and three long nails to the small, low attic over the kitchen. I decided to hang the herbs halfway along a rafter where the sun from the gable window would shine through the thin branches and tiny leaves: good for drying, pretty to look at. Kneeling down with my hammer, I saw to my amazement there already were three nails in that place—three hand-made cut nails waiting, who knew how long, to give me a shiver and tell me I am not the first in this attic with this idea.

Some people like newness, are proud of being the first, but being *not* the first to hang something from that rafter was happiness to me. My husband and I chose an old house for the warmth and comfort of being part of a human chain. We climb stair treads worn by other owners' shoes and discover evidence there once was a room off the kitchen exactly where we thought of adding one. What was its use? When was it demolished? Why? These mysteries are somehow as satisfying as the recoverable history.

When we opened a wall to put in a window, we found a family roster of the people who built the house firmly penciled on the inner side of a vertical siding plank with the date January 1, 1870. Before we closed the wall we left our own signatures and date for future owners we will never meet.

It was a cold April day when we first saw this place, after 11 years of renting vacation cottages in the vicinity. We were city dwellers with two small sons and a guilty fifties notion that we should be bringing them up in the suburbs, but one day of house hunting in Connecticut and another in New Jersey pitched us into such depressions that we decided on a double life with weekends and summers in a country town.

We had driven out to see something the real estate agent told us was "in the village and on the water," our difficult but firm requirement. The small bungalow had no age or distinction, and when I turned the door-knob to go inside I disturbed a wasp that stung my finger: a message.

But fate gave us a flat tire in front of that bungalow. Across the street from it stood an appealing shingled house that is kin to thousands of other farm and village houses on Long Island, and to millions in the United States: two stories high with a gabled attic facing the street, three windows wide with the front door to the side. Many of these houses are extended by one or two wings; this had a single wing set back about eight feet with an overshot roof above its small porch. The house sits so sweetly on the land behind its white picket fence and pair of American holly trees, a saltwater cove beside it, that it makes passersby smile—I see them when I am working in the front yard.

While my husband was changing the tire, I stood in the street hugging myself to keep warm. A white-haired woman was sitting in the kitchen window in the little wing, stirring cake batter in a big brown bowl. She took pity on me and called me in. The moment I entered the house, I felt as though I had already lived there. It felt like my house (a feeling we have learned is not unique; over the decades, at least once a year, someone leaves a note under our door expressing their infatuation and begging us to sell to them).

"Are you interested in the E___ house?" asked my hostess, motioning across the street.

"No, we want one like yours," I answered.

"We looked at it ourselves because I had a heart attack this winter and we need to live on one floor, but it's not big enough," she said.

There it was: an accidental meeting, a casual conversation, and my life changed forever. In June, when we moved to a summer rental a few streets away, I brought my little boys over to meet the couple (he was a retired carpenter), and from time to time—taking care not to annoy them—the four of us dropped by. We asked them to tell us if they found their one-story house.

The carpenter's wife called one day in July to ask us over to see an especially beautiful sunset. Then in August she called and said, "Tell your husband to come see my husband," and we were offered the property. No one else got a look; local agents were seething, we later learned.

We have always thought it was our boys who stole the hearts of the childless couple. It is a privilege to be able to choose your successors in a beloved house, one we will not have. When we leave it to our sons, will one of them want it? The elder has his own weekend house five miles away; the younger lives in California. I may have to haunt it to keep the next owners in line. Although we have taken the liberty of adding a small one-story wing, there is some tampering I will not allow.

I had a lifetime feeling about this place from the start. When the owners took us upstairs the day they offered to sell and we came to the room my husband and I chose for our own—not the largest but the one with the most windows looking out on the cove, the best water reflections on the ceiling—I remember saying to myself, "What a nice room to die in." It seemed such a bizarre and morbid thought for a healthy woman of 30 that I never mentioned it to anyone, but I think it was simply a promise of fidelity.

We didn't just acquire a set of rooms on a piece of land; we acquired 100 years' worth of other people's artifacts. The old couple left us three packed outbuildings—a chicken house turned carpentry shop, and two garages, all adjoining. The star piece in the workshop is a black walnut tool chest two feet high and three feet wide. When you lift the lid, you see that half the inner space is made up of a tier of shallow drawers with white porcelain knobs. The open half of the space contains a big collection of maple molding planes. Elsewhere in the shop are huge antique wooden clamps, wooden nail kegs, broadaxes, oil lamp brackets, a two-man cross-cut saw. Enough planks, two-by-fours, and moldings were stacked in the rafters to supply my amateur-carpenter husband for three or four years without his having to visit a lumberyard.

Among the garden tools in the garages were a thatching rake, hay and manure pitchforks, a seeder, an assortment of curators and hoes; also a device to mount steel-rim automobile tires, a coal scuttle, several sets of oars, a bee smoker, a Little Princess glass washboard, carding paddles, and a hackle for breaking flax. In the house we were left a Boston rocker, a brassbound camphorwood chest from the China trade, and a Hoosier kitchen cabinet.

Many of these things we use; all of them we keep and safeguard. They are our museum, handed down to us, the temporary curators. Another new owner on seeing all this stuff might have had a yard sale or called in a country auctioneer, but it is our strong feeling that these objects belong to the house as much as—actually more than—we do. A friend says we have the only kitchen in town that has not been remodeled, but we will never change it. Although a more efficient work arrangement would be easier for us, I couldn't part with the Hoosier cabinet or the huge cast-iron Glenwood stove that once burned wood or coal.

After more than 30 years in the house, we are still discovering significant objects. When my husband ran some wiring in the attic three years ago, he discovered between the floorboards a perfect inch-big, heart-shaped brass lock with its tiny key attached by a twisted wire; we knew it was English and Victorian by the coronet and VR engraved on it. In a cellar crawl space last year we found a tissue-wrapped roll of a late-19th-century floral wallpaper border, hand-painted and now very fragile.

We spent our first night in the house before we owned it. Our summer lease had ended, the sellers had moved before the closing, and they offered us the key and their blessing. Our first supper has become a family legend.

The four of us were sitting at an old round dropleaf table made of walnut with sturdy turned legs on casters. We had spotted it in the cellar—crowded with pickle jars, its dulled surface covered by white rings. Surprised that we wanted it, the couple sold us the table for $10 and, eventually refinished by my husband, it is still where we eat, read the paper, drink coffee, and visit with friends who may drop in for an hour and never leave the kitchen. (This is a kitchen-door town.) There are tables just like it all over the Northeast and probably farther afield.

I had just served the lamb chops and baked potatoes that first night when I noticed that a corner of the washable, canvas-backed wallpaper was loose. My husband and I did not care for that paper. The background was a pinkish gray and on it were green pine trees, red roosters, and red-and-green rural mailboxes in odd proportions, the roosters larger than the trees.

I picked at the corner and found that I could easily rip off the whole sheet. The ripping made a satisfying sound. I picked another corner loose and our six-year-old jumped up to help. I don't remember that anyone spoke. While my husband watched, finished his dinner, and poured himself another beer, and our two-year-old sat wide-eyed in his high chair, my older boy and I stripped those walls clean in about 45 minutes of feverish work. The floor was knee-deep in the heavy, heaped-up material over which my son and I looked at each other with triumphant eyes.

Later that night I asked my husband why he hadn't tried to stop me. "I wouldn't think of it," was his answer. "You were possessed."

Our kitchen has three windows and six doorways, leaving meager space for storage. The handsome four-panel outside door has a brass box lock and a texture to its old paint finish that speaks to every amateur photographer who sees it. This is a funny door. For years it used to like to open itself. We would sometimes arrive for the weekend and find it wide open; neighbors or the village police would tell us they had closed it for us. I decided it could be a ghost at work—I knew that leaving doors open was a popular ghostly prank. Maybe it was the person who hung things on rafters. I was convinced it was a woman. I did not share this theory within my super-rational family circle, sparing myself the inevitable "Oh, Mom."

I did decide to so something about it, though. One Sunday evening when we were leaving for the city I made sure to be the last one out and gave whatever hovered in the kitchen a stern talking to. "I know you hang around this house because you love it," I said, "and you are certainly welcome to stay, but surely you don't want to cause any harm here, so you have got to stop opening the door after we leave. Please?" Then I said thank you and closed the door. It hasn't been found open again.

Unfortunately this would prove nothing to most people because at the same time I spoke to the ghost we began to test the closure with a good hard push. In the Long Island dampness, a swollen door can appear to be closed, then later shrink and blow open. But I believe it was my little scolding that solved the problem.

Although we do some gardening—a 20-by-20-foot vegetable plot, a small perennial bed, a few new trees—it is the cove, our extended backyard, that we treasure most. The volume of empty air above the water *where no one can ever build* offers more light and sparkle and spatial freedom than an empty field would. It is an old habit to open the bedroom curtains and scan the waterfront in the morning, but it gives me a flash of gratitude every time.

By now we know the cove the way you know a longtime spouse. We have looked at it in every kind of light and weather and season: fog so dense we can't see the water, calms that make the surface a perfect mirror, storms that whip up whitecaps and even breakers. We learned that in the famous hurricane of 1938, which struck at high tide, a great bite was take out of the bank below our house. Our predecessor said there had been a grassy terrace with lawn furniture—all gone in one surge. Roses from that terrace still bloom in the weedy, brambly tangle on the scooped-out bank—'American Pillar' is one I have identified.

If the winter is cold and the cove freezes over, and if the ice is solid enough, some of the local men venture out toward the center and chop open a few holes. With tridentlike forks at the end of long poles, they poke for eels lying dormant in the mud. Thank God they do. Because one day when our younger son was 14, he was crossing the frozen cove alone and got too close to the dangerous ice where the tide was the strongest underneath. One of the eelers heard the dreadful cracking sound and ran over to where the boy had fallen through.

My booted son could not get out of the hole but the eeler pulled him free with the help of the pole. Neither my husband nor I saw any of this. How did I not sense danger, I thought later—what kind of mother is that? When I got back from an errand, my husband said our son had come home soaked and shaking; his socks instantly froze as they were pulled off his feet. I found him reading in bed, bundled up after a warm bath. He didn't want to talk about the accident, and I had to get his permission for a hug.

We did not know who had saved our child until the next winter when the eelers came back. I went out on the frozen cove and approached one after another, saying, "I'm looking for the man who pulled a teen-age boy out of a hole in the ice last winter." Finally I was given the name of a roofing contractor from the next town who had told such a story. I wrote to him; he wrote back—two emotional letters that my son didn't want to hear about—and the man came by in his pickup truck one day so we could meet. His company has done our roofing work ever since, of course, and when my son became a father I sent our benefactor the baby's picture as a reminder of what he did for us.

Not only did he prevent a tragedy, he made it possible for us to stay in our dear house. And my son is not going to be the next ghost here—that will probably be me, a link in the chain, a curator of this property. If those who follow (and that includes relatives) try to take away my Glenwood stove and my Hoosier cabinet and put in an island counter and banks of plastic laminate cabinets, doors will be found open. At the very least.

The 49th Parallel

STACY SCHIFF

TWO OR THREE TIMES A YEAR, I PACK UP—LOCK, STOCK, AND half-size hockey sticks—to move between New York and a much smaller city on the Canadian prairie. These are seasonal migrations, which if not orderly are at least perfectly regular. By mid-June, our family has retreated north; before the Canada geese, and in time for Labor Day, we have headed south. My Canadian husband's business and the children's school vacations determine the itinerary. When the New York sidewalk clots with holiday shoppers, we are once again on the airplane north. And when the mountain ash drips with orange berries, when the pods on the caragana hedge crackle like popcorn, it is time to head south. With the luxury of two addresses comes the realization that ours is an imperfect, nostalgia-scented world. We arrive in Canada in time for the peonies, but we miss the lilies of the valley. September offers something of a consolation: we have two autumns, just as every self-respecting Canadian-American family can claim two Thanksgivings. This constitutes my sole attempt to compete with the lucky children of divorce I knew in high school who got Christmas twice.

In the absence of any parental elucidation, my children, who have participated in this constant commute all their lives, have made their own sense of the arrangement. Their friends sometimes retreat to weekend houses outside New York; our nine-year-old has been heard to refer to his Canadian residence as his "country home," despite the fact that it happens to be 2,000 miles away and in a city of 750,000 people. If he could live there year-round he probably would. Even a die-hard Yankee fan knows there is something to be said for a triple-A baseball stadium ten minutes from the front door and adjacent to a grass parking lot. And even I have to admit that the game is exponentially enhanced by being able to see the players spit and hear them swear, all from a $5 seat. Our son considers himself every inch a Canadian (to his mind a football field should be 110 yards long); the seven-year-old considers herself a New Yorker, which by some definitions qualifies as an American. To her mind civilization has something to do with bright lights and soup dumplings and alternate-side-of-the-street parking. There is no reason to Rollerblade on a lovely wooded path when you can do so on a concrete sidewalk and terrorize pedestrians of all ages. Like her mother, she feels safer in New York, where you are never alone. Moreover, if you are going to get out of bed at an ungodly hour to play ice hockey, you may as well do so in 50-degree weather. The baby is yet too young to vote, but not too young to have formed an opinion of the two health care systems, which she will divulge as soon as she can talk.

As it happens, our corner of Canada more closely resembles the heartland of America than it does New York, where phoning out for a video is considered an inalienable right. It is doughnut country; it is right-on-red country; it is not paralyzed by security details or water-main breaks or rumors of an errant snowflake; golf is discussed at dinner. But the beauty of this dual life does lie to a large extent in the cultural differences. The American-Canadian border might appear to be one of those cartographic conveniences, a poor relation of the equator and the Mason-Dixon line, that belt drawn across the stomach of America, south of which everyone prefers Miracle Whip and north of which they prefer mayonnaise.

Yet anyone who has ever crossed the 49th parallel suspects that America and Canada do occupy separate continents. That border is a very serious matter indeed; football fields south of the demarcation line really are too short, and there are too many downs to the game. If you are flying from the U.S., you know you are headed toward a kinder, gentler place the minute you board the aircraft. A hush descends in a Canadian plane. Once after a long research trip, I had the scare of my life when an immigration inspector invited me to step out of the line. I could think only of the new computer over my shoulder, which I had not altogether planned on declaring. He was thinking of the new baby in my arms, on whose account I was escorted to the head of the line. In the opposite direction the impression is no less distinct: It is one of unbounded energy. (I should add that no Canadian customs inspector, however considerate, has ever addressed me as "Honey" or "Dear." This is the sole province of New Yorkers. It makes an American of me every time.)

The world may be getting smaller, Canadian culture may well have been obliterated by its neighbors to the south, the global village (the term is Canadian, for the record) may claim us all, but it will always be half past the hour in Newfoundland. Separation by a common language is but the tip of the—I apologize to a particular Alberta reporter who throws fits when I mention the cold—iceberg. To life's eternal mysteries, add the question of why sterile cotton balls aren't sold north of the border. Why do Canadian infants get solid foods earlier, and is this in any way related to the fact that there are six Pop-Tarts to a box in Manhattan, eight in western Canada? Why is the alcohol content lower in American beer? Glossettes don't seem to realize that an entire American market awaits their chocolate-coated peanuts. (It does! It does! And send Coffee Crisps, too!) If you walk at a New York clip toward a Canadian automatic door you risk having your nose smashed. If you walk down a New York street at a Canadian pace someone—my very own seven-year-old, if no one else—will mow you down. I rest my case; talking about Canada is something even a convert can never do correctly, and I was born in Massachusetts. Of course, anyone is entitled to say anything he wants about New York, where nothing ever needs to be preceded by that self-defeating adjective "world-class." New Yorkers don't have anything to prove and they know it. The only thing less attractive than a Canadian's inferiority complex is the arrogance of a New Yorker.

Which is not the only reason the backing and forthing requires a certain degree of adjustment. Some things—I'm thinking of a particular little black dress—just don't translate. To live in two places is to sprout two selves, or at least it is for those of us superficial enough to feel we are colored by our context. And after enough adjusting, it is difficult to say which is the true self, which the reengineered one. Travel renews and reinvigorates, which means it is easy to live in the perpetual hope that you might shrug off parts of your personality, or acquire new ones, in the relocation. You too can be Jack in the town, Earnest in the country.

All of which begs the question, that stumper of which immigration officers are so fond: Where is home? We can't even figure out who is the "us" and who is the "them," something that works well if you feel it an advantage in life not to know if you are coming or going. After 15 years I still fumble with the answer as much as with our stack of passports; at the border we embark on our homegrown "Who's on First" routine. I am unbalanced for all kinds of reasons, but especially because in the back of my mind is a thought Edward Hoagland has so perfectly articulated: "To feel at home is the essence of adulthood." To live in two places is generally to feel at home in neither, to wind up the perpetual insider-outsider. Is home where the espresso maker is? Is the native language the language to which you default when counting? If so, I am a Fahrenheit girl in love with a Celsius country, willing to attempt all kinds of mathematical conversions, even if I'll never be able to order confidently in grams.

The fuzzy insider-outsider state has its advantages; the perspective is always better. There is a very great deal to be said for living somewhere most New Yorkers can't locate on a map, for raising children in a place where you can rent an apartment for what in Manhattan passes for the garage bill, where the custom is to sit in the front seat of a taxi alongside your driver. And therein lies the real issue: it all comes down to space, hence the averted eyes and the extroverted elbows in the elevator. New Yorkers have had to adapt to dealing with others in a confined space. They are greedy for their privacy; they are by necessity territorial. Canadians have had to adapt to dealing with others in wide open spaces. The luxury is in the embrace of others, huddled together against the elements. The charm is the same Antoine de Saint-Exupéry observed in Patagonia, where he celebrated the glow that humanity emitted in a cold climate: "It would be difficult to find elsewhere so developed a sense of society, of cooperation; of so much serenity." The climate is enormously hospitable because it is so very inhospitable. It would be difficult to think of a place where a foreigner could feel so much and so immediately at home. Except maybe for a provincial city of eight million people to the south. Because, as everyone knows, no one is as polite as a New Yorker.

The Smell of Mint

MICHAEL PYE

I'D SHOW YOU THE PHOTOGRAPHS IF I COULD; WE SHOW THEM constantly to everyone in New York. They are what we have left of the time before we belonged in Formentina.

You won't know the name, nor did we ten years ago. Formentina is the end of a string of villages in the middle of the forest in central Portugal. Our tiny dead-end hamlet consists of 12 houses on the first of the hills that lead to the great mountain barrier with Spain. It has one shop, which sells bottled gas and hot sauce and firelighters but makes its money as a bar. The small white chapel was built when Formentina declared its independence from the bigger, neighboring village. The issue was land, there was fighting in the streets, and the whole small war is proudly called "the revolution of 1989."

Our house is in the middle of all this: my house, with my partner, John. We are journalist and professor, writer and academic: mobile people, inclined to end up in the fuss and bother of big cities. For a long time we took that for granted—home was work.

But I'm European, and I had been writing columns about American politics for so long I felt like a tourist on my own home turf. John is American, but with a history of living in other countries. We started to talk about finding our own joint place in Europe: a roof at least, ideally a garden, and in some country that neither one of us yet knew. It couldn't be in England, because I come from there, or Switzerland, because John taught there, or Italy, because I studied there.

We might never have found our house, except that we found Portugal. We had needed a cheap break from London and spent a week close to Lisbon. We found odd shrines and Gothic mansions and cisterns of dark, still water. We found surf and woods and castles. The Portuguese, we discovered, garden with light and shade as well as brilliant bougainvillea and geraniums and lemons and morning glory.

We came back one summer to learn the language, all triply-embedded pronouns and future subjunctives, and swallowed in the speaking so nobody knows if you get the grammar right. After a month at the University of Coimbra, I was confident in restaurants and in the present tense.

We came back to Portugal the next summer to find that European house. John set a deadline to make sure it happened: a week. By the last day we were dashing from collapsible courtyards infested with ticks to a ruin by a waterfall with seven terraces of olives and a view like postcards that lacked only one thing: a road within a mile. We hit our heads in neatly, meanly restored stone cottages where the bathroom ran into the kitchen ran into the bedroom.

We despaired. At six in the evening we were in the shop-cum-bar at the end of what is now our road, huddled over beers. Experimentally, John said out loud: "We are looking for a house." Assuming he had mastered those few words of Portuguese, it couldn't do any harm.

"I've got one of those," said a square-shaped man called Antonio. "Follow me." He had a motor scooter fitted out with a cart. We walked behind him up a lane of olive trees, through a narrow gap between houses and into a rough kind of square, more of a clearing. They were building the little white chapel, I remember.

Antonio opened the gates to our house.

The courtyard, long flooded with water from the village washing trough, was a brilliant green. Chickens ran about. A pig sulked in a corner. The building itself was half-hidden. We could see golden river stone where the walls had escaped the limewash brush, and a roof like a land-slide of mossy and fragile tiles. There were also clues to the past life of the house: a cool room for making wine with a still in the corner, a huge pink chandelier in the room upstairs, a brick oven for making bread.

We took many photographs at that time, but they can't give you what is most unfamiliar of all: the smells. You step, and you bruise mint. It seems Portugal is one gigantic root system for mint, inter-rupted at times by cities, forests, or farms. The air is full of the scent of the woods, too, baked by summer: the pine trees and the eucalyptus. In early evening, when the cooking fires are lit, the village smells subtly like a smokehouse.

We found a calendar for 1988 on the floor—three years before we bought the house. The place had been empty since then. We found a single baby's shoe, so there had been a family here.

We don't have pictures of the handshake, but I remember that people were smiling. Antonio explained that if you leave a house like that much longer, water gets into the rubble and mud and stone walls and they dissolve away. Nobody wanted the house to become a ruin.

Antonio asked 1.2 million escudos, which was $7,000 or so. We didn't even argue; it was a fair price for a gesture at being Europeans. It was only in New York that we began to puzzle over exactly what we should do next.

We puzzled so much the house became an occupation. We discussed it endlessly: what windows, where to put the living room, what trees could be planted, whether to put out money for solar energy or a wind-mill or a well. It was more than a fantasy now. We were talking to builders.

The animals were evicted, although the chickens still scratched hope-fully by the gate. Every three months, when I was working in Europe, I'd go down to shout at the workmen. The old walls turned new and white. The old tiles disappeared. One August day, just before the annual village *festa*, a huge log of eucalyptus became our roofbeam and a new terra cotta roof started forming across it. We missed the old patina.

We were still just visitors, of course.

But the first summer in the house we found peaches on the doorstep, then plums. We saw our neighbor Zulmira arrive with a bucket of potatoes. Sure that men wouldn't know how to store them, she laid them out for us. Once her husband, Alcino, came with a piece of the liver of a pig that had just been killed. We heard the racket. Sometimes we could do something in return. We would be driving to the market in the nearby town Tuesdays and Saturdays and someone would need a lift with some buckets of green beans and cilantro and tomatoes to sell.

We started listening to our neighbors. Francisco, in his 70s, kept lamenting the dust and the quiet in the country; he once worked in Paris. "It's the quiet," he said, "which kills you." He explained who owned what, how to deal with the wandering grinning dogs that hung around, where to get water from a good spring.

The next year the house was three-quarters done. The living room was still unfinished, but it was covered and cool. The courtyard was blank concrete like a rough dance floor, which suggested a party. It was John's 50th birthday and the 50th for some of our New York friends, so we proposed one grand joint celebration: a housewarming, a birthday party, and our personal festa.

For a party like this, in our part of Portugal, you need *leitao*, roast suckling pig. My mistake was to think that you started by buying a pig. I invested in a small but growing sow. It took me and a farmhand to muscle Miss Piggy into the car, the lady complaining bitterly about being trapped in a sack. I began to think this pig might be, in every sense, too much. She was certainly lively. On the drive back, she settled reluctantly in the back of our ancient hatchback. Suddenly, she rose like a shark from the waters, stared out of the rear window and snorted regally at the cars behind us. One of them ran off the road with laughter.

The villagers pointed out, tactfully, that she was too large for any oven, at least in one piece. We pensioned her off to a good home and started again, with proper *leitao*, cooked crisp and gold from the *leitao* man, and a barrel of good red wine. Our builder, who was not a very good builder ("He's interested in electricity," we were told. "He's not interested in plumbing"), turned out to be a fair disc jockey. He brought his own six-foot speakers.

Our friends came from Zurich and New York, from London and Paris and Lisbon, trailing children and spouses and new lovers—that was the easy part. The question was whether guests would come from our village and those around us.

At six in the evening, Zulmira told us to go and invite the people in the *baixa*, the lower part of the village, for our 12 houses divide into an *alta* and a *baixa*, upper and lower, just like Lisbon. Apparently the *baixa* weren't sure they were welcome.

The outsiders arrived first—the Americans and Europeans with their eight o'clock party habit. Then, for hours, everybody was careful not to mention that nobody else came. By 11 there were villagers standing outside the gates, but nobody wanted to be the first to enter. We held our breath. We dreamed of mixing our worlds, big city friends and farmer neighbors, and we were now so close.

Then Tinita arrived. A small, fiercely bright woman. She snorted at the sight of everyone holding back. She gathered her relatives, and she has many relatives, and she swept through the gates with a convoy behind her.

By midnight, we knew people who had grown up in our house, one who had been born there, people who remembered when it was the local tavern. Tinita and her husband danced in the courtyard—fast, boxy athletic steps—joined by the Swiss and the English and the builders and the neighbors.

I had brought the collected works of Motown, which seemed right for a 50th; the builder refused even to think of playing them. Instead, the house rang with brisk, plangent, very foreign tunes. By one o'clock we had run out of glasses, which meant that somewhere in our house, chewing the bones of the suckling pigs, drinking the good red wine, there were at least 120 people.

We just meant to introduce ourselves, perhaps to make friends. We were only going to come in the summer, of course. This was simply a *casa de ferias*, a holiday house. But we were drinking, we were dancing, we were talking—somehow, in fractured Portuguese—and the next morning we had a brief bit of fame: "a festa de Joao e Miguel" was known all up and down our valley.

We have the photographs from the party, too.

We didn't know all the names at the time, let alone the intricate family relationships, so the pictures tend to be: men talking, children dancing, women talking. I do remember that Zulmira's daughter Irene came and seemed to listen to the music, which was remarkable; she is deep in Down's syndrome, and at 37 she screws up her eyes so as not to misunderstand the world. Where I come from, all too often, we set people like Irene aside.

Although the courtyard was a perfect dance floor, in the next weeks it started to look to us like some dry, distant planet. We started digging, paid people to help us dig, pulled muscles shifting barrow-loads of stone and concrete (and, for some strange reason, quantities of unmatched socks). We planted grapes to make shade for the house. Then we thought of planting roses along our blank white wall facing the chapel, the dark red roses that flourish everywhere here at tree height. Our neighbors approved.

The next year one of them, Jorge, a small smiling man with a whole horizon between his two front teeth, turned up unannounced in a kind of deep sea diver's helmet and a mackintosh. He carried a tank, a pipe, and a nozzle. "The grapes," he said, with great authority, and began to spray sulphur on their leaves. He pruned them for us, too. The grapes in our house, Zulmira said, had once been "uma meravilha"—a wonder.

Nothing very bad happened in New York, not to us. A man downstairs got his throat slashed lightly. An older man died and his body was found days later. The block association turned political over a sick tree. But somehow I began to notice the fact that I said "Good morning" to only a few people.

We found excuses to spend long summers in the village: books to be written, projects to be thought out. We said we had so few distractions, although the social calendar is packed with expatriate dinner parties, a birthday party at an endless table in a garage, village festas, obligatory openings (art happens all over the place, even here).

Walking the village street is a social event. You say "Good evening" and you are offered wine from a barrel, thin red stuff. You drink and you talk; that's how things are done.

In time, the grapes met the wisteria over the windows of the living room and made an intricate shade. The roses boiled up in unexpected neon colors. We bought the disused schoolhouse next door, which had lost its roof and its floor, and turned it into a place for guests.

We took far fewer photographs, I noticed.

One Saturday, the square by the chapel filled up with most of the men in the village. They had concrete mixers, terra cotta blocks, metal girders, windows and doors. By midday, they had made a skeleton for a *Casa do Povo*—the "House of the People" that every other village has, a place to drink, play cards or skittles, have a meeting, or in larger places use the pool or the gym.

The women arrived with meat, wine, salad, and tables, and the village ate. Then the skeleton was filled out with blocks, plastered over, and the *Casa do Povo* was almost ready: a box with a stage for the music at the festa. John and I weren't expected out on the square with the bricklayers. Unlike our neighbors, we are not construction workers, so we stayed in the house. But it was a dazzling day, a whole community deciding what they wanted and making it. We offered, tentatively, to do the painting. The offer was accepted. So day after day John was out and I was out, turning the Casa—and bits of the road and the rosemary bushes—an immaculate white. Jorge walked by and said it was well done, really well done. He smiled generously.

One summer, John stayed on to teach at the medieval university some 15 miles away. We commuted between New York and Formentina, from rush and menace to a community that felt absurdly safe. The house was entirely finished now, the marble hearth ready to use, the wood ceilings and floors varnished like mirrors. It had become a work of art: our work of art.

Then our neighbor Francisco died.

We were used to his wit. When we left windows open for our cat, he warned the wild cats would come, too. "You'll be the Feline Society of Formentina," he said. "Famous for its cuisine." He explained everything in French when our Portuguese stopped working.

He fell one afternoon. His wife wailed and people came running. His face was green-white. John asked the proper questions: Did he have pains in his chest or in his arms? He didn't, but he still died. A stroke, they said.

That night, the village assembled, blankets over their shoulders, to sit up with his body. The next day he was buried from the great monastic church nearby.

His house next door, with the wild ivy flourishing over a roof of ridged old tile, was shut up for a while. In the careful garden, the beans dried up on their poles. We went to the masses for his memory, the little white chapel overflowing with people, neighbors and family, under the glint of supermarket chandeliers. We talked about Francisco endlessly with neighbors, about the blow to the village.

Then his widow came to see us, wrapped in proper black. She brought potatoes. She was sure two men wouldn't know how to store them properly, so she showed us. She kissed me.

"When we live here. . . ," John said one evening, as we were packing to go back to New York.

I said, as though I knew it for the first time, "We already do."

"Got a House, a Showplace"

FRANCES KOGEN

WE BOTH AGREED. WITH RETIREMENT APPROACHING, IT WAS time to sell our big family home, time to find "a last house," as M. F. K. Fisher used to say.

"Buy whatever you want," my husband told me.

"But you don't even want to see it?" I asked.

"You're the Realtor," he said. "Surprise me."

My husband had his hands full in those tumultuous days 15 years ago. He was a criminal defense attorney in Miami. His clients included politicians, judges, child molesters, drug dealers, doctors, movie stars, rock singers. Nights when he was not trying a case, he was off to the dog track, where he ran a kennel of racing greyhounds. He named his dogs after old songs: *Ain't Misbehavin'*, *If I Didn't Care*, *Moonlight Serenade*. He claimed the dogs kept him sane.

My husband loved the house we were ready to leave, with its deep front lawn and winding drive, although he was rarely home and took no part or interest in its maintenance. He loved the sauna and swimming pool deep enough for a diving board, although he could not swim. He especially loved competing on the tennis court and thought himself a great player in spite of a bad leg, the result of a World War II wound that had kept him in the hospital for a year.

We had met on the deserted campus of the University of Michigan during spring break of 1949. I was from California, his family had recently migrated from Brooklyn to Florida, and neither of us had the money to go home.

Two years later we were married by a justice of the peace in the courthouse in downtown Miami. Our first home was a rented efficiency on Miami Beach, one stifling room and kitchenette with a starter set of Franciscan Ivy dishes, an assortment of jelly glasses, and a Murphy bed. Until he passed the bar exam, my husband worked without salary in a law office on Lincoln Road. I found a job selling tickets on non-scheduled airlines in a newly opened storefront on Washington Avenue. So many planes crashed in 1951 that I felt guilty every time I made a sale.

One thing led to another: a one-bedroom apartment, three babies, a three-bedroom split-level tract house. Word got around that juries listened to my husband. "They feel sorry for you when they see that hearing aid sticking out of your pocket," the other attorneys joked. He made money.

"Go find a big house," he told me. "A place the kids can be proud of." Us, he meant. A showplace, he meant. My husband, like me, was raised during the Depression. He grew up in a succession of rooms behind or over mom-and-pop stores. The last time I saw my childhood home, a stucco duplex my father built in Los Angeles, I had to ask the taxi driver, "Will I be safe going there?" "You will if you're with me," he said.

My husband was proud of the sprawling five-bedroom ranch-style house we bought in 1962; he cherished it like a prize credential, like his All-City Latin medal, like his beloved law degree. The house made him feel important. No use to point out the floor plan was too chopped, ceilings too low and closed in; that I would have to chauffeur three girls to school, albeit excellent schools, five days a week for the next ten years. I hired a decorator; tinkered with the kitchen; lugged in an 800-pound gas range with eight pilot lights, two 26-inch ovens, and a salamander, but never got it right. It was never really me.

Where did the time go? For me: Girl Scouts, PTA, reader at Recordings for the Blind, chauffeur. I turned one bathroom into my darkroom for black-and-white photography. I copied Fragonard and Renoir paintings in needlepoint, gave sit-down dinners for up to 100 people, got a license to sell real estate.

My husband's law practice exposed him to adulation, bomb threats, men who made toys for nephews by day and raped women at night, children who murdered their mothers. We managed to raise three daughters—two attorneys and a speech therapist—who married good men.

Then it was time to move on, time to find that "last house." As a real estate salesperson I saw lots of places and I knew the rules: location, location, location. Never fall in love with one house. Be able to walk away at the bargaining table. One glimpse of the unpretentious little green house crouching alone and undefended at the end of a dead-end street and I forgot everything. I did it all wrong.

A sophisticated airline pilot and stewardess owned the property. Bill and Barbara. Their baby was less than a year old. The hybrid structure was started in the early 1950s on an isolated acre of pines, live oaks, palms, gumbos, frangipani, and fruit trees, hidden from the street and neighbors by a high cherry hedge. A succession of owners had grafted on rooms, pruned away walls—one of the three tiny bedrooms had been a utility room, the living room was once a breezeway.

All in all the house was nothing much except for the kitchen. It was 15 by 30 feet with a massive brick fireplace, a large cooking island, three skylights, and a cathedral ceiling. Standing by the range, you could see treetops bobbing beyond three clerestory windows on the west wall. It was just what I wanted.

Off the brick-floored screened porch at the back of the house was a wooden deck with built-in benches, an antique rooster weather vane, and red geraniums in terra cotta pots. The deck overlooked a serene kidney-shaped pond on the west. A picket fence curved along a leafy 15-foot incline; a gate opened to coral rock steps leading down to a wooden dock, two benches, and a picnic table. Tied to an enormous banyan tree festooned with tropical vines was a Huck Finn raft.

I loved it. Living in the little green house would be like camping in the woods. (When the girls were small, I badgered my husband into buying a tent, but camping to him conjured up memories of life in the foxholes in Germany's Hürtgen forest, of collecting dead bodies in the rain under gunfire on his 21st birthday. The tent ended up at the Salvation Army.)

Now I envisioned my nine grandchildren sitting on the dock nibbling bologna sandwiches, or fishing, or sprawled on their stomachs watching tadpoles move in the cool, deep water. I pictured Walden Pond, Hiawatha's "green and silent valley." So what if the house lacked central air conditioning? We could put that in, but I preferred the idea of controlling the temperature with individual room units and old-fashioned jalousie windows. In our big house we rarely opened windows, never heard birds sing or leaves rustle, never smelled gardenias or night-blooming jasmine.

What about the location? What about the pile of rusted appliances in the carport of that untended house on the corner? Ignore it! I told myself. Don't look!

Barbara airily dismissed worries about the railroad tracks, hidden by pine trees on the east side of the property. "We love the train. It runs only twice a day three times a week. Two minutes and it's gone! Come over tonight. We'll open a bottle of chardonnay and listen to the 7:13 go by." I went and the three of us talked more: of moonlight streaming through the pines, cries of red screech owls hanging on sweet-scented night air, squirrels, painted buntings, red-bellied woodpeckers, raccoons, possums, turtles. We talked of butterflies—giant swallowtails, red admirals, Brazilian skippers. We talked of Wallace Stevens's "dew of old devotions."

Considered hinterlands in 1952, and largely overlooked in the subsequent rush to all-house, zero-lot-line suburbs west of the Palmetto Expressway, the area was now classified as "close in." Land values were beginning to rise. Barbara said a physics professor from the University of Miami lived in the house with the pool and tennis court across the street, a French teacher in a private school in Coconut Grove owned the house out of sight on the other side of the pond.

Barbara said, "A friend told me she sat in the bathtub last night trying to figure out how she could come up with the down payment to buy our house." I pictured my competition pondering, tendrils of damp hair curling about her face, the bath water growing cold. I bought the house for the asking price. It was January. Renovations took six months.

Workmen gutted one bathroom, laid old Chicago brick on the living room floor, slathered on fresh wallpaper and paint, enclosed the screened porch with sliding glass windows. A painter lay on a scaffold for a week scraping bubbled varnish from the beams of the uninsulated ceiling in the kitchen; a cabinet man built 12 feet of floor-to-ceiling bookshelves. We got a new roof, new wiring.

One Sunday in June while we were still renovating, the *Miami Herald* printed a map with dots showing where dead bodies had been found in Dade County that year. Two dots adorned the driveway of my soon-to-be-home. A neighbor across the street told me about the white Mercedes abandoned with the motor idling and bodies of two young women stuffed in the trunk.

The neighbor behind me phoned me to announce her Doberman pinscher had given birth, and I should have a Doberman, or at the very least a German shepherd. She said Barbara's Irish setter slept through the last robbery. Bill was not home. He had the gun. (When I pointed to iron window guards stored in the garage, Barbara said, "Oh Frances, we can't live that way. We took them off.") I put the bars back on the windows and installed a state-of-the-art burglar alarm.

In August I took my husband to see the house for the first time.

"I hate it," he said.

Two weeks later, the driver of the moving van shook his head. "You're moving from there to here?" he asked.

In October a tall, thin man, dressed in a powder-blue pullover sweater and a ginger-colored stocking mask, stood under the floodlight on the rear deck. It was 3 A.M. I watched him from the darkened hall, wondering if I should push the audible alarm button and wake up my husband and have him yell I told you so, or push the silent alarm and wait for the police. I pushed both buttons. The thief ran away with a broken recording machine and two eight-inch reels of intermediate French grammar I had left in the garage.

There were other disturbances of the peace: a kitchen door was kicked in while we were away (nothing taken), a stolen Ford pickup truck was abandoned in the driveway, kids smoked marijuana in the woods by the train tracks and started fires, and motorcyclists careened and zoomed along the railroad right-of-way.

Aquatic weeds threatened to choke the pond, and there was no access for heavy dredging equipment because of the trees. No, the gardener didn't know anyone who wanted the job. He mentioned seeing a cottonmouth snake in the rushes and two little foxes. I bought Wellies, heavy gloves, an oar, and a rake three feet wide with eight-inch teeth and a long rope attached to the handle. One of my sons-in-law helped me drag weeds out of the pond, up the stairs, and out to the street to be hauled away by the county. It was hard work.

I got a permit from the Florida Game and Fresh Water Fish Commission to stock the pond with 15 triploid grass carp between 8 and 11 inches, as a "viable control of bladderwort, spikerush, and filamentous algae." (A few years later our two-year-old granddaughter invited a friend to "come and see Grandma's whales.")

Pine needles and dead leaves littered the yard and decks; roots of the banyan tree made pretzels out of plumbing pipes; armies of termites, palmetto bugs, and ants—fire, sugar, and carpenter—beset us, lured by dampness and leaf decay; algae and mold glazed the decks. I hired an exterminator and hooked up the hose to a six-horsepower pressure cleaner. We stopped parking our cars overnight in front of the house because thieves broke the windows and stole infant car seats, Raggedy Anns, strollers in the car trunk.

Thieves also made off with our barbecue and lawn furniture. I gritted my teeth and hung staghorn ferns and orchids—rose-purple cattleyas, and pink vandas and dendrobiums—in the trees, and wind chimes by the back door. I added a heavy stone table and benches, and swingsets in cement in the backyard for the grandchildren. A department store in a nearby mall did a promotion on Ireland; I bought the stone walls from the display department and lined the narrow path between the west side of the house and the pond.

Hurricane Andrew had other plans. It blew all the trees into the pond. The morning after, the place looked like *Little House on the Prairie*. Neighbors' houses stood naked and flawed beneath the cloudless, unbroken sky. One house had no roof. President Bush posed for pictures in its front yard. My grandsons, three of them under eight, came over to watch cranes, backhoes, and Bobcats clean up the mess, hoping to glimpse the remains of a possum we buried among the ferns.

I scoured nurseries and garden stores, carted home double hibiscus, Japanese fern trees, live oaks, black olives, Roebelenii palms. Hired men propped up the fence, the swings, repiped the sprinkler system, laid new sod, smoothed out the lumps with sand and topsoil. Life returned to normal. Ruby-throated hummingbirds and bees twittered over flowers, resilient squirrels crept along power lines, mallards tipped white tails and metallic-green heads up and down the pond; anhingas perched on the dock and spread their wings to dry; silky moonlight came in our window, as it had before.

We have lived in the little green house 14 years now. Our three girls and their families live within an hour's drive. We no longer give catered sit-down dinners, but our snug little guest room has housed former neighbors, college roommates, expectant fathers, relatives, and assorted grandchildren in cribs and baskets and sleeping bags.

All the previous owners have visited us. One woman recalled family cookouts in the backyard—her dad set up a smoker made out of an oil drum down by the gate. She remembered lying in bed terrified, listening to the rumble of trains carrying troops from the Homestead Air Force Base during the Cuban war scare in 1962. Another couple made the sentimental journey from Tampa. The wife told me how happy she had been living in the house, and asked did the multi-colored bird still come around? Bill drove down the East Coast from Stuart. Without Barbara. They were divorced. Their daughter, almost a teenager, was with him. Bill wanted to show her where they lived when she was born, and to see how the house fared during the hurricane.

Along about October of last year my husband started in again about the rusted appliances in the carport down the street. "All right," I said, "let's sell the place and find another." I lined up four or five elegant houses in "good" locations and showed him house after house. No, he didn't think so . . . No. An ad appeared in the Sunday classifieds: "Open House. Picture perfect Country French Acre Showplace! Five spacious bedrooms, three sumptuous baths, soaring ceilings, walk-in closets galore, sparkling pool!!!" The property was located in a gated and guarded, meticulously manicured and "structured" development. There no one broke the rules, painted the house purple, let weeds get the upper hand. But no, that house wasn't right either.

In fact, my husband changed his mind and didn't want to move after all. Our little green house had finally cast its spell over him.

Different things bring happiness to different people. Maybe he just likes where I moved his treadmill—out in the garden room, where he can see the sparkle on the pond in the early morning light while he works out, where he can sing along with Frank Sinatra or Tony Bennett as loud as he likes and not bother anybody.

So set 'em up Joe, I got a little story you ought to know . . . or . . . *I've got a house, a showplace, but still I can't get no place with you.* I can hear him now.

The Company of Raptors

JOSEPH GIOVANNINI

I HAVE NEVER RETURNED, BUT SLEEP OFTEN TAKES ME BACK to what my subconscious insists is the house of my dreams—the one-bedroom cottage I rented 20 years ago in the Los Angeles hills, not long after finishing architecture school. At $250 a month it was hardly a Hollywood glass-and-steel dream house overlooking an endless carpet of sparkling lights. But the modest, shingled, one-story structure did sit at the crest of a canyon on Mount Washington, where it not only presided over a panorama but also nested in a zone between untamed nature and sophisticated city.

There is in Southern California an invisible membrane between the last house at the top of a canyon road and the hillside around it: a little-known realm where Volvos and BMWs give way to raccoon, coyote, and rattlesnake. This territory of encounter between the raw and the cooked is where pedigreed Siamese cats leap off terraces to hunt lizards, quail, and mice, and cultivated bougainvillea creeps among the native manzanita. During a lonely period when I had few friends and a clandestine romance, this territory proved my refuge, my companion, and the centerpiece of my solitude.

Film, literature, and song have perpetuated the notion of Los Angeles as a fast-lane, high-octane society. But the easy, glitzy image persists at the expense of an almost unrecognized Jeffersonian ideal that quietly plays itself out in many hillside communities—in the San Fernando and San Gabriel foothills as well as the parts of Los Angeles and Malibu that lap the sides of the Santa Monica Mountains. Electronically equipped, college-educated, two-car households coexist with the indigenous flora and fauna just out the back door.

If I coasted down the east side of Mount Washington in my '59 Studebaker, I was only ten minutes from Zubin Mehta's Mahler at the Music Center downtown, yet I lived in a zone where hefty possum fished in ponds for carp and koi and rolled back newly laid sod to lunch on creatures exposed in the earth. From my desk, where I wrote architecture criticism for a Los Angeles daily, I could hear the wind against the wings of my personal hawk diving from a nearby eucalyptus for prey. Ripe, heavy avocados thumped the roof as I played the Waldstein Sonata on the piano.

I was reared nearby in a place appropriately named Arcadia, a town in Pasadena's orbit. Bucolic Arcadia had plenty of land, much of it on an alluvial fan at the base of the Sierra Madres. Peacocks escaped the local arboretum and strutted freely and raucously on our streets. The Arcadian character certainly made my childhood and adolescence happy, but when I left for college in the East and graduate years abroad, I acquired an irreversible taste for cities. Back in the land of suburbs after more than ten years, I was at a loss for where to live, especially since my high school friends had long since dispersed to careers in the four corners of the country. I was free to live anywhere and decided that L.A.'s canyons offered an interesting alternative to the overgroomed houses and yards of communities like Brentwood and Beverly Hills. I picked L.A.'s cheapest, most Bohemian canyon.

Miraculously rural Mount Washington lies off the Pasadena freeway, midway between downtown Los Angeles and downtown Pasadena. Its winding, uncurbed roads and its houses dug into hillsides or perched over slopes have attracted the kind of people who want to be alone—artists, writers, and garden-variety eccentrics: Greenwich Village West.

Mount Washington gives the lie to the myth that L.A. has no history. Developed in the early 1900s, when a funicular took residents from the trolley at the foot of the hill to the top, Mount Washington acquired over the years a yeasty collection of domestic styles on its saddleback ridges and in its canyons. Near the base, boulder houses were built with water-rounded stones plucked from the nearby arroyo. Higher up, several woodsy Craftsman-style houses reminiscent of Greene & Greene had sleeping porches announcing that Angelenos lived in sympathy with nature. Affluent areas of the canyon boast designs by second-generation Modernist Harwell Harris, with horizontal lines and glass corners inspired by Frank Lloyd Wright. Dozens of simple stucco buildings that elsewhere would be tract houses are adapted to the slopes in irregular, often quirky configurations. As in many Los Angeles neighborhoods, trees like the pomegranate and kumquat speak of L.A.'s botanical history and signal that the California yard, before it became decorative, served as a productive garden yielding fruits.

About my plain-Jane cottage I knew only that my landlord had lived there many years, and that he kept two monkeys who loved to flush the toilet to see the water swirl. But because the house occupied a choice lot at the tip of Mount Washington Canyon and commanded a long view through the spurs that framed it, I surmise that it was one of the pioneers on the Hill, built at a time when emigrants from the East came to dry out their tubercular lungs in the arid climate. (A sprawling former sanitarium, now the Self-Realization Center, still stands just down the street.) Before its image became swamped by Hollywood, Los Angeles evolved as a city offering health and resort-style living.

In this older, bypassed section of town, I rediscovered L.A.'s original character as I invented the way I wanted to live: this was the first freestanding house of my own. For nearly three years I witnessed the ebb and flow of city and country around me as I lived through my long-delayed rite of passage from student to adult. Somehow the house deepened the rite. Although in Los Angeles you are where you live, the uniqueness of this place was that it defied social labeling. I could forge my own identity.

At night, when I garaged my Studebaker and walked by the lone palm planted squarely in the middle of the lawn, I passed through suburbia into rusticity. The building was sited on a ledge terraced into the slope. The roof was lower than the front lawn, so it could not be seen from the street, and the surrounding eucalyptus trees shielded it from the lower canyon roads: the house was so secret that I often left the doors unlocked, and in the time I lived there no one ever trespassed. After I stepped down the stairs to a narrow forecourt, shaded by a wood trellis and monster ferns, I occupied an island of rented solitude. Coming home at the end of the day I would just shed my clothes and walk straight into the outdoor shower to wash away the day's toxins and ease into my private Eden. Lathering, looking up through the lacy leaves of a centenarian pepper tree, I could ponder the stars. In its isolation, the house formed a zone of reverie in a field of suspended time.

At 700 square feet, the house was not impressive. A small bedroom lay to the left of the front door, under a shed roof shaded by the fecund avocado tree. The dining area seated two; three was a crowd. The kitchen hung out the back, an architectural caboose. The wood paneling on the walls and sloped ceiling were painted white. The single item a real estate broker might charitably call a feature was the brick fireplace, which provided the only heat. When I moved in, I placed my bed in the living room so I could fall asleep sandwiched between the warmth of the fireplace and the romantic, untamed canyon just the other side of the plate-glass window; the bedroom became a study. Life here removed me from the city: torrential spring rains lashed it like a ship at sea and deepened its isolation. During the intense heat of the Santa Ana winds, the shaded house seemed to occupy an utterly still void. Any updraft channeled dry, penetrating herbal aromas into the interior.

The penalty for this raw Western beauty was the threat of fire, and the need to protect the house drove me outside into the yard. Houses at the tops of canyons are more vulnerable than those at the foot, and even if the flames don't touch residences, they generate 1,500-degree temperatures in which houses combust spontaneously. In my new role as a householder, I cleared the underbrush and planted vegetables on plots that had been terraced into the hillside decades before by someone who was evidently a serious gardener. Working the landscape, however, was not like placing a flower bed in a lawn. Judiciously chosen plants could defend the house against fire, so I tried to figure out what would cheat the flames but reinforce the wild character of the canyon. I cut back the oily, highly combustible chaparral—Southern California's matchstick—usually substituting fennel, which does so well in this climate. Fennel was fresh, fragrant, and a little unruly, and it yielded a potent health drink. At first I disdained the mangy black walnut trees with the sickly limbs that are so prolific here, but I came to respect their tenacity and recognized they had a place I shouldn't disturb.

As a budding gardener, I did flirt with the notion of transforming the yard and adjacent canyon into a micro-farm that would make my homestead independent. Though the idea satisfied my sixties sensibilities, I never pushed my lot and canyon to self-sufficiency. Managing the canyon was the course I chose, and with dirt under my nails, I developed an emotional connection to the landscape, the kind of feeling I presume is common to people who really live in the country and depend on the land for their livelihood.

I lived with a privacy that intensified any relationship. I had met a beautiful Eurasian and the isolation of the house suited a long, off-the-record affair with this woman who was, technically, already spoken for. We could not be seen together in public, and she brought no friends to my house. I might have had an emotional life, even a very emotional life, but little social life. I continued to cultivate my connection with the outdoors.

In my outback I discovered a society of animals, part of a tiny semi-rural ecosystem with a close relationship to the city. The great raptors in the eucalyptus and sycamore were there because the unspoiled canyon was a supermarket of fowl and rodents scurrying about. Juicy little quail, sometimes trailed by chicks, evidently felt exposed in the sun, so they raced across the patches of light to safe havens under bushes. The owls, which pair for life (and terrified my paramour, who considered them ill omens), came out in the evening and enjoyed a cocktail conversation before the hunt; the droppings they deposited on the chimney and roof peak, with half-digested little bodies, chronicled their sprees. I came to spot dozens of bird types, especially in the spring. Never was I bitten by any insect when I worked the yard, but one spider did find his way to my bed and thigh, where he made his presence painfully felt. My doctor, a fan of arachnids, seemed more interested in identifying the spider than in treating the bite. The culprit, evidently, was rare.

One night as I went to sleep, I doused the lights only to see the white walls glowing red. "Strange," I thought, "the fireplace isn't lit." I looked down the canyon and saw distant flames. The fire seemed safely removed, and I started to fall asleep until I realized, "No, this is life-threatening—I am the logical conclusion of that fire." I got up, called the fire department, and started packing my letters, photographs, and slides until, peering down the long canyon, I saw a convoy of trucks arrive. The firemen extinguished the blaze impressively in a matter of minutes. I was lucky, this time.

Domestic cats, including my dear long-haired Herman, would move freely through the membrane into the canyon where I could see them stalking and freezing as they hunted their quarry. Herman's transformation from a gentle bundle of black-and-white cashmere into a killing machine, emitting primordial clicks from the back of his throat, alarmed and fascinated me. Endearingly, he regularly deposited half-dead trophies of his hunt at the back door. Cats, in turn, were the natural prey of owls and hawks, which swooped down and carried them off in their talons to drop them to their deaths and pick at their corpses.

Raccoons were the most conspicuous of my furry neighbors, and because these little bandits with the bright eyes were cute, I made the mistake of feeding them scraps as though they were pets. They ate anything, even the soap on the tray at my outdoor shower, with incredibly articulated, rather human little hands, and eventually invited themselves into the house through the unlocked kitchen door. I walked in on one 20-pounder raiding the cupboards, and he stood his ground in the kitchen sink, wringing his hands, hissing at the showdown. There weren't many possum, but the one ill-mannered, long-toothed oaf I did see waddled off, confident in the knowledge that the inedibility of his meat protected him.

Every once in a while my yard drew unexpected visitors. Kids returning from the nearby grammar school occasionally hiked home single file through all the backyards along the canyon edge, using branches as machetes to whack their way through. Their shouting announced their advent, and usually there was a ripple of wildlife that cleared out in advance of their comically heavy-footed arrival. A smile always came over me as I saw children turn into Huck Finns for an afternoon in this canyon that I tended. They of course remained city kids, but like me they were charmed, charged, and changed under the canyon's influence.

Writing is a solitary task, but my interviews did introduce me to many people, and gradually I made friends. Increasingly I pointed my Studebaker west for my emerging social life. I found that I was coming home later and later and seeing my canyon menagerie less and less.

It seemed, finally, that I was living on the freeway, and I realized I had to give up one end or the other. After years in the company of raptors, I finally decamped for a much less interesting house near the beach and the company of people. The commute defeated the idyll but did not terminate it. The canyon house remains my only recurrent dream.

Losses and Recoveries

Belongings

HOPE COOKE

My mother piloted her Piper Cub one January night into the side of a mountain in the Sierra Nevadas. As my father had already left us, a baby nurse brought my sister and me back East, my mother's remains at the rear of the train.

My sister and I moved to my maternal grandparents' apartment in New York, and the endless traffic hum outside became my earliest Manhattan memory. A year or so later, I had my first epiphany in the hall of the apartment when I sauntered into a shaft of yellow sun wearing a yellow smocked dress and realized I felt yellow, part of the light. I was conscious the moment would pass, that I would always want to know what it was like to be three. I must feel this way hard, I thought, so I will always remember.

The following year my grandparents bought 8B, the apartment across the hall from them, and sent my sister and me to live there with a nanny and a Swedish cook. The room where I stayed was near the elevator, which rattled at night; it was furnished only with a low cot, scratchy carpet, and curtains patterned with what looked like bats but probably were butterflies as they had belonged to my mother, an ardent lepidopterist.

My grandparents seldom crossed the hall to see us. Though loving to each other, they remained virtually silent with us during our goodnight visits to their apartment. We would sit primly nibbling cheese and crackers as they worked on crossword puzzles, kissing their cheeks and leaving when they turned on the news. Their emotional distance stemmed perhaps from an outmoded upper-class belief that a separation between children and adults was correct (unless the latter were servants). More likely the pinched affection came from my grandmother's rage over my mother's death, and her hatred of my father.

When I was six, an English governess arrived to replace the many illtempered Scots nannies who had passed through the household, running 8B. I was afraid she too would leave. On her days off I counted the dresses in her closet, making sure she had not packed. But she stayed and began to furnish my room from her salary, framing the *Cries of London*— sentimentalized pictures of street hawkers—from a Yardley's calendar, hanging ruffled curtains, and giving me a reading chair. The room's transformation made me feel like Sarah Crewe, the Little Princess.

At night before sleeping, I made up stories about families swaying their way across the country in covered wagons, shipwrecked children weaving shelters with rope and thatch. The first filled me with a sense of loss as the families jettisoned furniture to lighten the load; the second thrilled me with the notion you could make a house from leavings. I sometimes couldn't sleep because I was too busy fashioning stumps into tables, making little mossy chairs, lining up driftwood shelves with gourds for cups. I determined I would one day create a home with my own belongings.

In the summers we went to Long Island to a big clapboard house built before the Revolution. I spent the daytime in an outbuilding turned into a little playhouse, my governess reading or sewing on its porch, me fussing over dolls inside. I felt huge there. If I needed to feel my right size, I'd go to the unoccupied guest room of our main house, drink in the silence, comfort myself with how everything fitted together: the light curling over the four-poster beds, the grain of their golden wood like brushed fur, the silk counterpanes embroidered with hard, raised monograms.

My grandmother sold the house after my grandfather's death, when I was ten, asking my sister and me to choose the things we would like to keep. It was then I saw my mother's furniture, which had lain crated in a shed on the grounds. Out of the boxes it looked new and unused, like merchandise in a shop. I didn't want any of it and there was an auction. What I did want, insisted upon having, were my books and the guest room furniture, including a mahogany highboy, tiger maple bureau, pie-crust tea table, and poster beds. Now it was my turn to have possessions boxed and stored, this time in a Manhattan vault where they stayed for years, a dark, unattended party.

I went off to boarding school and later to college, living by now like the proverbial Collyer brothers in a flood of books, records, and clothing, losing all sense, or even memory, of furniture. Having no interest in objects, I skipped the hefty chunks on interiors and dowries in books assigned for my French and Russian literature classes. For that matter, deeming it realist trivia, I skipped objective description of any sort, speeding through tomes in a matter of days. And I was enraptured and curious about travel: ever since high school I had been going back and forth to the Middle East and India, visiting an aunt and uncle in the diplomatic service who became my guardians after my grandmother's death.

The week after college ended, I left the country to get married. Packing cases full of childhood paraphernalia followed me to my new home in Sikkim through Suez, around the Indian Cape, and up the Himalayan foothills. One crate became a clubhouse for my stepchildren—the realization of a fantasy I had held since I was their age. I even made a sign saying "Grown-ups keep out," though now I was the adult.

My new home, the Palace, a clumsy turn-of-the-century stucco building with about 15 rooms, posed a challenge—a satisfying, even thrilling challenge. My husband, the country's crown prince, was a widower when we met in Darjeeling during one of my summer trips to India, so there had not been a *kim-ki-Am,* mother of the house, as they say in Sikkim, for some years. Also we were cash poor, an attribute we bore proudly, most Asian royalty being venally well-to-do. On top of this, an elder royal half-brother had retired to Tibet a generation earlier, taking all the palace furniture except a Victorian buffet too heavy to move, even meanly stripping the rose-patterned English paper from the drawing room walls.

The furniture I brought was assimilated into the musty, sparely furnished rooms, which lent themselves more readily to my Early American pieces than to the Sikkimese cabinetry already there. The mesh of styles reminded me of old houses in Salem and Newburyport, where China goods blended with Colonial tables and chairs—houses my mother's seafaring family had lived in long ago.

For the ten years I lived in Gangtok, the capital of Sikkim, I had not only the satisfaction of being involved in the country's push for development in health, education, and welfare, but also the daily pleasure of a cozy, child-filled house. Despite a sometimes strained marriage, I exulted in finally having a home of my own, the rooms assuming their own traits, which all of us knew like family secrets: the children's hide-and-seek spot under the table; Old Faithful, the guestroom urinal that gurgled all night; the fire-lit nursery, snug as a tent. When I finally had to leave that house as violence ripped the country apart during its merger with India, I said farewell by sitting down in each room, as the Russians do before making a journey. Partly because of the suddenness of my flight with the children, partly because of my decision not to disturb the harmony the house had achieved, I took almost nothing with me.

My two children, five and nine, my teenage stepdaughter, and I came to New York on visitors' visas, though we were not visitors; neither were we immigrants, nor were we homecomers. We were displaced people. Except for my sister, with whom I had scant ties, I had no immediate family here, no visceral sense of belonging. The few trips I had made back to the United States from Sikkim had always been cocooned, ceremonial, speaking for and of my new country, even the long dresses I had worn setting me apart.

For months before leaving we had been threatened by armed gangs as turmoil in Sikkim grew; for years before we had been censored, bugged, and intimidated—so now I had a released P.O.W.'s sense of relief, exhilaration, weightlessness, and disbelief at being here, along with an overwhelming sense of loss for the country we had left.

I rented an unfurnished apartment by the East River. The dining nook had a tiny crack of a river view—a crack of freedom. Though events unfolding in Sikkim often loomed larger than our life in New York, the precariousness of our existence here made me wide awake to connections, awed by the city's plenitude, its hurly-burly freedom.

On weekends I took the children to every block party, street fair, and community dance in town. Sikkimese and American friends joined me. My friends and I were like a tribe, sharing hardships, celebrating good times. The rest of the city seemed in the same mood; we had returned at a period in the early seventies when people were hungry for shared ritual, linkage.

Memories slowly surfaced, fall being one of them. Fall was American, and I had missed it more than I had known, even Macy's Thanksgiving Day Parade reducing me to tears. By spring, our friendly Yorkville apartment house had begun to feel homey although, reflecting our uncertain tenure, I had outfitted our apartment minimally. I had enough inheritance left for our rent and the children's school, but except for mattresses and plank bookcases we had little furniture. Occasionally I would bring back something found on the street. Children from other floors gravitated to our apartment to jump on our mattresses, exuberant at the absence of belongings and constraints.

Despite their lingering grief at leaving Sikkim and their longing for their father, my son and daughter were learning city skills, swaggeringly independent with their bus passes. My son became a soccer star and we went to all his Randalls Island games. Every holiday our mattress-filled living room filled up with Sikkimese students who had no place to go. We were extended family, in any case; exultant in our growing friendship, franker than we would have been at home, as we always called our old country.

But even as we racked up months, got variables in order—school, pediatrician, bank branch, supermarket—my days were alarmingly unstructured. Respites reconfirmed our rootlessness. When we returned from weekends visiting a married friend in Connecticut, we felt the loss of her big frame house, her husbanded life. Visits to my aunt in Washington, where we ate dainty, balanced meals off bone china, left me weak-kneed getting out at Penn Station, all defenses gone, only yellow cabs as armor. Our apartment would look so bare, but some part of me was proud to be a standing vertebrate, which New York requires of you, as opposed to curling up in a crustacean society, which official Washington can be.

Traumas afflicting our family in Sikkim strafed us every few months—big ones like attempted murder, house arrest, illness, death. Every time I got a little vantage here, took a New School course, published a story, some far larger reality there wiped it out. Sometimes I would start to snivel on the street and go into a dark restaurant until I got a grip.

Though I eavesdropped intensely on our neighborhood, major national events passed by almost unnoticed. I missed the '74 recession except that suddenly the remainder of my money was considerably reduced. I heard the muffled clapping of the gloved White House servants saying good-bye to the departing Nixons but only vaguely understood the cause. I was aware of the Embassy rooftop helicopter exit from Saigon but couldn't share the shame. So I began to read up on the years I had missed, to trek city streets in a conscious way. Every weekend saw me heading out on a social history walking tour, the local reality giving me ground under my feet.

Tragically, my husband died of cancer in New York soon after he was released from house arrest and we had to struggle with that loss, but eventually the roil in Sikkim ended. As the children came of age, I was far more in charge of my life than before. Now that my son had finished high school and my daughter was away in boarding school, I moved to Brooklyn to a neighborhood as gracious and quiet as parts of London, but with New York's flair. At first going from our Manhattan high-rise aerie to the Victorian enclave felt like a retreat, but my new neighborhood enfolded me, its streets as cozy and tended as rooms.

My wisteria-entwined brownstone turned out to be near Greenwood Cemetery, where my mother was buried, a strange coincidence and satisfying closure. I had not known she was there until some time after moving to Brooklyn. There were other coincidences too, including the auspicious Buddhist symbols on the Victorian fence and the Asian bamboo grass in the backyard. My old furniture, sent back from Sikkim ten years after I left, settled itself into the sitting room warmed by a fireplace, and upstairs in my bedroom and library with their scrolled plaster decoration. I realized I had missed the familiar pieces like limbs.

A year after moving in, I met a man who lived nearby. "Where do you put your Christmas tree?" he asked the first evening he came for dinner. I liked the question.

Now we are married and proud grandparents of two little girls who visit often. Though my son and his wife, a childhood friend from Sikkim, live nearby, he still stores his comics and soldiers in our crowded basement. My daughter goes back and forth to Asia, sometimes taking her possessions, sometimes leaving them here. I ruminate on her midden of goods—her children's books, her shoes, her four-poster bed stuck with decals—missing her nearness, knowing that her life and belongings will fully intersect before long. Often it takes time, but it happens.

A Room at the Inn

CYNTHIA ANDERSON

NOT LONG AGO I SLEPT AS A PAYING GUEST IN THE HOUSE where I grew up—in my old room under the eaves.

The murmurs that drifted upstairs that night could have been those I had fallen asleep to for 18 years: my father's even bass, my mother's throaty chuckle, my grandmother and aunt. When I was a child the voices sometimes drew me from my bed, down to the foot of the stairs to peek into the living room through the curtained French door. My sister Gillian often joined me there, as did our small cousin George, a boy everyone called a genius who was known to us for the collection of rabbit bones beneath his bed and the butterscotch smell of his breath.

Nothing was happening in that room, everything was. We studied the way Aunt Elaine inclined her head when she spoke, the flash of my mother's rings as she shuffled playing cards, the smooth circuit of my father's Scotch from table to lips to table. If we waited long enough my grandmother would get up to stir the fire. The room would brighten and we would be comforted even as we shivered in our pajamas. Sometimes one of us would sneeze and the door would swing open. We would be shooed back to bed or, if we were lucky, brought to the sofa for a cuddle and a round of bridge, which George always won.

Instead the voices I heard that night were those of strangers, other guests at what recently had become a public accommodation—the Center Village Inn. Downstairs the fire was lit against the cold Maine night, at least it had been when I arrived. Otherwise the living room was unrecognizable, the wall to the dining room knocked out and the new space filled with needlepoint rugs and a careful arrangement of overstuffed chintz.

Elsewhere the changes were equally dramatic. New windows ran the length of the kitchen. In the old utility room, where we used to sit on the agitating washer to play a game Gillian invented called Blast-off, steam rose from a recently installed hot tub.

I had arrived late from Boston, done a hasty inspection of the downstairs—didn't want to see, wasn't ready to see—then returned to the foyer to retrieve my bag. The new owner sat at a desk beneath the chandelier my mom took apart each spring to wash, 100 soapy prisms in a towel-lined sink.

Mrs. Keaton looked up from her ledger and smiled. "Finding everything you need?" Her eyes were welcoming.

"I think so," I said. "Thank you." I had registered under my married name; she wouldn't know me unless I introduced myself. Even so, my stomach was tightening.

She pointed behind me. "We have a big-screen TV and lots of movies in our game room. Did you see it?"

The game room had been my grandmother's first-floor bedroom. "Yes," I said. "I guess I'll pass on a movie tonight. I think I'll go upstairs."

"First door on the right, a single," she said, smiling again. "It's open." My old room. The tightness spread into my chest; I hadn't slept there in ten years.

In my bedroom the odor of fresh paint and lemon polish replaced the wet-dog smell of our boxer Gulliver, who spent much of his indoor time on my braided rug. The horse wallpaper I chose in third grade was gone, as was the ceiling-to-floor corkboard where I had pinned pictures of John Travolta, my skiing medals, and the limerick Gillian wrote for my 12th birthday. The room had been made into a smaller version of the ones downstairs: bright and countrified, like a page from Laura Ashley, like any of a dozen inn rooms I have slept in before.

But the biggest change was the air itself, which felt warm and muffled. When I lived here, the inside temperature rarely exceeded 60. My grandmother's almost religious belief in the curative powers of fresh air had been passed on to my father, which meant the downstairs was only marginally insulated and the upstairs not at all. A glass of water left beside the bed could form a skim of ice by morning. A stiff wind would rattle the windows and seep through the walls, resulting in a draft strong enough to blow out the candles on a birthday cake. "Heavens," my grandmother would exclaim, pulling her knit shawl closer. "It certainly is outdoorsy in here."

I turned out the light and, too warm, lay on top of the comforter. The moon shone through the window. I recognized the place where it hit the wall and the trapezoid it made. The shape would flatten, I remembered, and disappear as the moon rose. I wished for sleep, but felt lonely, and uneasy about what I was doing. Of the people who once lived here only Gillian, who backed out at the last minute, knew I was coming. My parents would disapprove, especially my mom. Why go back? she would say. Why not leave the past alone? But I had to see what had happened to our house.

My father would probably understand my visit. After all, he lived here almost his entire life, as did his father and his father's father, who built the place in 1872. But even my dad might question my tactics. The anonymity, the way I just showed up: one person, one night, please, filled out the registration and parked my Subaru alongside other out-of-state cars in the new lot carved out of the lawn.

For three generations, while our family was growing in size and prosperity, the house grew too. My great-grandfather built it with the future in mind. The original structure was simple: five large rooms with a central chimney and a south-facing porch. A second floor with bedrooms followed, then a two-story wing and another kitchen. The house filled and swelled; at the start of the 20th century its 14 rooms held a dozen members of extended family. Photographs from that time show the place to be lovely and meticulous, the faces of its inhabitants content. My father spent his childhood hunting salamanders in the brook, climbing the quartz-streaked ledges that rose beyond the back field.

By the time Gillian and George and I lived here, the house was in decline with its unused beds and closed trunks, with the presence of lives already lived. Not that we sensed this often. To us it was just our house. If there were too few people for too large a place, if the shadow of the dead dwarfed the living, we saw it only through the eyes of others—when a playmate turned quiet inside the big rooms, or once when the housekeeper swept cobwebs from a corner and muttered "mausoleum." Mostly we were absorbed by the immediacy of childhood, by a new litter of kittens or a fort in the woods.

All that would change. Two weeks after his 15th birthday, George fell 60 feet from the roof of a college observatory. He did not die in the accident but slowly, over a month's time. At the hospital, when it was my turn to read to him, I took his hand, now bigger than mine, and tried not to look at the swollen mask of his face. We read, but I thought he wasn't listening, that he was already in another place.

The day after the funeral, on a warm May morning, my mother and Aunt Elaine began the grim job of putting George's things away. His rabbit bones and plaid shirts, his assortment of astronomy texts—all were packed into trunks, which my father stored with the others in the attic. But I still felt George everywhere, and each morning at breakfast I sat beside his empty chair.

The losses, though smaller, continued. My aunt went to live with a cousin, and Gillian and I left for college soon after. That fall my grandmother slipped getting out of her car and fractured her hip. She entered a nursing home and would never return to the house. At Christmas my mother delivered a final piece of unhappy news: she had accepted a job in Portland and was looking for an apartment there; my father would not be going. I felt sad but not surprised. I knew about my mother's longing for the urban life she left when she married, and about the nights my father drank too much.

For ten years after my parents' divorce my father remained in the house, closing off one room after another until he was inhabiting just the original core. During that time I often visited my mother, who was content in her new condo, but I did not enjoy going back to the house. My dad would stay up too late—reading in my grandmother's chair by the fire—and I would lie in bed listening to mice in the walls and worrying about the plaster that had fallen from the ceiling.

In 1993 my father finally moved to a smaller place. When I sat with him at night on his new porch, relocating Orion and the dippers in the dark sky, I mostly felt relief. Even so, my father and Gillian and I cried at the closing of the sale of the house to a lawyer and his family. We felt sadder still when we heard about their financial trouble and the quick resale to a retired couple from Pennsylvania, who wanted to turn the place into an inn.

I awoke early the next morning to a tapping sound in the spruce outside my window. When I crossed the floor, it groaned in a place I remembered. The tapping stopped and a bird flew off, but not before I saw its red cap—surely not the woodpecker that woke me so many mornings when I was a child, but maybe one of its descendants.

In the kitchen a half-dozen guests sat around a pine table. Mrs. Keaton stood at the stove, pouring batter into a skillet. "Good morning," she said, gesturing toward a seat with her spatula. "There's coffee and juice on the table."

Gray skies and snow banked partway up the windows darkened the room. When I was in seventh grade, a series of blizzards dropped so much snow that the windows were blocked completely. Gillian and George and I would go down to breakfast and the lights would be on. At the same stove where Mrs. Keaton was standing now, my mother would fry eggs and issue admonishments: no playing in snow tunnels, no sliding off the roof. By March the windows offered a cross section of winter: two feet of packed powder, an inch of ice, a layer of leaves and twigs from a wind storm, two more feet of snow.

Mrs. Keaton set down a platter of pancakes, steaming and fragrant with cinnamon. I reached for syrup but did not pour. I felt queasy in this house that was no longer mine, trying to eat breakfast with strangers. Mrs. Keaton pulled up a chair, poured herself a cup of coffee. The man beside me asked her about cross-country skiing. Did she know any trails? Mrs. Keaton said no, but her husband might. I knew. The trail I trained on during high school began in the back field then ran along the brook. I said nothing.

Another guest mentioned the quilts on the beds. "They're beautiful," she said. "You have so many nice things."

"Thank you," said Mrs. Keaton. "It's been a lot of work. The place was empty when we moved in."

"When did you buy it?"

"Almost two years ago. From some folks who hadn't owned it long."

"It's lovely."

Mrs. Keaton sipped her coffee. "I think we'll be happy here," she said.

I thought about happiness as I tied my boots to go outdoors. In the years before George died, were we happy in this house? Certainly Gillian and George and I were loved. We were the center of life here, and we felt it—the source of my mother's laughter, the wearers of the sweaters my grandmother knitted. At night, after my father finished reading to me, he would kiss me on the forehead and say, "I love you, pup."

But there had been other things: the uneasiness between my parents, and the house itself, in need of constant repair. If the furnace wasn't broken, then the roof was leaking, and if the roof wasn't leaking then the water in the well was low. Still, the size of the house, and its age, and the fact that it always had been inhabited by my family made for a sense of belonging that absorbed everything else. We handled the arrowheads my great-grandfather had collected, and searched for our own in the back field. "You have your great-grandmother Elizabeth's eyes," someone would tell Gillian, and the proof would be upstairs in a portrait hanging on the wall. We knew who we were in this house, I thought.

Outside, the air bore traces of sulfur, the way it did when the wind shifted before a storm. It would be snowing by noon. I crossed to the spruce where the woodpecker had been drilling earlier. There was no sign of him but the top half of the trunk was pocked. I stepped closer; maybe he was hiding.

I saw the scratches on the bark before I remembered their meaning: G.E.B., C.L.B., G.P.P., G.B., 6/11/72 . . . The club had been George's idea, founded the week school let out when I was in fourth grade. George carved his and Gulliver's initials; Gillian and I signed our own. We draped old sheets on the outer branches to make a tent and met there each morning to plan the day—damming the brook for a swimming hole, or bicycling to a nearby peacock farm where, if we were lucky, one of the males would drop a feather or two.

One morning we collected quartz from the base of the cliffs. Back under the tree we sat on the prickly ground and wound wire around the stones to make jewelry. After lunch we set up a stand in front of the house. Bicyclists and other passersby stopped, but our best customer was our grandmother, who added earrings and necklaces to her already substantial collection of things we had made. As the coins accrued, George sat and calculated our gain at varying rates. $11.23 at seven percent for one year; $11.44 at nine percent... George droned on, and Gillian and I rolled our eyes. Why couldn't he be a normal seven-year-old?

My eyes filled. George is still here, I thought, he will never be anyplace else. All of us were still here, a little bit, the selves we left behind when we moved away toward the rest of our lives. In a couple of hours I would get in my car and drive to Gillian's house on the coast. My father would join us there, and we would sit at my great-grandmother's kitchen table and eat clams my sister had dug that morning. My sister's cats would settle on our laps, and we would talk about the snow tires my father recently bought for his mountain bike, and my brother-in-law's new job. My mother would call, for the third time that day, to talk about the baby girl Gillian is carrying: Do you have a car seat yet? she'd ask. I saw some nice ones today. When it was time to go my dad would kiss me on the forehead and say, "I love you, pup."

Near the porch the cross-country skier was knocking snow off his boots. "I used to ski around here," I told him. "There's a great trail if you go through the field and cross the brook. Turn right, then left when it forks."

He reached for his poles. "Thanks, that sounds great."

"Just keep an eye on the weather," I said. "I'm pretty sure it's going to snow."

The weekend after I went back to the house where I grew up, I was rummaging in the attic of the house where I live now, in a suburb close to Boston. I opened a trunk and set some photographs aside: a sepia print of the house just after my great-grandfather finished it; a shot of the garden bursting with hollyhocks and phlox; the family on the porch during a 1960s reunion; and George on Mount Katahdin, the last picture we have of him.

I had copies of the photographs made on Monday. When I finished packing them, I found some paper. Dear Mr. and Mrs. Keaton, I wrote. I used to live in your house. I don't know if you remember me, but not long ago I stayed there overnight, in the room where I slept as a child. I thought you might like some of these things . . . I put the letter inside and sealed the box to mail it. One more picture, of Gillian and George and me in bathing suits, arms looped around each other's shoulders, I set on top of the piano.

Three years ago, when we emptied the house, there was enough to furnish Gillian's place and mine twice over. Much of it we stored, for our children and our children's children. Still I read by the light of my grandmother's lamp, serve Thanksgiving dinner on the same china I grew up with. When my dad visits us, he says he feels as if he's back in the old place. "The house is here," he tells me, and I know he means more than just things.

A week after I mailed the box, a letter came from Mrs. Keaton. They were having the pictures framed, she said, thank you. Come back and see us anytime, she wrote. We will have your room ready for you.

I don't know when I'll go back, or if I ever will. But sometimes I think about the photographs hanging in the alcove off the foyer. I imagine guests pausing to look, wondering a moment about the family who once lived there.

Birth Mother

ROBERTA BROWN ROOT

TODAY IS MY DAUGHTER'S BIRTHDAY. KIM WILL TURN 33, BUT we have only been together for her last three birthdays.

On a shelf over my kitchen counter, next to a small ceramic doll that has topped every birthday cake of mine as far back as I remember, stands a framed photograph of my newfound daughter. She is wearing bib overalls, a baseball cap—worn backward—and red high-top sneakers. She sits on porch steps, elbows propped on knees, chin resting on balled fists. This picture of my daughter was taken the day we met. In it she looks much younger than her years, as if she has saved her childhood for me. For her birthday celebration, my daughter has requested cinnamon rolls, which I am baking. When I finish, I'll top the sticky buns with the little blond doll in the pink dress.

The sun is coming up over the Cascade Mountains. My daughter and I were both born shortly after sunrise. That, however, is the only thing the days of our birth have in common.

My parents were high school sweethearts—he a football star, she a drum majorette, along with her twin, Betty. Dad came from the Browns who owned the local paper, and Mom from the Browns who had the electrical business. When they wed, the newspaper headline read

"Brown Marries Brown," and as the time drew near for my mother to give birth to her first child—me—both families insisted that she come home to Minnesota from the small college town in South Dakota where she and Dad lived. Only Doc Ben could be entrusted with such an important delivery.

Listening to this story told to me repeatedly as a child, I visualized the day of my birth as a festive event with only the fireworks missing, the trip to Waseca Memorial Hospital a parade: Mother, always the majorette, led the way, screaming, "Hurry, hurry, the baby's coming!" while Betty pushed the wheelchair and echoed the cry. At this point in the tale, someone always mentions that Mrs. Downey, who had her baby the day before, recognized the voices, and shouted, "God be with you, Bonnie!" from her bed. By the time I was born, the news had spread and seven Brown grandparents—greats included—were on the scene.

How different was my own birthing journey, leaving months in advance, traveling 2,000 miles from home to hide while I awaited my unwanted child.

The sky is clear outside my kitchen window, the lake a deep blue. A heron stands on one leg at the end of my dock, fishing. I stop to watch him, pouring myself a cup of warm milk to which I add a splash of coffee, a tradition handed down from my great-grandmother. My daughter wasn't present to acquire my family's traditions, and she has rejected those of her adoptive family. Instead, she creates her own, abandoning them when she finds new, more interesting ones.

I reach to the top shelf for my grandmother's footed cake plate. Next to it sit large white enamel bowls with dark navy rims and two lidded square containers, matching—also hers. My daughter throws things away. Recycling, she calls it. She then buys new. "Things are things," she says. "They don't mean diddly." She has nothing from the family that raised her. "They wanted a real heir," she explains. And she must think, if a baby can be given away, what should be saved?

How often I had run across Elm Avenue to my grandmother's, where those bowls were filled with potato salad, or fruit salad loaded with whipped cream and red maraschino cherries. The little square enamel boxes were packed with side dishes—the cucumber slices Grandma called bread-and-butter pickles, and dark red pickled beets, which smelled strongly of vinegar and cloves.

Kim pushes pickled beets to the side of her plate. "Beets," she says, scrunching up her face endearingly, like a four-year-old. "I hate pickled beets."

"Didn't you have pickled beets as a child?" I ask.

"My mother didn't cook," she says. "She drank. Remember?"

She says this matter-of-factly. Without self-pity. But her mood has changed. It's not about the beets—I know that, yet I want her to eat them. I want them to be a potion for her. I want her to swallow them and be filled with the women who came before us. The grandmas, the great-grandmas, the aunts, the great-aunts.

The adoption agency had promised a good home. "Teachers for parents," they had said. "Four children—she'll be the youngest." I had pictured trips to the beach, big family picnics in the park, and birthday parties, lots of birthday parties with balloons, hats, and noisemakers, maybe her own cake-top decoration. This imagined childhood had offered me solace over the years. But now there is a real face and a real voice to tell me otherwise.

"Did you love my father?" she asks.

There is no easy answer. If I say no, I will sound irresponsible. If I say yes, she will wonder why we didn't marry.

"It was a summer romance," I say, finally. "We were devoted to one another, but I wouldn't call it love." A summer of grief was what it had been. My darling grandmother dying, my mother huddled over the deathbed. Then the casket, open in front of the living room picture window, me crying in the yard, not caring that the minister promised heaven. The big house on Elm Avenue to which I had run on my way home from school was vacant now, a For Sale sign punched into the front lawn.

"In your father's arms," I tell my daughter, "was the only place I felt alive." For a while, anyway. "We couldn't get married," I say. "I hadn't even finished high school." We agreed to my parents' request that we never see each other again. "There were no choices in those days," I tell my daughter feebly—my reasons sound like excuses.

My daughter absolves me. "I don't blame you—I understand." She never gets angry with me, no matter how much I encourage her to. There is no room for anger in our relationship—she is too frightened that I'll leave her again. But she must be angry. How could she possibly understand that to be pregnant and unmarried then was a scandal, when today single women can become pregnant by choice, and if they are celebrities, can parade their babies before the public.

Pregnant at 17, I sit solemnly next to my mother. "Don't tell a soul—not even your friends," she says. "If they guess, don't admit anything." We are on our way to California, where I will stay with Aunt Betty until I show, then I will move to The Door of Hope. Unlike my mother's first delivery, mine would end not with a celebration but would take place in a labor room containing one single bed, no chair at its side.

In that room, my child, eager to be born, forces her way into the world while I, frozen with fear, resist every contraction. A woman in a uniform sits at a desk in the dark hallway outside my room. Periodically she administers an injection that induces confusion but leaves the pain undiminished. Maybe this will give you something to think about, she seems to say. My daughter is born the following morning. I remember shame-filled screams, a whirling delivery room, cold forceps, numb muscles that couldn't comprehend PUSH.

Three days pass. Three days I have slept through. I sit on the edge of the bed, gingerly. Sun streams into the room. It's hot. I'm sweaty. A woman from the adoption agency has awakened me to sign papers. She reminds me that if I care for the child at all, I will do the right thing and give her away. She deserves a decent life with decent people. This is not only for the good of the child, she tells me, but also for my family who have done nothing to deserve this embarrassment.

"Have you named her?" the woman asks. "You know that you need a name for the birth certificate." She tells me not to waste a name I might want to use later.

"Wendy," I say, after the Peter Pan character. It's a never-grow-up name. I allow myself this sentimentality. The woman tells me that I should give her the father's last name, "Just in case she someday sees the birth certificate. She doesn't need to know she's illegitimate—she might think you died. It's better that way." I do exactly as the woman says.

A nurse comes into my room. "Follow me," she says. "You can hold the baby." I feel weak. The nurse turns the key in the nursery door. I have stood here before but the glass was curtained to keep the sinful mothers from seeing their babies. "Sit," the nurse says. The rocking chair, wooden, is unforgiving against my ripped and stitched bottom. I wince.

The nurse picks up a child, mummy-wrapped in a receiving blanket, and hands her to me. I take the sleeping baby, sigh, and close my eyes. I don't want to feel anything. When I open my eyes again the nurse is standing in front of me holding out a bottle of milk.

I know what to do with babies. I was ten when my brother was born. Every morning I got him up and dressed him before I went to school. My parents worried that my hip would become deformed because I spent so much time carrying him on it. I was crazy for babies. I wanted four. I had the girls' names picked: Hannah and Isabel—my grandmothers' names. The boys'—movie star names—kept changing.

I touch the rubber nipple to my sleeping baby's lips. Moving it back and forth, I try to wake her. It's obvious she has just been fed and this is some strange formality The Door of Hope believes in. The baby stirs on my lap. I should be talking to her, telling her things, enough to last a lifetime. I know I will only hold her this once. I study her face. She has more hair than any child I have ever seen, dark brown hair that stands on end. Her face is tiny. She looks like her father.

I stand to the side as the nurse diapers my baby, then she hands me a white kimono. The baby suddenly startles. I wrap my fingers around her little arms and hold them securely against her body. The gesture calms her. I lift my baby onto the kimono, pushing her arms into the sleeves, tying the little pink ribbons in front. I am intent. My hands, remembering my brother, work deftly, automatically.

Before putting on the booties, I quickly count my daughter's toes. They are identical to mine and to my mother's, second toe longer than first, baby toe nearly nonexistent. Her tiny foot is slender and perfect.

I wrap her in the receiving blanket, snugly so she'll feel safe. I pick her up intending to give her to the woman from the agency, but instead

I bring her to my breast aching with milk, kiss her cheek, push my face into her neck, smell the powder. The woman holds out her arms. "You'll soon forget," she says, taking the child. "Better not to get too attached."

The woman turns and walks away. Suddenly, I am running after her. "One more thing," I say. I pick up my daughter's hands and look at her fingers—they are long and tapered, the fingernails are square, like my grandmother's, my father's, mine. I tuck the hand into the receiving blanket. I want to kiss it, but I feel dirty in the eyes of this woman, and I know the kiss will not be enough. I would need to gobble her up to be satisfied.

I telephone my parents. "It's over," I say. "They took her away." I hear tears in their silence. They, who have raised four, understand more than I what it means to lose a child. I go back to bed and fall into a sleep deep enough to last for 30 years.

I lift the risen dough from the bowl. When I was a child making bread with my grandmother, I would watch her hands at work, pushing, pulling, rolling the dough. How often I repeated these motions with my other children helping—the three I raised. When I knead, I always think of my grandmother's hands, the hands my first daughter inherited, but she and I don't have warm memories of doing things together. Our history is pain. We must create a future that will fill in our past.

"Let's bake bread together," I say to her.

"I'll watch," she says. "You bake." Her mother criticized, she reminds me. "I could never do anything right, and I hated to make her mad. When she was mad, she drank. When she drank, she reminded me of my adoption fee—she called me her $1,000 mistake."

At home, alone in her own apartment—which, since she has moved to Seattle, is close to my house—Kim rehearses what she has watched me do. In the safety of her own kitchen she bakes bread, makes jelly, freezes pesto and sun-dried tomatoes. She is still afraid to work with me. I might find fault, abandon her for some blunder, but I see that she is beginning to trust me. "It helps," she says, "that you came looking for me."

Three years ago I wrote a letter to the adoption agency giving legal consent for my daughter to make contact with me. They would need two letters, they said, one from each of us, to arrange a meeting. Within a week I heard from them, within three, we had met.

Driving to our reunion, noting the landmarks on the route that Kim gave us, I felt so still inside that it frightened me. Anxiety would have been preferable. I asked Randy, the man I have lived with since my divorce many years ago, whether he thought I was okay. He smiled and nodded. The brown motel my daughter drew on the map whizzed by on the right but I was lulled by the tall redwoods, and when the balloons appeared at the side of the road, just as she said they would, I was taken by surprise.

The car rounded the corner of her driveway—I was unaware that it was still moving. I pushed the door open, Randy shouted, "Wait!" but my foot hit the pavement as if the car was a scooter. Randy slammed on the brakes as I lunged, leaving him and the car in the middle of the turn. Without warning a sound rose from within me. I didn't notice it at the time; only later did I remember. I have never before made this sound. It had an inhuman quality, the wail of an animal, the cry of labor. My daughter heard me before she saw me from the open window where she sat waiting. Our embrace was a desperate clutch. The noise stopped as abruptly as it began, and Kim, taking me by the hand, led me into the house.

She showed me her room. The walls were lined with Gumby dolls, teddy bears, a clown with a sad smiling face. Such power, I said, in a never-grow-up-name you didn't know you had. She rolled her eyes, shrugged her shoulders, threw back her head and laughed a silent laugh. I recognized the laugh, complete with the mannerisms. It belongs to her father. Thirty years ago, I thought it unique.

Before long we were ripping off shoes and socks, pointing at the long middle toe. "What a relief," she said. "We're alike."

My three other grown children used to refer to their newfound sibling as "my mother's daughter," but now I hear them talking about their sister. They have adjusted to the unspoken lie from a mother who preached honesty. At first Kim wanted to call me Mom but I couldn't bear it. What kind of mom hands her child over to a stranger? On their birthdays, I tell the others the story of the day they were born. To my newly found daughter, I say simply, "You were born at The Door of Hope. You had hair. So much hair. More than the other three put together." I know it's not enough, but I have nothing more to offer.

I take the cinnamon rolls from the oven and arrange them on my grandmother's footed cake plate. With a knife I make waves of white frosting, one cresting the other. When I have finished, I reach for the little girl in the pink dress and place her squarely in the center. She stands there precariously; her balance is off. With a firm hand I push her deeper into the sticky buns, until I'm sure she's safe.

Solid Gold

STARR COLLINS OSBORNE

I AM STAYING AT THE HOUSE I GREW UP IN SO I CAN HEAR MY father lecture about his childhood at the annual Mark Twain Memorial Luncheon. It's the last night I will ever spend here.

Daddy grew up in downtown Hartford on a big city block that was home to some 85 of my relatives around the turn of the century. They occupied 12 Victorian houses whose backyards—and children—ran together. In 1938, when my father was a junior at Yale, the family sold out and moved to the suburbs. The houses were demolished to make way for a hospital; the main driveway gates were moved to the entrance of the West Hartford reservoir. Gone forever are the days when cousins would go to Europe and bring back Italian coffered ceilings to install in their living rooms, when my great-grandfather, president of a trust company and chairman of the city parks department, could have the clanging trolleys rerouted during his daily afternoon nap; but the block has become part of our familial DNA.

Of the nearby writers' colony only the houses of Mark Twain and Harriet Beecher Stowe remain. The Collins family name is found only on a few street signs and some stained glass windows at the nearby Asylum Hill Congregational Church, of which my great-great-grandfather was a founder. We still have more windows dedicated to our dead than any other family at the institution Mark Twain called "The Church of the Holy Speculators."

At the lecture, my father describes the architectural and human history of the family block, recounting how Twain, Sam Clemens to his neighbors, came to call on my triple-great-aunts. The author and former riverboat pilot was a bit too casually dressed for those Yankee spinsters, and the visit was not a complete success. Later that afternoon, a box arrived from Clemens, in it a bow tie. The note attached read, "This is the tie that should have called with Mr. Clemens." Booker T. Washington also visited the block, staying with my great-grandparents when he lectured in Hartford. According to family lore, the Irish maids refused to wait on Washington because he was a Negro. My great-grandmother, in what was probably a political statement as well as simple courtesy, cooked and served all of the great educator's meals.

The Twain Memorial Luncheon is oversubscribed, by strangers who want to hear about my father's early days and by cousins who actually remember them. And here I am, age 31, having driven five hours to hear my father speak of his childhood just when I feel that the sale of his house is irrevocably drawing the curtain on mine; I am surprised about how childishly petulant I feel. Already our rooms are being stripped and packed. By next month my parents will be living in a condo.

My childhood was spent in West Hartford on Sunset Farm, one of the first planned communities in the United States. The land, a large horse farm when the area was still country, had been bought by a friend of my grandfather's in the early thirties. My grandfather was one of the first to settle on this parcel, with its widely separated Tudor and Colonial Revival houses behind their fences on a system of winding private roads and riding trails. The beautiful landscape, much of it wild, is dotted by ponds and streams, every inch of which I still know by heart. Even today I can find where the lady's slippers bloom.

The Mark Twain lecture went well because my father is a wonderful raconteur. I remember that when we were little he used to give us back rubs before bed and tell us "Apple Tree Stories," a serial drama he created about Foxy and Coonie and the other animals who lived in the crab apple tree in our front yard. One May night we looked out into the branches and there, in a cloud of blossoms, nine pairs of eyes shone back at us, reflecting the lights of the house like a string of tiny Christmas bulbs. Mrs. Coonie had had babies, and because my father had not included them in our stories, she came to show them to us herself.

Our brick house, built around 1940 in the William and Mary style, generously wrapped itself around our lives. In this place I was always a girl. It was safe home, where I could slam doors, read in the afternoon sun, disappear for hours to work in the darkroom. My father lived here 45 years, my mother 32; my grandparents once lived three houses away, but by the time I was born my grandmother occupied the bedroom next to mine. We wandered in and out of each other's worlds, down corridors covered in Williamsburg reproduction wallpaper.

Now the extra andirons and crystal and my old bedroom furniture have been tagged for sale, and the refrigerator, covered with bumper stickers—"Luray Caverns," "Palm Beach Polo," "Old Friends Are Worth Keeping"—is destined for the basement of the condo.

The house is stained with our tears, but I like to think our laughter will still echo in the halls. My parents were married in the tiny front garden in June 1962. It was the second time for each of them. My mother's son, Faulkie, my father's son, Woody, my mother's poodles, and various family members in Jackie Kennedy–style suits and white gloves were in attendance. This I learned from looking at the large leather-bound picture albums in the study, which I memorized during the cocktail hours of my childhood, the one time of day when all the children and grown-ups gathered together. I was born the June after the wedding, my sister Natalie in October the year after that.

One spring night when I was three, I must have been drifting off to sleep, smelling as always the dampness of the brook outside my windows. Faulkie and my father, whom Faulkie had asked permission to call Dad, were in the driveway trying to fix the radio in my father's Jaguar. They had no luck—the Jag was always broken in one way or another—and Faulkie drove off on his motorcycle to meet his pals at Friendly's, the neighborhood hangout. He had an appointment to sell the bike, but he never got there. Someone going 50 miles an hour drove right through him while Faulkie was at a full stop. My father was still tinkering with the cars when he heard the ambulance a mile away on Farmington Avenue.

Hundreds attended Faulkie's memorial service, most of them kids, but I wasn't there. No one explained his death to me, why Faulkie didn't come back. I guess they thought they were protecting me.

I was hurt that Faulkie had left me. They tell me I wouldn't sleep and wandered the halls calling for him at night. The remedy was a summer of phenobarbital, which made my understanding of the loss even hazier. My two teenage half-brothers had doted on me, exhausting their sibling rivalry impulses on each other. Woody was home only on vacations, pushing through his last years at Hotchkiss and first years at Yale. But Faulkie, for whom boarding school was but a painful memory, had lived at home. Although he was only 19, he was engaged. I don't remember his fiancée; I didn't think about his world beyond me. When he wasn't working at the gas station or studying for his high school equivalency exams, Faulkie played with me. I taught him how to play dolls. He in turn would strap me into his Corvette and drive at high speed around Sunset Farm's curving roads, telling me about handling and traction as if it were a bedtime story. I followed him around everywhere. He taught me to dance to the Beatles and how to shave, lathering up my cheeks every morning and slicing it off with his finger. Perhaps I remember more than a three-year-old usually does because I lost him.

Now, whenever anything happened, I silently wondered what it would have been like if Faulkie had been there. We children spent endless winter evenings eating at the kitchen table while Mom prepared the grown-ups' dinner, NBC news always in the background, until my father's headlights swept the driveway and the electric garage doors swallowed him back into the house.

Life went on without Faulkie. The youngest two in the household, my sister and I were simultaneously adored and forgotten, a tightrope we walked easily. Our place at a grown-ups' dinner was under the table, studying adult knees, trying to make the dogs lie on the buzzer under the Oriental rug that was designed to summon a maid. We were routinely put to bed with the same relaxed affection shown the dogs when they were put out to do their business.

At holidays and every Sunday for church we had to dress in velvet and patent leather. But we were also free to explore the brook leading to the upper pond, to wash cars, to bake marble cake in our turquoise Easy-Bake oven with its exceedingly powerful lightbulb heat source and offer morsels of it at cocktail time to our parents and grandmother. On Christmas Eve, Santa (a chubby friend of Faulkie's in costume) would visit, leaving packages with Dawn dolls in them, smaller versions of Barbie. He once dropped a sleigh bell on the brick front walk, excellent evidence to bring to school as proof of the mythic visit. Every Christmas breakfast, after stockings and before the tree, the rare pileated woodpecker would arrive. At the first BB-gunlike sound in our cedar tree, my dad would grab the binoculars, scanning the woods for the big bird. We would all watch until it flew away, knowing we would not see that flaming head blaze through the morning until next year when he would come again to celebrate Baby Jesus's birth.

In our house we never had rules, but we could sense them. We were taught responsibility, respect for others, and common sense. One summer night I awoke to yelling in the backyard. From the window I could see my father and Woody running across the backyard in their shorts waving brooms. A fox had gotten into the duck house. Someone had forgotten to lock the door after feeding time—me. I was so ashamed I couldn't even speak. I knew I had failed and caused the deaths of two of my ducks, but nobody scolded me.

Most of my friends lived in conventional households, and I reveled in how different my family was. The major figure keeping things lively was my mother. One of her typical games was testing how soon she could hit the switch on the car visor that closed our garage doors—loads of fun until the ski rack was ripped off the car roof. Probably the most expensive amusement she schemed up for us was painting her bedroom and sitting room. "Go wild," she said to Natalie and me, "the painters come Monday." We made bold yellow and black smiley faces and daisies and horses. The workmen painted the rooms an icy celadon and our images showed through. In the end it took three extra coats to cover our schoolgirl pentimenti.

My mother's greatest ally was our middle-aged housekeeper-nanny,

Gwen. She had worked as a young woman at the foundling hospital my grandmother established. Gwen could answer every *Jeopardy* question, all the while preparing the children's dinner. I can still feel her laugh vibrate as I lay against her bosom listening to her read a cowboy book.

My grandmother used to sing us to sleep with terrifying lullabies about a black fox that she had learned in her Edwardian English childhood. I knew this fox lived underneath my bed and would grab my ankles given the chance, which caused me to use a triangular reading pillow as a springboard to my mattress every night. Later Gram's round-the-clock nurses came into our young lives. When round-the-clock nurses are present, children have no need for cross-cultural school programs. Viola, a Jamaican nurse, taught us how to cook with coconuts, siphoning the juice and broiling the meat. She believed in hell and told us about it in delicious detail.

Nurse Louise would play with us like an older child during my grandmother's naps. Looking back I realize she was probably younger than I am now. She taught us to use stilts on the asphalt driveway, sometimes refusing to share them until my mother intervened. One winter, Bunny, the night nurse, was the main topic of conversation among the females of the house. Everyone wondered when she would tell us she was pregnant. This would be the eighth child born to Bunny and her husband. "True to her name," I heard Gwen say. Natalie and I would try to wake up before Bunny left in the morning so we could scrutinize her stomach. One night when I couldn't sleep I went to the nurses' room, lay down, and talked to Bunny till morning, and finally she told me. I could hardly wait for her to leave so I could spill the beans. I was the honored one. The next day she told my father, but she had told me first.

We didn't have Mark Twain, but we had our own colorful characters, and I learned to love them all for who they were. I learned how to play one against the other and which one to ask to get what I wanted. I learned about community, about social survival. I learned that no two people see things the same way.

What makes me saddest about the sale of our house is leaving the scene of my few memories of Faulkie. When my mom next walks down the path in our woods to plant bulbs around his memorial stone, she will have driven from a home my brother never knew. I have taken my last swim in the spring-fed pond near his stone, and I didn't know at the time to mark the occasion.

But it is comforting to hear my father lecture about his history. His vanished childhood is still very much with him, as mine is with me. Although we no longer have the material details of this house or his previous house to prompt us, I realize we know our stories by heart. My life was like liquid gold, cast in the mold of our house in Sunset Farm.

Eldor's Hut

SHARON WHITE

I SAW ELDOR'S HUT FROM THE OUTSIDE FIRST, A SMALL, ROUND building made of rough wood with a sod roof. Through a square window the size of my face, I could see wooden benches built into the walls for beds and a tiny wooden table pressed under the window. The hut was perfect, sitting in a cluster of slim birch trees in a forest in northern Norway. I could hear the sound of a large waterfall. Men who fished for arctic char in the nearby lake used the place, and sometimes people went there and picked cloudberries, that sweet, spicy, salmon-colored fruit of the north.

I slept in the hut years later. I was a young widow. My husband had died a year after we were married; he was 33. Two years later, I flew to Alta, Norway, because I wanted to be happy again. I was traveling to spend a few weeks in Båteng, a place dark most of the winter, blazing with sun all summer. A man I had met 12 years before wanted to marry me. I had written to Harald after my husband's death. Harald wanted a child. He wanted me to live with him in the town where his family lived and worked on the fertile banks of the Tana River.

It was my second visit to Båteng, a small village in the part of Norway that curves above Sweden and Finland and touches Russia. When I first went to Båteng, I was very young. It was a year after I graduated from college. I was going to work on a farm for several months in a Norwegian program called International Youth Work. I had asked to be placed on a farm as far north as possible. I took the mail boat up the coast past the Lofoten Islands and their turquoise sea. I saw a herd of reindeer swimming across the harbor at Harstad and watched as the landscape flattened and grew long and dark at the edges.

In Båteng, I lived in a house with a farmer and his wife and two of their three sons. The farm was a cluster of buildings: a barn; a dairy with a stone floor; a split-level house painted lime green; the original house, tall and narrow, now an office for a Mazda dealership; and a red sauna shed with one round window. The middle son lived with his wife and two children in the basement of the new house. My room upstairs was small with only a single window. The family farmed fields by the river and on the edge of the forest.

The fields were bare and cold in May, with snow in patches on the low hills across the river in Finland. My favorite places on the farm were the sauna and the dairy. I liked the way the calves bit at my arms and licked my shoulder with their rough tongues. I got used to the smell of cow dung as I shoveled it clear of the stalls. I walked up to the forest where the birch trees were leafing out. When I ran above the town on the paved road, I could almost feel the earth turn.

As the days grew warmer I began to like my life in Båteng more and more. I knew something was happening to me. After a month working on the farm, I fell in love with Harald, a bachelor and the eldest son, ten years older than I was.

He managed the farm and owned the Mazda dealership with his two brothers. Harald could speak several languages. He knew where to find the bird he called the English eagle and showed me where foxes lived in a sandy esker near the village. He was a sportsman, he told me, and proved it in long walks across the forest and, on my second visit, in his skill at skiing. I was 22 and in a strange and beautiful place. Harald was powerful and mysterious. I was afraid of him at first.

We picked cloudberries in the forest and ate them with fresh cream and sugar. I swam in the Tana, a river that flows into the Arctic Ocean but warms quickly, its shallow, clear water thick with salmon as large as a small child. I started to learn a few words of Lappish, the language of most of the people along the river.

We walked hours into the forest to waterfalls lit at night with the low sun of the north. The light glowed under the birch leaves and illuminated the tiny red spores of moss. Sometimes we slept on reindeer skins in a cottage his uncle built for the harvest. After days of work in the barn and the fields, we took saunas in the little shed. I shook sweet branches dipped in cold water on my body, soft in the steam from heated rocks.

When the weather was clear, I pulled cut hay to be dried on wires strung across the fields. We ate pieces of salmon grilled over a fire of sticks gathered on the riverbank, where slim black boats were tethered. In the evening I would hear Harald walking across the gravel of the road, a white pitcher in his hand, to collect milk from the dairy for dinner.

After a party one night, when people were dancing near a blazing fire by the river, Harald told me his uncle had said to him, "You will lose the American girl."

"You see," Harald said, "I don't know what it is—this word love. I feel for you a little more, not less."

One morning I got up and fainted onto the kitchen floor. I cut my head, and Harald's youngest brother, Knut, who was visiting from Bergen, patched up the gash. Later, Harald took me to the clinic several miles away and I was stitched up and bandaged.

I told Harald I was leaving soon. It was early September and already the birches had turned their brittle gold. I imagined I would return. I could see myself living in a house above the town.

When I got home in the fall, I knew something was wrong with me. I thought it was a broken heart. My doctor performed several tests. He told me I had a parasite from eating uncooked salmon. I wrote to Harald. He sent me a silk shawl and photographs of the new shop he was building.

"When will you come to visit us in Båteng?" he asked in his short letters.

I was not convinced that he loved me. I was swept along into another life and I stopped thinking I would go back to Norway. I married at 30.

When I returned to Båteng, I was 34. I woke that first morning in a new cottage Knut had built on the edge of a small field opposite his parents' house. Black shiny crows skimmed the white field. I admired the practical beauty of the cottage: sleeping closet in the kitchen, the boards of the walls washed with white paint, rag rugs scattered on the floors.

Some days, as I lit the stove at four and waited for Harald to finish working, March's early darkness frightened me. I called my mother in a panic. I wanted her to tell me to come home. All I could feel was the whiteness of those hills, the gray edge of the water, the smooth stones of the Arctic beaches. They were so smooth—sometimes I thought I too would like to be ground like that by waves and put to rest on some gritty beach.

One day we watched Harald's father stuff a paper sack full of candy in his pocket before riding his snowmobile to Eldor's hut, cutting a trail for us, dragging a pack wrapped in skins on the back of a track setter. We were skiing to the hut I had seen 12 years ago. Finally I would open the little door and sit on the bench and look out through the square window the size of my face.

We skied to the clearing where the hut sits beside a frozen lake full of char, covered with snow and prints of reindeer, the tracks of a wolf who called out at dusk. We kicked off our skis and stooped to enter and threw our gear on the wooden benches. I felt their worn wood, rubbed my finger on the glass of the window, peering out this time at Harald splitting wood. He knocked an ax through the slim birch logs for the little stove. I could hear the trickle of water under the frozen waterfall. When he opened the door I held his cold hands against my face. Soon the hut was warm.

My trip to Båteng seemed to finish something started 12 years before—it broke the spell. I made a list of the attributes of the child we might have. I thought about commuting between this world and the other.

After I spent two weeks in Båteng, Harald drove me to the airport in Lakselv.

"You have a problem," he said.

"Which one?" I asked.

"About living in Båteng."

I took the mail plane out of Lakselv and flew south. The plane was small and there was only one other passenger.

"We will fly low," one of the pilots told me. Below there were glaciers, reindeer running, half buried in windblown snow.

I did not return to Harald. I put away the silk shawl he sent me. I continued my life in a place far away from the dark winters and blazing summers of Båteng. Three years later, I married a man who had grown up 35 miles from me. Now we live near another wide shallow river. Our eight-year-old son believes in magic doors to wild lands. Sometimes I think I would like to take him to Eldor's hut.

Watching the Longhaired Fawn

STEVE ELLIOTT

I HATED THE FIRST NIGHT I SPENT HERE, EVERYTHING ABOUT IT.

I hated that I lived in a single-wide mobile home a mile down a dirt road. I hated that everything I owned fit inside with room to spare. I hated that I now lived alone. I do not have a TV and on that first night I had not unpacked my radio. The phone was not hooked up either, so there was no way I could call or make Internet contact with someone—anyone.

All I had was me, and that was not company I was real fond of at the moment.

This is starting over, I told myself. Millions of people do it, some after real tragedies. And this is not a tragedy. This is a marriage ending for reasons right and reasons wrong, actions taken and actions not taken. It was necessary, I told myself. None of that matters, of course, when you are alone and the tears won't stop.

The next morning I saw the deer for the first time. Or maybe it was the day after. There are four deer that live on the hill here with me, although I have seen as many as seven at once. They come out every morning and evening to graze on the sparse grass that grows outside the living-room end of the trailer or on leaves that have fallen to the ground.

The ones I see most often are two does and two fawns, one still a spindly-legged baby. The little one's coat is not smooth and short like the others'; it is long and shaggy and multicolored. I always look for the baby first and smile when he comes close.

The second morning I saw them, the fawns were playing. The little one was running laps as near as I could tell, bounding down the hill at full-tilt, circling around and coming up on the other fawn from behind, then tearing off to do it again. The older one played like a kitten, pawing at the ground, leaping straight-legged in mock surprise, rooting and pawing again. I had to stifle my laughter so I would not scare them away.

When I realized that I was seeing the same four deer day after day, my thought was to give them names. Almost immediately I realized how stupid that would be. The deer certainly would not care, and it was not as though naming them would make them "my deer" somehow. I don't want that anyway. I just want to share the hill with them and watch the long-haired baby grow up. I want never to lose the sense of wonder I feel seeing them walk by so gracefully. Today they were lying together in the morning sun. I made coffee and sat at the window, just watching.

After the marriage fell apart, I took a transfer with my company from our main office in California's Central Valley to a small branch in the Sierra Nevada foothills, the mother lode. It is beautiful here, destination country for skiers and hikers and campers. I am 70 miles from Yosemite, 20 miles from a national forest, and ten miles from the mine where they dug up a 300-pound gold boulder a few years ago.

It took me a while to find the single-wide. There were not many rentals available, none that I could afford anyway. I looked at a couple of apartments, but the thought of moving to this lovely area to live in an apartment in town just didn't make sense. I looked at one property that advertised itself as a "small country cabin in rural setting." Translation: shack. I couldn't even stand upright in it. So when the single-wide showed up in the local want ads, I called and got directions.

I almost didn't see the place. As I switched from one bad dirt road onto another, I was ready to turn back. I thought it was too far out and I wasn't even there yet. But at last I got to the trailer on top of the hill and my opinion changed. The view looks back over the area I had just driven through—its name is Peaceful Valley. The trailer is at the end of the road, surrounded by oaks, a few pines, and manzanita—squirrels were chasing each other through the branches. It is a small trailer, ten feet wide and 40 feet long, but it was clean and seemed solid.

At the house my wife and I had shared, there is a workshop in the backyard that measures ten by 20 feet. When the landlord told me the dimensions of the trailer, I could not suppress a bitter smile. My wife and I did not live in a palace, but our house was nice and roomy, with vaulted ceilings and a fireplace. It was our first home and we thought it was perfect. And now I was considering a trailer that looked a lot more like my old shop.

But the ride back to town did not seem as long as the ride up, and the rent was affordable, so when the landlord called later that week to offer me a lease I took it.

One of the first things I came to appreciate about living here was the silence. The woods at 2,800 feet can sound like a symphony during a storm, but when the wind is still, the silence is amazing. At first, my brain kept trying to fill it. One day when I was sitting on a moss-covered rock by the dry stream bed on the back of the hill, I heard a low sound, almost a hum, coming from everywhere. It was not really there. Silence is the total lack of sound, but when your ears and your brain have never been this far out of a city, have never really experienced absolute quiet, they do not know how to process it. The hum is a phantom noise, like the pain an amputee feels in a lost limb. The hum fades as you grow used to the stillness, and I have come to appreciate that stillness greatly, both outside and inside myself.

Slowly I started getting stuff I needed. I didn't buy much; one of the things wrong with the marriage was the amount of clutter we had let into our lives. I would not allow that to happen again, but I did not plan to occupy an empty box either. I didn't want to feel like a guest, as though I was camping here. This is where I live now, I told myself, so it may as well be home. Yet I still did not believe that in my heart. Home was still the place I had left—the wife, cats, and 100-pound dog

I loved, the house we all shared. This was an address, basic housing, more than anything a reminder of everything I had lost and left behind.

I started small: a set of dishes and flatware for four. The dishes are plain off-white stoneware with simple green rings around the edges. There were other colors to choose from but green suits the location. I found a teapot that matches. I bought a small, unstained wood table and two chairs and set them beneath the window that looks out over Peaceful Valley. It is a wonderful view, even during the moments I am not aware of it. I am at the table a lot, reading or writing or just watching the sun stream through the oaks. I paid bills here once and won't do that again. I have a desk and a room without a view in the middle of the trailer where I prefer to pay the bills and do my taxes and handle all the other business of living.

The window I save for inspiration.

A friend of mine gave me a small couch that fits perfectly against the wall opposite the table, and in the afternoon the sun pours across it like syrup. If it catches you there, you stay and finally get an idea of what it must be like to be a cat on a warm windowsill. That is about all the furniture that fits in here. I made a list of other things I wanted and some of the items surprised me. Like kitchen knives. My mother-in-law had given us a set for Christmas a few years ago, and they turned out to be maddeningly mediocre: just bad enough to always bug me, just good enough that I could never justify throwing them out. So as I made my list, I discovered I wanted a good set of knives.

I didn't buy them, though. I shopped several times, in several places, but could never bring myself to put some decent knives in my shopping basket. At least I could not bring myself to settle for a lousy cheapo set, either. Partly it was the money. Starting from scratch costs a fortune, even when you don't buy much. Mostly it was guilt—an ugly little voice inside me saying things like, "Why the hell do you deserve good knives now? You didn't get them before. You didn't buy them for her, to share. But now, after you walked away from your marriage, a failure, now you want good knives." To make matters worse, I had brought some of the old knives with me. Not even the whole set—just enough of them to make it difficult to buy new ones.

My mom finally got me out of that spot. She had been worrying about me since things got rocky, and wanted to help any way she could. When I moved here, one of the first things she said was that she would come up and help me stock it. It took a few weeks to make our schedules work out, but finally one Saturday, after I gave her careful directions, she made the hour-and-a-half drive.

I was worried that she would think I was too remote, too far out on a bad road. I was afraid she would be polite about my trailer and say something like it would be OK until I could find a real house. But when my mom got here, she surprised me. She liked it. She didn't mind the road, and I could see her breathe deep, inhaling the clean air I already loved. "This would be a great place to be when it rains," she said. I made her a key so she can come up here and sit in the silence—or the rain—whenever she wants.

That afternoon she took me shopping and bought everything that was left on my list. The knives I wanted are on my counter: black handles, full tangs, stainless-steel rivets. I oiled the block and sharpened the blades and I love reaching for them, picking the right knife for the job instead of the only one left that doesn't have a loose handle. When I am done with them, I wash the blades and wipe them dry and put them back in the block immediately. They are never lying around on the counter. They never sit in the sink. They are not taken for granted. I wish I had learned that lesson sooner, when I still had a marriage to apply it to. Start with something good and take the time and make the effort and learn how to care for it. The little things do matter, in a home and in a life. I am learning that here.

I remember the first time I thought of the trailer as home. I was driving up after work one night, late. It was already full dark. The last bit of road is an S-curve, around a granite boulder, then you are on the hilltop. When I made that turn and my headlights found the trailer, I smiled. It surprised me. But I have since discovered that when I go back into the city where I used to live, I can taste the air. Everything is hazy, dirty somehow. I can't breathe as deeply.

It was the storm that really convinced me, though.

The storm came on a Friday. I was lucky to be here. I should have been at work, but I had to go in Sunday instead. Having a day to relax and think sounded really, really nice, so I just stayed put. Earlier that week, my therapist (another new thing in my life since the split) asked me about home. I had told him that was one of the hardest losses, one of the things I really missed, the home I left.

"What does home mean to you?" he asked. It took me a while to answer. The important questions always do. "Home is where you are safe," I said. "The place where you belong." Not much of an insight, I know, but I had never really thought about it before and that was the best I could do.

I was thinking about it that Friday as I watched the storm move in. It built slowly, from the west. The sky changed from smoke to slate to gunmetal, and the wind appeared in a moment, like someone hit a switch. The rain was everything my mom imagined it would be, dancing on the flat metal roof, tapping out rhythms and patterns only the gods can sense. I sat on the couch as the storm built and wrote letters with my favorite fountain pen on the last sheets of stationery I had. I wrote to the important people in my life—my mom and my sisters, a college friend, a special co-worker, telling them where I was. I described the sky and the rain and the personal discoveries I was starting to make.

I sat and listened to the storm and looked at the simple things surrounding me—a good set of knives, a green teapot—and I wrote about my small mobile home at the top of a hill a mile deep on a dirt road. I wrote about the silence and the deer and told about a longhaired fawn who lives on this hill and is learning to make his way in the world.

Femmes Seules (Women Alone)

ANN PRINGLE-HARRIS

"YOU'LL NEVER SEE THE INSIDE OF A FRENCH HOUSE — THE French don't invite foreigners." That prediction, volunteered by a friend long ago, is in my mind as I look at a faded snapshot a real estate agent once sent me. Instead of washed-out colors, I see my house in all its Provençal brightness: dazzling white walls, red-tile roof, a mass of pastel flowers in a stone enclosure, ripening tomato plants on terraces rising from the back lawn. There is a leafy tree just outside the doors leading to the kitchen, a spot of incredibly brilliant blue sky behind it.

In this house I intended not just to learn French but to become French—for a while. The intention was partly subconscious and totally irrational, but then there was nothing especially rational about the whole enterprise. Renting from photographs a house in a country you have never lived in, whose language you speak only haltingly, and whose citizens are not known for their kindness to strangers, is in any case risky. Leaving your husband behind and taking with you three children aged five, seven, and 11—well, I was warned that I would spend the summer trying to find peanut butter in the store and English-speaking children on the beach.

I had some rapturous memories that spurred me on. This summer was to be Chapter Two in a romance that had begun some years earlier on my first post-college visit to France. I had fallen in love with a place where schoolchildren exchanged handshakes as they greeted their friends on the street, where everybody seemed to argue heatedly, but not fight, over political issues, and where a young man might try to strike up a conversation by murmuring of the colors of your costume, "Ah, le rouge et le noir."

The children and I lived in a renovated farmhouse outside Sainte Maxime, then a picturesque village with a quiet beach; a busy square with shops, cafés, obligatory merry-go-round; and a casino that I suppose provided a certain amount of elegant night life, although I never investigated. My terrace after dark, with flowers glowing like pale stars and a sky as deep and soft as navy blue velvet, would provide elegance enough for me.

After I had stocked the larder, arbitrated disputes over bedrooms, and learned to light the gas oven without singeing my eyelashes, I explored our domain. We had a garden, a spacious patio with table and chairs, a front lawn for a croquet set the owner had kindly left for us—and there was a house next door. This long, low structure caught my eye right away. Each morning I could see two women who looked to be somewhere near my age—one small and blonde, the other dark and taller—taking their coffee outside. A little boy who played around the table belonged to the taller woman; I could tell from the maternal pats, kisses, and very occasional corrections she bestowed on him.

Maybe, I thought, the way to be invited into a French house is to invite the French into your house. These women didn't seem to have much company except for the two men, presumably their husbands, who arrived on weekends. And so, after practicing my invitation aloud several times, I introduced myself and invited them for a cold drink that afternoon, which happened to be July 4. It was our Independence Day, I explained, and since the French had helped us win our independence, we could celebrate the day together.

Looking back, I marvel at how much we talked that afternoon. I had no idea that my vocabulary would support such an exchange of information. Both women—I'll call the dark one Madame D, because it was years before I even knew, let alone used, her first name—were from Lyons. "It's called the gastronomic center of France," Madame D said, pointing to her sturdy, round-cheeked son as living proof that this label was apt. The little boy was the youngest of her four children. The others were at a summer colony, somewhat like camp. It was clear that she missed them. I did, too. They would have been a perfect match in age for my three.

As we sipped our cold tonic water, Madame D volunteered that the Lyonnais had a reputation in France for being stiff and formal. She flashed a smile, as if to indicate how little credence I was to put in that judgment. And indeed, before our modest party broke up I had learned about the blonde woman's hopes for children, about water shortages in the Midi, and about the mistral, a cold wind from the Rhone Valley that can conveniently be blamed for any mental or physical ills one may suffer in southeastern France.

Neighborly chats became a feature of our life at Ste. Maxime, along with excursions when I took the children to 13th-century churches, Roman ruins, coves hidden in the shadows of the Mauresque mountains. On Bastille Day the four of us went next door for a small celebration at which we drank mineral water with grenadine syrup and toasted one another's native countries.

France was a contender in the World Cup soccer match that year, and our household had a television set. With charming formality Madame D presented herself at our front door and asked if she and her husband— the other couple had left—might watch the match that weekend. And so I met Monsieur D, who turned out to be good-looking, with easy manners and, like his wife, a sense of humor. By that time my husband had joined us and we were in the process of planning a tour through Italy. Before we took off, Madame D and I exchanged addresses.

"I'll write," I said, "and please correct my French!"

We both kept our promises, exchanging cards and notes at Christmas and Easter. I admired Madame D's cards with their thick, tissue-lined envelopes, and I admired even more the way she would very subtly use—correctly—a phrase or verb form that I had used incorrectly. No, the Lyonnais weren't standoffish, but yes, they were in some respects formal: one should use the right words in the right way.

Three years after our summer in Sainte Maxime, I persuaded my husband to pass through Lyons before we took our two younger children to a camp in Switzerland. This time we were entertained not simply in a French garden but in a French home, the Ds' pleasant four-bedroom house with a prettily planted terrace from which you could see a silvery slice of the Saône River. For each course of the three-hour lunch we received fresh plates, with clean glasses for the accompanying wines. One wine had been bottled at the family's vacation cottage. Another was Beaujolais, the wine of the region. The last glass was for champagne.

By that time, all of us, adults as well as children, were laughing and talking like old friends, we in whatever French we could muster, they rattling on as if we understood every word instead of one in three or four. It was a mystery how Madame D, helped only by her two daughters, managed to keep up a steady flow of food, plates, and glasses from kitchen to terrace while at the same time being a relaxed and charming hostess. I could never have done it, but it made me happy to watch someone who could. Now that I had met them all, I fleshed out my imagined picture: a happy family, religious Catholics, educated, sufficiently prosperous, settled in the community.

I was surprised when almost a year went by with no word from Lyons. The letter that finally came was so shocking I read it several times to make sure I had understood—although I knew I had. "Mon mari m'a laissé. C'est triste, et difficile pour moi et les enfants." My husband has left me. It's sad, and difficult for me and the children.

My image of a happy family fell apart. My faith in my own judgment dissolved. I could only justify myself by reflecting that one often fails to see the signs of marital tension even among one's closest friends. Each time I read the letter I was struck by the simplicity, the directness, the Frenchness of it. Americans in such situations, I thought, try to explain events for which there is no explanation. They refer to problematic relationships, a partner's need for space, and so on. I was touched by the elegance, the eloquence, of Madame D's bare facts, and by the confidence in me shown by her letter. This confidence, in view of our long-distance relationship, puzzled me until I remembered that I sometimes told total strangers what I hadn't told my best friends.

Of course I wrote back. I don't recall what I said, but I recall very clearly our next meeting. My husband and I planned to drop our older girl at a language program in the Loire, then drive through Provence and into Italy with our two younger children. Lyons was on the way, and I had written asking Madame D and her children to be our guests at dinner the night we would spend there.

Did I expect to see a woman depressed by divorce, worn down by the demands of single parenthood? What I found was an object lesson in what to do when your husband leaves you after 18 years and four children. Madame D had a new, very becoming haircut, and a new job at the local ministry of education. She was clearly touched by our having taken the time to visit her and her children.

We drove to the inn outside Lyons, where we were to dine and where we and our children would spend the night before going on to Provence. That was the plan, but from the whispering and giggling that went on at the children's end of the table, I could see that it was undergoing modification. Madame D presented her proposal: might our children spend a few days with hers while we toured Provence? We could pick them up before going to Italy.

And so it was that two American children became, temporarily, French children. They went to school with their age mates, because the French scholastic year ran longer than ours. They spoke only French, because the second language of the D children was German, not English. When we picked them up five days later, they seemed at ease with their new friends and with the language, which they both studied in school. The youngest of Madame D's children, the little boy who had been at Sainte Maxime, was close to tears as my son, older than he but not too old to be a playmate, said good-bye.

"He was very good to him," Madame D said, referring to my son's treatment of her son. She filled me in on what the children had done on their free days, what they had seen of Lyons, what they liked best to eat, all the details mothers hope to have when their children go on a visit.

As I listened, I marveled: a job, a household of six children for five days, and no help.

Years passed—how many?—between that visit and the time when I wrote a grieving letter, with news that perhaps shocked Madame D as her news had once shocked me. What did I write, and what did she write back? I have forgotten, although I remember suddenly seeing a new significance in her long-ago letter to me. I was a link to a happy summer she had spent at Sainte. Maxime before her marriage ended, just as she would now be forever linked to the happy summer I spent at Sainte Maxime before my marriage ended.

For the most part, the last years of that marriage became like the rain-damaged portion of a book. You can read what went before and what came after, but the damaged pages are stained and stuck together, illegible. Yet I recall thinking how ironic it was that I had faulted myself for not sensing trouble in Madame D's marriage when I had been totally blind to trouble in my own. I remember, too, almost envying her having been divorced when her children were still young, still living at home and needing her. I was left with two children on their own and one away at college. The empty rooms in my apartment seemed to mirror the empty spaces in my life that I didn't know how to fill. For all but a few of my adult years I had been a member of a twosome.

That thought sent my mind back to Sainte Maxime. Yes, my children were with me, but I had negotiated that adventure on my own. On my own I booked passage on a transatlantic liner. On my own I picked up a new French car and drove it in the nerve-wracking Paris streets and on the high-speed auto routes of the provinces. I alone had tracked down the real estate agent, made arrangements with him and the owner of the house, inquired about beaches, shops, and restaurants, all in French. It was I who bundled the children into the car and searched out clear mountain streams to bathe in. And it was I who made friends with the next-door neighbors.

I had made myself at home in a stranger's house in a foreign town in a country I had never lived in. A woman alone. *Une femme seule*. Why did it sound better in French? Might it be better in French? I agonized for a long time over that question. I felt I could never go back to Sainte

Maxime. And after I found a full-time job it was easy to dodge the challenge of solo vacations taken anywhere. Still, somewhere inside me, fear fought against desire and caution against impulse until, finally, desire and impulse won. For my three weeks off I booked a round-trip flight to France.

Solitude in the romantic French countryside would, I was sure, be unbearable, but I thought I could manage solitude in a big city. And so I chose a walk-up studio in Paris that had no associations whatever. Instead of lazy days at the beach, I spent busy days at museums and theaters and language schools. I haunted the Métro and roamed through all the neighborhoods I loved. I went to services at Nôtre Dame. I shopped for melons and cheeses and crusty baguettes just as I had at Sainte Maxime, but I prepared my meals for one. And I pondered an invitation I had received from Madame D.

Over the years our children's paths had crossed, and she and I had seen each other two or three times. Mostly, though, we had kept in touch through letters that were like continuing conversations. My letter to her about my mother's death crossed hers to me with similar sorrowful tidings; our mothers had died in the same month of the same year. As only daughters we had each assumed caretaking duties, and for each of us those duties, now discharged, had left a void. There were happier exchanges: wedding invitations, birth announcements, family pictures.

As soon as I made my Paris plans, I wrote to Lyons, and Madame D's telephone call came the day after I settled into my studio. Would I spend the July 14 weekend at her cottage outside the city? It's very small, very simple, she kept repeating, as if I might desire something elaborate. But the smallness and the simplicity didn't disturb me. What I was asking myself was, would the past come painfully alive for me in a situation rather like the one at Sainte Maxime: two women keeping each other company on vacation, their husbands elsewhere—this time permanently elsewhere?

At the railroad station I instantly recognized Marie-Claude (after 30 years we were using each other's first names). We drove to the cottage, passing in less than 15 minutes from the urban outskirts of Lyons to a rolling countryside in which cows stood patiently in green meadows and the air was fragrant with mown grass. The cottage, once an out-building on a farm belonging to Marie-Claude's grandparents, was basically two large rooms. The living room had beamed ceilings, a stone fireplace, a kitchen at one end. In the garden was a table shaded by a tentlike canopy. We drank our breakfast coffee there as roosters crowed and small birds fluttered their wings against the tent roof.

Whether because of the quiet charm of the cottage, the peaceful countryside, my progress in the language, or all these things, on that visit Marie-Claude and I talked as if we had been college classmates instead of women from two different continents who had by chance ended up as summer neighbors. We sat up late and exchanged confidences about events in our recent history—an unsuccessful second marriage for me, an inconclusive love affair for her—and what we had learned from them. We spoke of our pride in, and our occasional worries about, our children.

Then she spoke of what I had deliberately not mentioned, letting her bring it up if she wished. The youngest child, the little boy at Sainte Maxime, had grown into a tall, handsome young man. I knew that because he and one of his sisters had visited New York. I knew, too, that although he was strong and fit, an athlete, he had not been strong enough to defeat the cancer that struck him at age 30. In a letter to me, Marie-Claude had described herself as inconsolable. The word, though blunt, seemed true and inescapable, like the words in which she had described the breakup of her marriage.

At the cottage she told me that she still had sleepless nights, and moments when she would find herself, in a shop or on the street, weeping and unable to stop. Yet she was joyous with her children, generous with her friends, at ease in her life. That strength came partly from her character, but it seemed to me that it was also a part of what I admired in the French way of living: grief is not hidden, it is acknowledged. And acknowledgment robs it of some of its power to destroy.

On Sunday, the third anniversary of the young man's death, there was a memorial mass at the local church, and an informal gathering afterward at Marie-Claude's, of cousins, aunts, uncles, children, and grandchildren. I, the only guest who was not a family member, received the family embrace.

As my train pulled out of the station the next day, I reflected that trains from Lyons went southeast as well as northwest. I could as easily take one to Sainte Maxime as to Paris. I made a promise to myself: one day I will go back. One day it will be time to retrieve my memories, time to revisit my house, the place where I made my French friends and where I first learned how to be *une femme seule*.

Garret Girl

KELLY CALDWELL

MY FIRST BEDROOM WAS A GIRLISH LITTLE SPACE, PAPERED IN pink and white stripes and decorated with prints of Renoir's *Girl with a Watering Can* and *Dance at Bougival*. My parents moved my sister Beth in with me when I was five, after our baby sister, Mary, was born. Each of us had a narrow white bed with our own cedar trunk at its foot. One of my amusements was waking up to see whether Beth was sleeping in a funny position—she favored one with her cheek on her pillow and her rear in the air—or whether she had crawled out of bed and slept in her toy chest.

Two years later, when Beth's charms were wearing thin, my parents saved me from her steady company. On my seventh birthday, after dinner and cake and unwrapping several new books and a Madame Alexander bridal doll, it was time for my big present. My folks made a show of it, tying a scarf around my eyes as a blindfold. Each parent took a hand and led me around, my sisters giggling behind. We went through the kitchen and up the stairs, then back down and around in a circle, until I was completely disoriented. Then we started climbing more stairs. When they whipped off the blindfold with a big "Happy Birthday," we were standing in the attic. They had cleared out the main room, making space for twin beds with nubby white spreads. My toy chest stood at the foot of one.

At last, a room of my own—with a lock on the door! It was only a hook latch but enough to keep out Beth and Mary, which was what really mattered. My literary heroines, whose stories I had listened to avidly slept under the eaves as I would. Sarah Crewe made her banishment to the garret into a blessing, and there she spun out tales of brave and beautiful princesses. Jo March retreated to her attic to invent villainous suitors and damsels in distress. I couldn't have had a better birthday present.

My new, long room had a big window on the west end and another on the east, and a set of drawers sunk into the wall. My own half-bath at the top of the stairs meant no more jostling with Beth to brush my teeth.

Sunshine was my roommate. It streamed in one window or the other all day long, but my mother worried that I would be cold when winter came. Dad p'shawed her. "Heat rises," he said. "She'll probably swelter."

I froze. My parents often tripped over me on winter mornings while I slept on the floor of Mary's room next to the heating vent. My mother sometimes suggested I move back in with Beth, but I passionately refused.

A few days after my birthday, I was inspecting my closet on my hands and knees when I spied a small rectangular opening low on the back wall. I poked my head into it and could have scooted right through, but the space beyond was pitch black and spooky. I backed out of the closet and started to look around my room for another way in. I saw a door tucked into the farthest corner on the same side, set unobtrusively into the wall paneling. I estimated the distance between it and the little hole and realized there must be a whole secret room! I grabbed the doorknob but found it locked.

I went downstairs to my mother, who was in the kitchen with the afternoon paper, drinking coffee and smoking.

"What's that locked room in my attic?"

"Stay out of there."

"But what is it?"

"Never mind."

"But it's my bedroom."

"And it's my stuff. I don't want you in it. Besides, you wouldn't like it. That part of the attic is unfinished. I don't want you breathing around exposed insulation. And the dust." Here, she shuddered. "It's so dusty I bet the room is full of pill bugs."

"What are pill bugs?"

"Those silver ones that curl up when you touch them. They really like dust."

It worked. When I stood before the door with an unbent bobby pin in my hand ready to pick the lock the next day, I couldn't make myself face those bugs. Then I spotted another mysterious door on the facing wall and somehow I was less afraid of that one. I quickly went to work on its lock.

Twenty minutes later, Beth and her friend Chrissy came up—Beth barged in whenever I forgot to hook my latch—and found me on my knees, struggling. Beth took over and opened the door quickly, as if my mangled pin were a real key. It was a closet with a single hanger dangling in the middle, on it a mink stole. We touched the fur and dust trickled out. Beth reached up to grab it and I stopped her. "I want to try it on," she said in that half-whine, half-shout with which younger sisters madden older ones. "It's dusty!" I replied. But the fight stopped before it could really get started when I sucked in my breath and pointed at something shiny on the closet floor.

"Don't touch it!" yelled Beth.

"Why not? It can't be real."

"How do you know?"

"Dad and Mom would never have a real gun."

So I picked it up. Unlike the toy guns I had played with, this one was heavy. Very heavy and very real. I shrieked and dropped it and the three of us ran screaming from the attic to report the big find to our mother. She kept us downstairs until Dad came home, and by the time I went to bed that night, both fur and gun had disappeared.

I knew my parents were deeply opposed to wearing fur ("It's one thing to kill animals for food, but it's another to kill them for vanity") and to keeping guns where children live. We weren't allowed to visit kids whose parents had guns in the house. I was flabbergasted to find these objects in my parents' possession, practically in the room they gave me for my birthday.

My mom explained that Grandpa Caldwell had given the fur to my grandmother when they finally escaped their cramped walk-up apartment on Chicago's South Side and moved to the suburbs. Grandma had treasured it, and Dad kept it to remember her happiest days. The gun belonged to my mother. All she would say about it was that she had two possessions Beth, Mary, and I could not play with and they were her father's World War I service revolver and the flag that had draped his coffin when he died in 1969.

When I finally pried these stories out of my parents, I lay awake trying to guess what other treasures could be hidden in the secret room and decided to brave the bugs. I got another bobby pin from Mom. Eventually I had to ask Beth, and we broke in together. My mother wasn't kidding about the dust—the air grew cloudy as soon as we started to move around in it. By the light of a bare bulb we found trunks of old dresses and trinkets, boring old papers belonging to my grandparents, books and notes from Dad's law school and Mom's nursing school. And there were boxes and boxes of family photographs. Like most children, I had never thought about whether my grandparents had known joy or sorrow, but after Mom told me the story behind the fur, I liked looking at snapshots of them with their feet up by a barbecue, napping in a hammock, fishing.

I experienced other revelations in my attic simply by gazing through my window. Our little white house with its forest-green shutters sat in a middle-American suburb where elms and oaks lined the streets. The houses were similar in size and shape but not identical. From my attic, I could see over everyone surrounding us, all the way to the high school two blocks away. I also looked down on the roof of our family room, which my parents had added, and on the nights I read past lights-out, I would watch for the family room to turn dark, then feign sleep until after my parents checked on me.

I was a student of the neighborhood. I could tell that the teenage Gaylord boy was out past curfew by the way his mother stood in the door, arms crossed. I could tell that the Woodstock Blue Streaks won their home football games by the surge in crowd noise. After the end of the game, I would watch cars race each other down our street, then listen as they screeched around the very tight corner. I often found it more fun to watch the show outside my window than to read.

One night when I was eight, I heard shouting from the street. I looked outside and saw no one, then realized it was my parents, arguing in their bedroom, their voices spilling out their windows. My folks were not-in-front-of-the-kids types, and it was the first time I heard them fight. I had nothing to compare it with then, but looking back I can say it was one terrible row, full of vicious swearing, and it ended with slamming doors. I crept down the stairs and heard breathing. It was Mary, waiting to come to my room. Beth tiptoed up the stairs a few minutes later. We pushed my two beds together and shared them.

My mom assured Beth and me the next day that all married couples fought and it didn't mean they were getting a divorce. But we knew lots of kids—including Chrissy, the daughter of our parents' close friends—who heard that line before their fathers eventually moved out. A few months and many fights later, Dad came home from work and didn't take off his tie. He and Mom gave the speech they had carefully rehearsed but it wasn't as comforting as they wanted—we were screaming and crying before they finished the first sentence. Dad fled to his car, I to my room, where I watched his car peel away from the curb.

The nights were quieter then, and the whole house seemed wrapped in sadness. My mom wandered around the rooms. Beth and Mary began creeping into her king-size bed after she fell asleep. I took to sitting on my bed imagining we were enveloped in fog, that when I looked out my window I couldn't see the neighbors or the street or even the roof of the family room. I pictured myself dropping out of my window and landing like a cat on that roof, disappearing into the fog without my family ever knowing.

I couldn't really escape, of course, so I did the next best thing: I took refuge in writing stories. Like Jo March and Sarah Crewe in their attics, I made up wild, fantastic tales. The continued adventures of the all-powerful Pippi Longstocking. A series of fairy tales ending in the demise of the same ugly witch, based on an awful first-grade teacher I still hated. All my stories had just and happy endings, and I convinced myself that eventually all of us would, too. When Mom bought a new, cherry-red Pacer, I figured that she was writing her own ending, one that would be happy even if it wasn't her original choice.

One night, very late, I was awakened again by shouting. I looked out and saw my mother on the sidewalk in her night clothes. Elegant even in a midnight crisis, she stood with her navy silk gown fluttering around her ankles in the breeze. Moonlight flashed off the robe's cream-colored cuffs and lining. Her voice, denouncing my father who was hidden from me in the shadows, had a hysterical pitch I had never heard. Suddenly she jumped into his car, parked at the curb, and drove off, roaring through the stop sign by the high school.

Dad came up to my room and I asked him what was happening to Mom. I could see by the panic in his eyes that he would not have a quick answer the way he usually did. Only once before had he failed to answer a question of mine—when I asked him why the soldiers shot the students at Kent State.

He left to find my mother while a friend stayed behind. I thought my heart would pound out of my chest. I had to do something, I thought. I looked up out of my window at the starry sky: "Please don't let anything bad happen to my mom." I fell asleep against the window sill, waiting.

My father did find Mom that night, but she didn't come home for two days, after which he drove us to Elgin to retrieve her from a gloomy psychiatric hospital. We waited in the lobby inspecting a model of a proposed expansion to avoid looking at the other waiting families. Dad and Mom emerged from an elevator and she kissed us perfunctorily, hustling us to the door at the same time. "Let's get out of this place," she said.

At a fast-food restaurant nearby, where our mother, usually a nutrition hawk, beamed as Mary ordered chocolate chip pancakes with whipped cream, Mom and Dad announced that Dad was coming home. They were going to work on fixing their marriage, and Dad promised to stay.

He lasted less than a year. Mom started talking about our post-divorce lives. We might have to move, she said. I told her I didn't want to give up my attic and lose my privacy. "Well, I don't want to move, either," Mom snapped. "This is my home."

Her home, her marriage, her calling as a stay-at-home mother, her dinner parties Martha Stewart would envy, her nights at the opera in sleek black dresses, her standing as the wife of the city attorney of our small Illinois town—these were the stakes that anchored her life. She had chosen them and driven them deep, and when they were wrenched out against her wishes, she didn't want to start over. Joining the growing throng of divorcées, going back to nursing the sick and the dying—that was someone else's life and she couldn't embrace it.

We found her on one of those perfect fall mornings when the leaves have turned and the air smells like autumn but is as warm as June. So silently had she slipped out of the house that I didn't wake up. Until I walked by the garage and heard the motor running, I thought my mother was out buying milk. When I saw her in the car, I thought she was sleeping.

My father told me she was gone, but for a long time part of me believed she was coming back. Still, that first night, in my bed, I knew one thing: my safe attic childhood was over. No longer would the intelligence I gathered there serve any useful purpose.

Dad moved in again and hired a loving daytime babysitter who broke through our pain and bewilderment with comforting food and hugs and help with homework. He took us to the circus one day with a friend named Linda, and when I saw how they kissed goodbye at her car, I knew I was powerless. That night I had the only dream I have ever had about my mother since she died. She came into my bedroom wearing her nursing uniform and cap and she was very angry. She chased me around and around and around, until finally I fled down the stairs and out of my attic.

Within a month of my mother's death, Linda was a regular fixture at our dinner table, and Dad ceded more and more parental duties to her. She combed our hair after our nightly baths and set it in rollers for us. She helped us pick out our clothes for school. Linda could be fun, capable of having whipped-cream fights with us in the kitchen. But she was unpredictable, sometimes launching into 30-minute tirades. We used to time her.

Dad and Linda had a Valentine's Day wedding four months after my mother died. Beth and Mary hungrily accepted Linda as their new mother, but the changes had come too fast for me. I missed my mother but was afraid to say so. Yet once Linda was in my life, I soon became just as terrified of losing her.

Linda was uncomfortable living in our mother's house, and when I was 11 we moved. Our new place had much more property—acreage for the horses Linda kept, a pool, and a deck—but there was much less house. Once again I shared a small bedroom with Beth and I gave up trying to write my stories. I needed a room of my own for that, and anyway I had lost the gift of inventing just and happy endings.

I learned to do my homework in the midst of chaos: Beth and Mary fighting, "Tom and Jerry" cartoons going full-blast, Linda on the phone, dinner bubbling six feet from my ear, two dogs barking and skittering across the kitchen floor. I was well prepared to eventually become a journalist capable of working in newsrooms despite blaring televisions and police scanners and raucous colleagues.

I got my own apartment at 19. The first night I lay in my bed and said, "This is my room," while in my mind's eye I saw pale yellow eaves and a window with not just a view but perspectives. Every time I moved, I would say those words and picture that attic.

Today I am lucky enough to live in an apartment with a big interior balcony. From my desk there, I watch the beagle across the street sleeping on the sunny side of the couch, my opera-singer neighbor warming up as she walks to work, parents next door filling an inflatable pool with water and half a dozen preschoolers.

Although I don't pretend I am in my attic anymore, I often say to myself, "This is my room," before I turn back to writing my stories—stories with satisfying endings.

Secrets and Mysteries

The Uses of Adversity

PHILOMENA C. FRIEDMAN

THANKS TO A FEW FOREBEARS WITH TASTE, MY MOTHER WENT
as a bride to live in a house that was pretty. With the help of adversity,
she turned it into a house that was beautiful.

A few years after the First World War, Mother began housekeeping
in a New Jersey countryside that was still rural, green, and leafy. She
and my father were given as a wedding present the white clapboard
farmhouse, built in the 1880s, in which my mother had lived as a little
girl during a half-dozen years when my newly prosperous grandfather
had set up as a gentleman farmer. All of their lives my mother and her
sisters remembered that time happily, but for their father the farm was
more biblical scourge than gentlemanly avocation. Silo fire, hailstones,
and his own incompetence as a farmer sent them fleeing back to the city,
and him back to business.

A good sweeping-out was all the refurbishing that the house was
given before my recently married parents moved in. They quickly whitewashed the solid plaster walls, which had survived without blemish the
dozen years that the house stood empty, and were ready when the furniture began to arrive from all the aunts as well as from my grandfather.

Excepting a maple trestle table that was 100 years older, almost everything was from the first half of the 19th century, though in varied styles. Into that roomy white interior with its big windows, quite different pieces of furniture came to keep good company. A pair of stenciled Boston rockers seemed comfortable with a carved pine chest thought to have been made in New Mexico, and both looked natural with a pine corner cupboard that had "Lott 1842 Grantham N. Hamps" burned into its underside. Whatever their provenances, they shared the fellowship of lovingly worked wood.

In this congenial mix of furniture styles and periods, my parents began to raise a family. We children—I was the last of five—deepened the patina of those old pieces, with dolls' beds in bureau drawers and homework on a wonderful drop-leaf table in the second parlor. The furniture became a little more worn, a little shinier where it curved, but not a piece was marred. There was no chair that we were forbidden to sit on, and none that we were permitted to climb on. Parents were in charge and children did not scratch furniture because they were not allowed to. Accidents were few, quickly repaired, and quickly forgiven.

For nearly a decade our family and its furniture lived and mellowed together. Then came our first experience of real adversity, the Great Depression. Like most people they knew, my parents lost whatever savings and investments they had. We were lucky because we owned our house outright and my father kept his job, though at a reduced salary. From our parents' conversation, from the frequent and serious patching of corduroy knickers, and from the occasional appearance of oatmeal at dinner as well as at breakfast, we small children gradually sensed more than we actually understood of hard times. We knew people who lost their houses because they could not pay the mortgage, and we knew that some of our schoolmates' families were "on relief," the 1930s term for receiving public assistance.

Even in that atmosphere, we were surprised when my mother said one day that she was thinking of selling the low-poster bed that was in our guest room. "After all, we seldom even look at it. Someone who uses it every day will enjoy it more, and the money would be very helpful just now." Probably none of us had ever slept in the bed and we had surely paid it no particular attention, so we didn't mind when it went away, leaving us with a clear view of a rug that was prettier than we had noticed before, and a pleasant new space in which to play.

Over the next two or three years other family pieces were sold. A Windsor tavern table that sat between two chairs in a little bay window, where we used to play Chinese checkers, was the second thing to go. Realizing that the departure of a table of which we were fond might upset us children, my mother set out to cast a certain light. "We know very well what that table looks and feels like. We don't even have to close our eyes to see it still sitting there. You don't lose something you love if you remember it. Our table isn't lost, it's just not here now."

In the calm certainty that she spread around us, worrisome ideas about having to sell the table to buy something we desperately needed just didn't occur to any of us. We felt that our table had gone out of the house to work for the family, just as we children would have done, had we been old enough. Our table was still part of our lives, which could go on in familiar ways because it was earning money for us.

Having faith in our mother, we saw through her eyes. We continued to feel the Windsor table was still ours, and the objects that followed it out the door. Principal among them were six slat-back chairs, a firehouse chair, some pretty Sandwich glass, and half a dozen pewter porringers that we always called "the hard plates," probably because one of us, learning to speak, had been unable to say "Hartford," the place where they had been made. My mother never replaced any of the things she sold, not even later when finances were no longer a problem. Even to think of it would have seemed disloyal. Nothing could replace the furniture that had helped us.

Anyhow, nothing was needed, for we still had the originals in our minds. The empty spaces where they had been took on a kind of glow. Very likely we came to remember them as finer than they really were and somehow to love them more after they were gone. Learning to see what was not actually there also made us look more closely at what remained. I am sure that we grew up taking more pleasure in fine furniture than we otherwise would have.

Visitors to our house sometimes commented on its simplicity, how pleasingly uncluttered it was. On those occasions my brothers and sister and I exchanged sly glances, loving the idea that the visitors could not see what we saw, the house with the furniture that my mother had enchanted us into feeling was still present.

The enchantment faded only a little as we grew up and married and moved away. My mother lived in the house alone after my father died, and there, when she was 80, adversity paid a final call: she began to go blind. Sparse furnishings were a help as she honed her perception of every household object's location. What had been familiar was now made precise to within an inch.

When her vision was almost gone she had bars installed, waist-high, on the walls of all the rooms on the ground floor. A breakfront sideboard and an oak cupboard had to make way. They went to the children for whom they had long been intended.

When I heard of the bars, I winced to think of Mother being forced to destroy her house. I was wrong. Though she could not distinguish visually between the heavy plastic and the aluminum of the bars that were recommended, she rejected both kinds. Judging from the touch of her fingertips and my sister's description of color, she chose bars of a very light steel in a matte gray that was the shade of modern pewter. And she was right. She could still see what could not be seen. The bars she chose did not reflect but softly absorbed and seemed to hold just beneath their surfaces the light coming through the windows and the colors of the big old rugs.

The house was more beautiful than I had ever known it to be. With the bars it seemed to stoop to lift up its friend, and in so doing it gained a wonderful, sad grace. I imagined an aged ballerina living out her days in her own studio.

My mother stayed in the house another 15 years. One hand resting naturally on a wall bar, she moved easily among the remaining pieces of her lovely furniture, undoubtedly enjoying them still. At 97 she died quietly in the spindle bed in which she had slept for three-quarters of the 20th century.

But my mother and the furniture that she had used to teach her children to be true still had something to teach me. I was surprised to see a crowd at the house the morning of her funeral. Several dozen people seemed to me a great many for a woman whose friends were long dead. A man whom I had not at first recognized introduced himself as an elementary-school classmate of mine. I thanked him for his kindness in coming to show respect for a woman whom he had probably not even seen for decades.

"I am here out of gratitude," he said. Oh? "In the Depression, your family had little, but mine had nothing. For three years your mother fed us."

He pointed to two men who were talking quietly on the other side of the room, identifying them as childhood friends of one of my brothers. "I expect that they are here for the same reason."

Beyond the two men was our parlor bay window. In front of it a little Windsor tavern table glowed.

The House of the Weeping Woman

ALEIDA ALMENDARES DE VILLALBA

TRANSLATED BY JOHN MATKIN

A SECRET TOLD IN A DEATHBED DELIRIUM, HIDDEN JEWELS, and a lost way of life filled my thoughts as the plane landed in Havana. My heart raced. Soon I would see the family home I had fled 37 years ago and yet had never truly left.

Together with my parents, my grandfather, and an uncle, I had flown into exile during the Revolution in 1961 with only the clothes I was wearing. I was 13 that summer and believed we were only going to Madrid for a visit, but we never returned. Seven years later, in accordance with my family's wishes, I was married to a Spaniard 20 years my senior. He had social position, a minor title, and considerable property. Eleven months later he was killed in a car crash near Marbella. And so, widowed and childless at an early age, I came more then ever to dwell in memories of my childhood home. In dreams and reveries, I climbed the steps and walked through the rooms and ran my fingers along the walls and furnishings.

The family called this "the new house," although it had been built by my great-great-grandfather in 1865. The original family home was an early-18th-century mansion in Old Havana, where for generations our extended family had lived together. But no one wished to remain after a day in 1864 when a young servant girl who had been entrusted momentarily with the baby of the family dropped a mango from her pocket through the balusters along a third-floor corridor overlooking the patio. Leaning over the railing, she lost her hold on the infant and in trying to catch it lost her own footing as well. Both servant and baby fell to their deaths.

From then on, the building became widely known in Old Havana as "The House of the Mango Tragedy." The family dispersed. My great-great-grandfather, whose son had been the infant killed, built a new house to the west near the sea. He chose a design of the last French Empire, and it was constructed in creamy golden Cuban limestone. He fancied anything French, so he gave this retreat from sorrow a French name, Sans Souci, "without care."

By the time of my birth, my mother had set the style of the rooms. The staid Napoleon III architecture made a perfect foil for the gilding, brilliant colors and florid exuberance of Mother's taste. The walls of the long stairway were painted crimson red. Each morning I would lick one finger and run it along the chalky red calcimine surface as I descended, and then rub it on my mouth for lipstick.

A very large standing portrait of my mother wearing a red moiré ball gown dominated one wall of the dining room. A well-known artist had come to our house every morning for several weeks. As my mother posed, he recited the poetry of Federico García Lorca to keep on her face just the expression that he wished to portray. A necklace of emeralds from the Chivor mines had been in the family for more than 200 years and was to have been worn in this painting. On the second morning, however, the artist exclaimed, "Take them off please, Señora. Your neck is much more beautiful than the emeralds!"

In the center of the dining room stood a long native mahogany table surrounded by high cane-backed chairs. The flicker of candlelight animated those at table, and reflections in the mirrors on opposite walls extended the family tableau to infinity.

The house was always alive with sound. The staccato of women's conversation amplified across polished tile floors in breezy high-ceilinged rooms as Mother met with her friends in the afternoon. Father's deep clear voice resonated down the hallways as he summoned his major-domo or whistled his favorite tune, "Always in My Heart." Long after I had been sent to bed, I would often hear the faint strains of Ernesto Lecuona's "Damisela Encantadora", or "Siboney", as musicians played from the loggia while guests in the garden talked and laughed and danced in the moonlight. Often, evenings were punctuated with the click, click of dice being shaken in a *cubilete*, a small leather box, as Uncle Rodolfo and his friends gambled.

At night, before I fell asleep, I could sense the city pulsing. The crash of the waves against the sea wall along the Malecón drive, the breeze that rustled the palms in the garden, even the passage of the moon seemed a symphony of sensuousness. Always, in the distance, there was the throbbing murmur of music, a mélange of melodies neither Spanish nor African, but a unique synthesis. Night-blooming jasmine and sweet aromatic cigar smoke, the scent of rum and perfume, all blended into the essence of Havana.

I never tired of watching Mother in her dressing room while her maid, Caridad, brushed her hair each morning or applied the flamingo-colored nail polish, careful to leave the moons and tips exposed. A half-high wall and a *mampara*, a double-swinging louvered door, separated Mother's dressing room from her bath, providing privacy while allowing ventilation in the tropical climate. On the evenings when the family entertained, I would often stand beside the triple-mirrored dressing table cluttered with perfume bottles and feather powder puffs. Burying my chin in the marabou collar of my mother's dressing gown, I would watch as she opened one jewel case or another and held the emerald necklace to her throat or a pearl and diamond aigrette to her hair.

"These will all be yours when I'm gone," she would sometimes say. "When do you think you might go?" I once replied. Touching the tip of my nose with her folded black lace fan and smiling broadly, she answered, "Not yet, my love," and swirled from the room to her glittering guests below.

Father noisily negotiated business by telephone from his desk in the library. He bathed morning and evening, changed his shirt three times every day, and smelled of the French cologne Jean Marie Farina, which he sprinkled liberally on his handkerchief.

Uncle Rodolfo had three rooms upstairs. He was unmarried and the handsomest young man in Havana. Unlike the rest of the family, he had green eyes of a brilliant intensity in which more than one young woman had become lost. He often dressed in silk suits the color of vanilla ice cream and as soft to the touch.

Before the Revolution, Cuban society was very elitist. The members of the old families moved within closed circles—the *gente conocida*— from generation to generation. Uncle Rodolfo rebelled against this and would sometimes appear at a social function at home, to everyone's distress, with a beautiful, bright-eyed country girl, or even worse, a tourist met over the tables of a casino—it didn't matter that her husband owned a chain of drugstores in Milwaukee.

Grandfather and his friends gathered each morning on the loggia facing the sea. All dressed in white pleated *gueravera* shirts and sitting in rocking chairs, they would have their dark strong coffee in tiny cups, check the daily *El Mundo* for the market price on sugar, and converse under the intoxicating cloud of smoke of their Larrañaga cigars.

Occasionally, Grandfather's friend Ramón Grau, who had twice been president of Cuba, came to dinner. Preparations were especially elaborate, and Mother personally supervised. Señor Grau had an inordinate liking for *diplomate*, fruit pudding. On each of his visits, this was served as dessert. So exacting were his tastes that his own cook came to our kitchen the day before to preside over the making of the pudding. There was talk of a secret ingredient that made it quite distinct from this popular dessert as served elsewhere. Despite my spying through a kitchen window, the secret was not revealed to me.

To a child this life seemed carefree, but there were mysterious happenings in the garden. One October night in a rainstorm, I was awakened by muffled voices beneath my window. As I watched from behind the shutters, three of the servants carried a small box from the house in darkness illuminated only by candlelight. At the foot of the ceiba tree in the garden, they dug a place in the earth and buried their mysterious parcel. Something was taken from a bag and scattered over the spot. Then, after some strange incantation, they returned to the house.

I was not alone in observing this ritual. The light of a cigarette drew my eye to a figure standing just out of the rain under the portal of the driveway. It was Uncle Rodolfo. I never spoke of this to anyone, but I always imagined it to have been a baby. One hot, humid night in summer, I was again drawn to my window by a faint sound—a woman's laughter. There by the light of the moon in the shadow of an old yagruma tree stood my father and the wife of a well-known Cuban senator. I watched for a long time as they talked in hushed tones and kissed. As I returned to bed, I heard the door to my mother's bedroom quietly close.

Nothing was said of this episode. Some weeks later, at a large wedding reception in a private club, this same senator's wife approached my mother and, as was the Cuban custom, attempted to kiss her on the cheek. Mother drew back and sharply said, "I do not kiss those who also kiss my husband." The room, filled with conversation and laughter, fell silent. Then, as if nothing had happened, all resumed as before, and so did our lives. Mother would never have permitted herself such a breach of etiquette as insulting a guest in our own home, nor would she have admonished my father in private. The reception was the best opportunity for her to make her feelings plain. Shortly after our departure from Cuba, we learned that the senator's wife had died by her own hand.

Mother never recovered from our departure from Sans Souci and from Havana. Like a plant whose roots are damaged in transplanting, she soon declined. In Madrid, she seldom rose from bed before noon. She dressed invariably in black, as if in mourning. The vibrancy of her personality became the confusion of a sleepwalker, and she died an early death. Grandfather died of lung cancer and, I always thought, a broken spirit. With the loss of the sugar fortune that had sweetened his youth, Uncle Rodolfo followed an eager American heiress, whom he hoped to marry, from Madrid to New York. She said yes. Her father said no. Not long after, he married a cashier from the Automat, and they had five children in a small apartment on Empire Boulevard in Brooklyn.

Although Father outlived both Mother and Grandfather by more than three decades, he was obsessed by a determination to return to

Cuba and reclaim all that had once been ours. As he lay dying in Palm Beach, his last fevered words were to me: "The emeralds and all the other things, I left them behind with Caridad. It was the only safe place." With a gasp as faint as a spider's breath, he was gone.

Four days later, I arrived in Havana to collect my long-dreamed-of treasure. Caridad had been not only my mother's personal maid but her confidante as well. Although she was black and we were white, it was as though the same blood flowed through our veins. Over all these years we kept in close contact. With her 96-year-old brother, she shared two small rooms in a crumbling white colonial house in that district of Havana called La Vibora. On my arrival, I went directly to her with the news of Father's death. She told me that he had given each of the servants a substantial amount of money before going into exile.

When I asked whether she had anything else, she pointed to a torn and faded photograph fastened to the wall with a rusted tack. It was of our family on the steps of Sans Souci with Caridad in the background holding me. Beneath it on the floor was a worn and dusty pile of Decca records and an old phonograph. These were Caridad's only treasures, the remnants of her life with us.

I told her of Father's last words. Smiling, she reminded me that *caridad* meant "charity." "Maybe he left the jewels with the priest to be used by the church," she suggested. Father Demitrio now had a church at Batabanó, and Caridad insisted on accompanying me there. We made the journey in a *guagua*, an old Cuban bus without glass windows. Across from us sat a country woman holding in one hand a live chicken with its feet bound and in the other a bundle of yucca root. Father Demitrio had no knowledge of anything being left behind by my father, but did recall that each year Mother had made a pilgrimage to the shrine of Caridad del Cobre in the countryside. A brief telephone call to the elderly caretaker of the shrine proved she had not left the jewels there. After a simple supper of black beans and rice at Father Demitrio's humble table, we returned to Havana, tired and dejected.

When at last I stood at the entrance gate to Sans Souci the next morning, it seemed like the remains of some lost civilization. I had expected a flood of emotion, but I felt numb. The ancient ceiba tree had uprooted the entrance walk, as if to defy anyone to enter. The great roots knotted and curled around one corner of the house in a possessive embrace, partially dislodging a corner of the steps. A tangled torsade of vines bound a louvered shutter against a pair of windows. In the garden, banana and banyan, copa de oro and sea-grape grew together in wild profusion.

In the cruelest joke of all, time and the elements had conspired to alter the name of the house to reflect its present reality. Two of the black iron letters that were mounted on the garden wall beside the entrance had fallen and lay half buried in earth and vegetation, so that the house name, Sans Souci, now read Sans Sou, "without a cent." How fitting.

Talking with people living nearby, I learned that over the years many families had occupied the house, always for brief periods. Most were simple people from the countryside who had been relocated to the city after the Revolution. Some had previously lived in *bohíos*—huts without plumbing, electricity, or floors. I was told that a pig was once kept in my mother's pink marble bathroom for weeks while being fattened for the table.

Each group of new residents would soon complain that the figure of Caridad del Cobre, patroness of Cuba, in a mural my mother had commissioned to be painted on the stair landing, would sometimes wail and weep. Believing that this image of the saint was unhappy with their presence in the house, and sensing it to be a malevolent omen, the superstitious squatters would soon move out. Eventually, the reputation of this "House of the Weeping Woman" caused it to be permanently abandoned.

I let myself in through a pair of doors that had been loosened by termites. As I walked through the rooms, I found only three objects that remained from our time there: A crystal chandelier that had hung above the dining table, now missing most of its pendants, held a bird's nest in one of its gilt-bronze arms. The mirrored walls were so dimmed by decades of dust that I could hardly see myself. And the face of the notorious mural on the stair landing did appear to be heavily tear-stained. On the floor, at the foot of the mural, remained three whole dried oranges and stubs of candles—no doubt an attempt to propitiate the unhappy saint. As a child, I had seen a similar offering left by one of the servants in front of another saint's picture on a shelf in our pantry.

As I stood in silence pondering the weeping and wailing that had been reported, I thought again of Father's last words. Could he have said, "I left the emeralds and everything else behind Caridad," instead of "behind with Caridad"? Remembering a trapdoor in my mother's bath that let plumbers in to repair the pipes, I apprehensively opened it.

Inside, I could see a black metal box forced between the wall and the pipes. No doubt this pressure had loosened the old lead pipes so that when the occupants turned on the water, a wailing sound was produced behind the mural. In addition, the pipes must have leaked and saturated the wall until apparent tears ran down the figure's face.

I could not budge the box, but with great effort I opened the lid. Inside lay three jewel cases and a leather pouch—all empty. Stunned, I sat on the steps for a long while as the sun streamed through a broken shutter illuminating the soiled and faded red wall. It seemed to me extraordinarily ironic that the place in which Father had hidden his valuables called attention to itself, that the wailing and weeping of a figure of Caridad would lead one or two peasants to a fortune in jewels.

As I left my childhood home, I closed the decaying doors as lovingly as I would tend a beloved's burial place.

The thrust of the ascent when the plane left Havana forced me heavily against my seat, as if the gravitational force of the house were drawing me back. Then as the plane leveled, I felt a great weight had been lifted from me. In revisiting Sans Souci, I had come to perceive a great reality. All possession is an illusion. Objects, property, and people are only ours for a certain time. The past is memory and the future is a dream. All we truly possess is the moment. That should be our passion, our obsession, and our treasure.

Who Loved Aunt Ella?

DALE MACKENZIE BROWN

MY FATHER USED TO LET OUT A WHOOP AT HIS FIRST SIGHT
of the farm. I share his exhilaration to this day, although I am not the
shouting kind.

I have been coming to the farm all my life. I know its fields and
woods, sounds and smells; there isn't a nook in the house that I haven't
investigated. My father's Aunt Ella lived here last. She was the prettiest
of four sisters and she preserved a certain comeliness right up to the end.
Yet she never married. She survived the Great Depression with the help
of a hired man, and doggedly reached the age of 86. Late in life she
painted a cardboard sign in big black letters with old-fashioned serifs:
"Farm for Sale. Inquire of Ella Neal, Over the Hill." She never put it up.
The sign sits in the pantry to this day.

Only death could separate Aunt Ella from the farm. She left it to Dad
and his younger sister, who lives three miles away and keeps a close eye
on it. Upon his death, Dad's portion passed to me. Thus I gained what
has become for my family—but never was for Ella—a retreat from the
everyday world.

The view is finer than the house. Painted white, with a silvery tin
roof to reflect the sun, the modest L-shaped building sits high above the

valley in the lap of the hill. A green lawn and shaggy-barked maples surround it. Two porches—one to the side draped with a grapevine, the other out front facing a road on which only half a dozen cars will pass in a day—invite sitting and dreaming. The nearest neighbors are a half-mile to the north and the south; to the east and west for at least a mile there is nobody.

My ancestors left their old Connecticut home and came to this perfect spot in New York's Chenango County in the 1820s, their possessions piled high in an ox-drawn wagon. They sheltered first in a house on a rise too wind-blasted for comfort and long since torn down; they built the present one in the mid-19th century, using local ash and hemlock for timbers and flooring.

I would like to think that not much has changed here in the years since then, but it has, of course. Most of the small outbuildings are gone, along with the sagging barn that outlived the cows it housed, lingering on for some years afterward, a drowsing memory of itself. The pasture that swept up the slope opposite the house has become overgrown with trees, and the site of the vegetable garden is now a tangle of weeds. But some of the fields are worked by a farmer in the valley, and the air still carries the smell of ferns, newly mown hay, and daisies.

One of my earliest farm memories is of riding a hay wagon, on top of the world. The farm was the first place I really saw stars, diamond bright in the blackness; the Big Dipper angled toward the pond where bullfrogs croaked, and still do, on summer evenings. Dad pointed to the sky and told me to watch for the star that would fall. No doubt I cherish the recollection because my relationship with him was continuously interrupted by his long spells away from home; he came and went all the years I was growing up, commanded by his job and whatever other need he may have had to be absent. We were never closer as father and son than when we were upstate on vacation. Mother did not always go with us; she said she had to look after her brother, but I suspect she really wanted to give us a chance to be together.

We would stay with my grandmother, Aunt Ella's non-identical twin, who lived in the nearby town. The treat for me was to go "up to the farm" as soon as possible. Aunt Ella was set in her ways, and there were chores that she and the hired man had to get done. We timed our visits to the hours when Aunt Ella was most likely to enjoy company, which generally meant after supper.

Sometimes she would be in a very good mood, ready for some fun. She might play the harmonica or her violin for us, throwing herself into the music, doing a little accompanying jig around the room. A woman of unusual musical ability and completely self-taught, Aunt Ella also played the piano, the guitar, and the autoharp.

I was a history-minded boy and loved to sit in the big kitchen, a fire burning in the iron range to drive away the chill, listening by the amber light of kerosene lamps to Grandma and Aunt Ella tell of the olden days. They would recall happy family evenings around this same stove in the company of their uncle and aunt and two boy cousins from up the road—popping corn, telling stories, laughing, singing.

As the old women talked, Ralph, the hired man, would sit in the corner in his rocking chair, smiling, glad as ever to see us. Dad was fond of him. Like Aunt Ella, Ralph had not married, and in some curious way these two castaways were suited to each other. He wound up working for her for 30 years and doing a good job, despite occasional bouts with booze and the fact that he had only one hand. In place of the other hand (lost in a mowing accident) a steel hook projected, fastened to the stump by a leather collar and straps; the hook seemed as useful a tool as his own five fingers had been.

These days when my wife, our grown daughters, Elisabeth and Marissa, and I come to the farm we feel a sense of reunion—with the past as well as with one another. We always enter the house from the side porch where carriages once discharged their passengers, the deep wheel ruts still visible in the lawn. A twist of the wobbly doorknob lets us into the kitchen, a plain, square, wainscoted room with an oilcloth-covered table, mismatched chairs, a wood box in one corner, Ralph's rocker in another. Its prime feature—indeed, the heart of the house—is the old black iron cookstove, squat on bowed legs. If there is a chill we build a wood fire in the stove's belly. The heat is a baking kind, good for the bones, and it consumes some of the mildew odor of closed-up spaces.

Soon the house is alive again. Door latches rattle as we plunge from room to room. A lot of the furniture—a great deal of it brought in that wagon from Connecticut—has gone to family members, but much remains, including the upright piano in the living room, the music cabinet with a mock-inlay front, and the Morris chair whose heavy lines and clawed dragon feet are so ugly no one wants it.

Though the interior is not as Aunt Ella left it, she is a strong presence in the house and I don't have to look far for reminders of her, or of the others who have lived here. The cabinet built into the living room wall holds visiting cards and leather-bound books bearing their names: Rosaltha and Rosetta (my great-grandmother and *her* twin), Lucretia, Artemisia, Huldah, Ora, Violetta Zepherine, Levi, Cassius, Orson, Wallace. A buttermilk-red blanket chest in the front hall contains pictures of many of them—formal portraits in velvet-covered albums or snapshots pasted down with triangular corners on black pages captioned in white ink. Buried among the albums are scrapbooks with clippings from the local newspaper describing the picnics, church suppers, and reunions they attended, the births of new family members and the deaths of old ones.

Even the drawer of the Mission table next to the Morris chair offers evidence of vanished lives. Reaching into it recently I came up with a round-robin diary kept by various family members who vacationed at the house after Aunt Ella's death, with several entries penned by my father. On one of our stays with my girls he entered something very important to him: "Elisabeth told me three times today she loves me."

And who loved Aunt Ella? Last summer I made up my mind to find out by tackling a task I had been putting off for years—to read her diaries, kept in a trunk in the upstairs south chamber, as she called it. Filling a cardboard box to the top, they begin in 1893, when she was 12, and continue off and on until 1967 when she died. The entries are scant and mostly unrevealing, with "Did up usual work," a litany, and the weather noted daily—Stormy and blustering, Rain, Pleasant. Yet as I fast-forwarded through them, I entered her life.

In 1893 she spends the winter cozily enough, visiting friends, having sugar on snow (hot maple syrup reduced to sticky chewiness by the jolt of sudden cold), and enjoying visits from her kinfolk up the road, but the winter begins to wear on her and April finds her running joyfully to the woods "after flowers." In 1898 a man enters the picture—"Went over town in the evening. Carl Loomis came home with me. Ha! Ha!" He is never heard of again in the diaries, alas, and in the meantime her oldest sister, Kate, marries and "has a kid." There is something defiant about that statement, a cockiness. What does she care? She's Ella!

Now a new name appears, Byron Brown—or Bike, as she sometimes calls him. "Byron came over in the P.M. in his buggy. Went riding." He is mentioned more and more. "Byron came over tonight. Tra la! Tra la!" She has some second thoughts and pencils out the "tra la, tra la." My grandmother gets hold of the diary and forges, "Byron came over in the eve and smacked me and smacked and smacked." Fussed, Ella adds a note and arrow. "Emma wrote this." But Bike is soon the person she wants notified in case of an emergency, or so she has written on the frontispiece of next year's diary, and there is a lock of blond hair tied with a thread and placed in a pocket on the inside of the back cover, his no doubt.

Several years go by, and though Ella and Byron are now engaged, references to him dwindle. According to family stories she couldn't make up her mind when to marry him and finally turned the patient fellow down, though she never mentions her decision in the diary. After marrying someone else and fathering three children, he went out into his barn and shot himself; the bullet passed through his pocket watch. Ella's diary merely mentions that Byron Brown "was buried today." Though people said he never got over her rejection, their gossip and her guilt go unrecorded.

The only daughter at home, she lives on with her father and mother. Grandma, her twin, is already having babies. My father, the first, is born in the front bedroom, on a January day so cold the runners on the sleigh creak when my great-grandfather goes to town to get the doctor. A year later Ella's mother dies at 60, a wizened old woman drained by chores and illness. Ella cannot bear to write in the diary, she just blacks out the day with a pencil. If ever she thought of leaving home, she cannot now. She takes over her mother's responsibilities, an endless round of mopping and washing and baking and milking, relieved for her by field work, at which she is good. Her father, a gentle, sweet man, adores her; he writes little poems to her, his "Jupe," which I found tucked away in drawers.

Her older sister Anna, whose marriage has failed, comes back to the farm to live, and she and Ella make good companions. The sisters share the chores, take and print photographs together, wash each other's hair, sing duets. Then grippe strikes the area. "Pa very bad," Ella writes, "Anna worse." And the uncle up the road is ill, too. The men from the church hold a wood bee at the farm, cutting and laying in a winter's supply. The doctor comes and goes; Pa improves, Anna and the uncle die. Now more lonely than she has ever been, Ella writes in the diary, "Lord, make me as good as Anna was." She tries; she is even born again in the fever that the firebrand preacher Billy Sunday has spread over the land. But the histrionics go against her Congregationalist grain and she settles back down, content to sing her solos in church—"Only Wait," "They Are Nailed to the Cross," and "No One But Jesus," and lets these be proof of her devotion. Frustrated as life passes her by, she gains a reputation for being snappish.

Ella's New Year's resolution for January 1, 1924, is "not to worry so much over things, as I have in the past." Wishful thinking. As her father ages, she must take on more and more the running of the farm. Ralph arrives to help out, and when her father dies, Ralph stays on. Her diary reveals that her pleasures have all become small ones: sugar on snow, the gingersnaps and wine drops she bakes, the first beet greens, peas, and string beans from the garden, her cats and dogs, an occasional letter from a friend or member of the family, a short week's visit from one of the boys up the road.

Ralph's pleasure continues to be the bottle; under her watchful eye, he can't get away with much, but he hides his whiskey in the barn and when he is unable to stand his life any longer he goes off on those toots she despises. She fires Ralph several times but always takes him back.

And then it is time for Ralph to go. "They took Ralph to the nursing home," she records. He is too sick to come back, and Ella is alone on the farm. Her two surviving sisters—her "darling sisters," as she now refers to them—eventually die. She begins to mention having pain. "Had backache all day." She takes to sitting in her rocking chair beside the stove, looking out the window, waiting for someone to come and see her. The cows are sold, the hens are eaten; she is down to one cat and no dog. Nature takes advantage and begins scampering back toward the house in the form of mice, chipmunks, and squirrels. When the mice get inside, she is alarmed. They are too much for old Tom, the cat. But Ella endures.

The winter before she dies, she looks on the good side of things: "It is nice and warm in the house," so she pops some corn after dinner, settles down into her chair and sews rags for a rug. Though her backache keeps up and her big toe buzzes, she shovels a path through the snow to the mailbox and she begins to crochet her rug. The snow thickens and deepens. There are no letters. "Terrible lonesome." But the first real spring day sends her to the pasture to cut pussy willows. And once again it is sugaring season. She desperately wants to taste the new syrup. "Come on, Ashville," she writes, referring to the man who taps her trees along with his own. "Bring me some."

She is hospitalized, then taken to the senior citizens home. "Awful homesick, but what can I do about it?" She worries about Tom. "Poor old fellow." And the diaries end.

I need relief. I go outside. It is late afternoon. The shadows of the ancient sugar maples stretch across the lawn in a direction opposite to the morning shadows—sundials telling time. I walk along the road breathing in the mingled scents of summer. I remember how someone thought to honor Aunt Ella after her death and put a new signpost at the foot of the hill saying "Ella Neal Road". The sign fell into the bushes long ago, and I think she would have been glad. To her this was the Old Joe Road, its name for close to 200 years; it always led home.

Reunion

LUCINDA PARIS

MEETING YOUR HUSBAND'S OLD GIRLFRIEND IS A STRANGE business. Meeting her in Japan, stranger still. Chloe and John had exchanged occasional letters for many years, since they were at university in London. When he wrote to tell her he was coming to Japan to give a series of lectures, one near where she was teaching English, she invited us to her house and reserved a place for the three of us on Shiraishi Island, in the Inland Sea, at an international villa run by the Okayama prefecture. It would be peaceful, she had written.

It was midnight when the high-speed train pulled into Okayama Station. Chloe was waiting at the platform. She had a wonderful face— blue eyes, aquiline nose, thin lips. Her hair was fine, with waves around her forehead.

The three of us piled into a taxi. Even in the terrible August heat, the driver was wearing white gloves. We reached Chloe's house where there was one dim bulb shining over the front door. The cicadas were deafening.

She made us leave our sandals just inside the door and put on cloth slippers. The walls were brown, wet-looking concrete; the floors dark wood. "It's my castle," she said, "with more room than anyone at the school believes. Two bedrooms, one upstairs for my very own." There was a living room, a dining area, a kitchen, a bathroom with a funny lime-green washing machine. I noticed a basket of wet clothes and realized they had been wrung out by hand. Our room was a six-tatami room, very posh, Chloe told us, by local standards. There was a futon to be rolled across the brown mats and a coil to light against the mosquitoes. She left us with sheets and towels.

"I can see how tired you are," she said. "We'll talk in the AM."

When John and I unrolled the futon, a two-inch-long cockroach unrolled with it, then fled to a dark corner. The coil wouldn't ignite. Once we had turned out the light, we lay without touching. I could not sleep and repositioned myself a hundred times. Hours later the room became cooler. As I pulled up the sheet to cover our shoulders, I heard Chloe coming down to the bathroom, a flush, then her footsteps back to her bed upstairs.

We awoke to sounds of Gerry Mulligan. A cotton-kimonoed Chloe was in the kitchen packing food to take to the island. There were quiches and five bottles of red wine on the counter. The kettle whistled. She had already set the table. There was Marmite, orange marmalade, real butter. She scrambled eggs. Over breakfast, she and John talked about how Marmite, that awful brown yeast paste, was food for the gods. I had no appetite but was happy to sit nursing a cup of tea, watching how well everything seemed to be going.

We talked about our grown children, all from previous marriages. From her wallet Chloe fanned out several photos of her sons, handsome young men in their early 20s. Among them was a snapshot of John at about the same age—lanky, all cheekbones, holding a cigarette at an elegant angle.

"You don't still carry that?" he asked her. "It's from another century."

"Yes," she smiled. "I suppose it is."

We took a bus to the terminal, then caught the local train to Kasaoka Station. From there it was a wild dash by cab to the ferry. Just seconds after we ran up the gangplank, the boat pulled from its slip.

The deck of the ferry brought little relief from the heat. I sat several benches away, next to the rail, half listening to John and Chloe talk about people they had known in London, friends with whom they still kept in touch. Without the smallest gust of wind, a heavy curtain of rain moved across the water, hammered on the tin roof of the deck, then moved on. The boat slowly glided through the fog, past small mountainous islands. The gray-green conifers that wreathed each shore were filled with white egrets, like candles on Christmas trees. When I pointed them out to John and Chloe, she hardly looked up. She had pushed her straw hat off. It hung against her back on its ribbons.

The passengers getting off at Shiraishi Island were young—children and grandchildren coming from the cities, possibly a few vacationers, Chloe told us. Most of the residents on the islands were elderly.

We made our way through narrow streets lined with ancient houses of crumbling stones and wattle, and newer ones built of weathering plywood. Every house had its raised garden of flowers and vegetables, its vines of bright orange trumpet flowers and bougainvillea. Swallow-tailed butterflies fluttered above the flowers. Overhead, among the electric lines and television antennae, hung cages of drying fish and whole squid strung like star-shaped banners. In the gutters on either side of the walkway, hundreds of tiny crabs raised their pincers in the collected rainwater.

We paused to catch our breath in front of a dilapidated house. An old lady came out to greet us. She extended her hand proudly toward a dozen pots of bonsai in the yard, then toward a large garden. She smiled.

"*Konnichi wa*," Chloe said, bowing deeply. Good day.

"*Konnichi wa*." More bowing.

Just over a rise, not ten yards from where the walkway narrowed to a footpath, we were suddenly at the villa. Even from its back entrance it was an architect's dream: one-story, serpentine. The walls suggested sliding paper panels.

We exchanged our sandals for cloth slippers at the door. The floors were polished slate, the furniture pale wood. The main living and dining areas and the kitchen opened to a curved deck overlooking the sea. We put the food we brought into the huge refrigerator. There was a new gas stove, a dishwasher, a microwave oven, and a Mr. Coffee.

To reach the bedrooms, we padded past a large bathroom with a shower and communal tub, then out into a small terraced courtyard. There were four Western-style bedrooms and one Japanese. Chloe chose the Japanese room, with its tatami mats and futon. When John and I opened the door to our room, I was struck by its beauty at the same moment I felt a blast of cool air. An almost silent air conditioner was mounted high on the wall, operated by a remote control. The walls were white. Freshly ironed sheets and duvets covered the twin beds. At the foot of each was a folded navy-and-white kimono, the man's decorated with a bamboo design, the woman's with vines. A window looked out on the Inland Sea.

We had very little to say at lunch. "Collective tiredness," commented John. "It seems a sacrilege to lie unwashed on that bed, but I can't stay awake another minute." We left our plates on the table.

When I awoke, it was twilight. John's bed was empty. I took my towel and went up to the bathroom. John and Chloe were on the deck talking. I called to them. They waved their wineglasses in reply.

After my shower, I joined them but they were reminiscing about people I did not know. Although they tried to ease me into their conversation, I was content to explore the kitchen. The shelves were stocked with cooking oil, coffee, salt, sugar. In the refrigerator, I found small cucumbers and lettuces left by previous guests, and a lemon. I began to put together a supper.

A warm breeze from the sea swept through the screen panels, carrying the sounds of Chloe and John's laughter. There was something familiar about working in the kitchen, hearing voices through the panels. I turned the oven on low for Chloe's quiche. I liked the kitchen: the fixtures were shining clean, the towels and pot holders soft to the touch. I ran the lettuces under the tap, then drained them. For one brief moment I thought polygamy could work like this. A woman would not have to be always in tandem with her husband. Or be alone. She could sometimes have this. But then she would have to share her husband's bed. A flash of what that intimacy might be—John with Chloe—what that intimacy must have been, caught me as if it were projected on a screen. No, not ever. I improvised a dressing for the salad.

We ate supper on the deck. The weather had cleared, revealing a crescent moon, a sky full of stars. There were few lights in the houses below on the slope to the sea.

When we were having coffee, Chloe and John discussed Gran, John's grandmother, who died alone in a nursing home in London. John's parents had been working in Rhodesia; he had been in graduate school in the United States. Chloe said she visited Gran just before she died. He had not known.

"Do you remember her ring you gave me, the gold ring with the jade shield?"

"I wondered what I had done with that." Then he caught what he had said. "I mean, I knew it was something significant." But she had gone on.

"I lost it when my boys were small. Throwing bread to the ducks. It must have just slipped from my finger. You remember it was always a bit large for me. I searched everywhere. I cried for days." Her voice dropped to a whisper. "Perhaps a magpie stole it. Such bright shining gold."

He nodded.

"But you do remember the bracelet you gave me?"

"I'm miserable at things like this, dear," he said, leaning over to pat her hand.

Chloe spoke, to no one in particular, "I kept thinking of the line, 'They fly from me that sometime did me seek.'"

"'Flee,'" I mentally corrected her.

The next morning, I woke very early. I put on an old sundress and quietly opened the door and went into the courtyard and up the terraced steps to the toilet. The morning was overcast and already stifling. I went to the kitchen but could not face tea or coffee. I ran the tap over my wrists, then drank a glass of tepid water.

I let myself out the front door of the villa. In the garden just below, an old woman wearing a pink sunbonnet right out of Thomas Hardy was pushing a hand plow. Was this the same woman who had spoken yesterday? Yes. She bowed to me. I bowed back. *Konnichi wa.*

I started up a clearly marked path. After the first turn, the path became grass dotted with tiny bright blue flowers. I knelt and picked one. It was the same flower I remembered picking as a child. Did we call it a bluet? Not bluet, a yellow-eyed something? I pocketed it to show to John and Chloe. The cicadas had already worked themselves to a pitch, sounds within sounds suspended in the damp air. There was a small power station hidden in the bamboo. After a few hundred feet, the path grew so steep I had to hold onto the branches of low scrub pines. Then it was easier, camel humps of sand, gradually rising. I found myself high above the bamboo, then high above the village. At the crown of the hill, I suddenly came upon two kites, large as eagles—like those in paintings I had seen in Kyoto—perched in a stunted tree. They did not startle but sat watching me. Then, as if signaled, they took flight, their outstretched wings catching the warm updraft, lifting them high over the sea. I sat on one of the large rocks and watched them. They seemed married.

I took off my sandals to brush my feet. One sandal slipped off the rock and fell into a crevice. I slid down three feet after it, then put it on. When I stood, just in front of me, eye level, was a Shinto shrine carved into the rock face. Stacks of coins had been left as offerings, and a child's straw hat with blue crumpled ribbons. I reached out to straighten the ribbons, a simple act that put my children, when they were small, before me. I thought of a line of poetry, "Whoever you are, come back to me," and tried not to cry. Down below, a ferryboat was coming into harbor. The only thing I had to place on the shrine was the blue flower in my sundress pocket. It was folded upon itself, limp, but I left it there.

At noon we walked down to the village. It was almost deserted. The flimsy houses overhung the walkway. The conversations inside, the intimate clatter of dishes and pans, were so close I felt I was eavesdropping.

Worn stone steps under shade trees led to a group of weathered buildings, their tile roofs gracefully tilted up. A Shinto shrine, said Chloe, or perhaps a monastery. There was a waist-high basin guarded by a diminutive iron dragon, its mouth a spigot of running water. Chloe took one of the tin dippers and poured the cool water on our hands: "ritual cleansing." Then she climbed the steps to the giant temple bell and, with no hesitation, swung the heavy wooden clapper. The sound was deep, harmonious. It faded gradually, summoning no one. All was quiet except for the hum of insects and an occasional bird call.

Up more steps we came to another group of buildings. In front of one were three Buddhas, each carrying an infant in the crook of an arm. I remembered my father, dead so many years, carrying my infant son in just that way. A cloth pinafore had been tied to each infant. Dozens of bright plastic pinwheels stood in wooden holders, like flowers in vases. Behind the statues were two long rows of stone children, each crumbling little effigy wearing a sun-bleached apron.

Chloe spoke softly: "The pinwheels are offerings. Women who can't conceive visit this shrine, I think, and women who have lost children."

We sat on a wooden bench, looking at the Buddhas. We talked about our hopes for grandchildren. I was surprised when John began telling Chloe about a pregnancy scare when he and I had first lived together, about his going with me for my test, to a family planning clinic in London. It was a funny story—all the women, and him the only man in the clinic, but halfway through, I wished he had not begun.

"God knows what we would have done if there had been a baby," he said. "We weren't married yet and our children would have been horrified. But it would have been wonderful, too."

Chloe turned to me. "You're younger than I thought."

"No, not young. It was too late." I felt something inside me pull back.

We retraced our steps down through the roses. I left the two of them behind, talking. Bright blue-tailed lizards, the skinks from my Southern childhood, darted along the spillways. I spotted a small brown viper, its head shaped like a miniature anvil, and watched it zigzag along the hot concrete for a few seconds before I called to John and Chloe. By the time they caught up with me, the viper had disappeared into the grass.

That night we ate at a restaurant in the village. An old woman ushered us to our table; several other women stood in the corner, bowing. The menu offered shashimi covered in a pale pink jelly, strips of octopus, watery tofu, cold tempura, pickles. Chloe ate with obvious enjoyment.

"My Western friends think I am mad, but do you know, from the moment I stepped off the plane at Narita, I felt at home. Japan reminds me of wartime England. Austere."

"Just the words to describe the food," John said. We laughed. In the far corner, the old ladies joined in, a show of good manners.

Chloe did most of the talking. After John had gone to Boston and she had learned of his first marriage, she fled to Poland to teach. "Talk about austerity, postwar Poland was that. But I found solace in helping other people."

John concentrated on the grains of rice left in his bowl.

"After Poland, I came back to England and made that hopeless marriage. Then the babies." She smiled, "And all that."

It was a relief when she began talking about her English classes in Okayama.

The three of us walked along the moonlit path back to the villa.

Later that night, John climbed into my bed.

"You're very good about all this," he whispered. "I had no idea I meant that much to her, that I caused so much pain."

"We all do," I told him. "I just think she has to let you know."

Later, I left the bed and opened the window to the cool air, the muted keening of cicadas. The houses between the villa and the sea were in darkness. There were long strings of green lights in the distance, on the mainland. Tomorrow will be like rewinding a reel, I thought. The ferry, the train to Okayama, the train to Kyoto, the taxi to the hotel.

It was.

Almost ten years have passed. Chloe is still in Japan but about to retire to England, to a cottage in an orchard. We meet her in summer when we are on family visits to London and she is bringing her adult Japanese students abroad. We are easy with one another now, but I have moments when I see the three of us on Shiraishi Island, in that landscape of alien beauty so suitable for our first reunion.

Children and Elders

The Luxury of Order

SUZANNAH LESSARD

NOROTON, AS IT WAS UNIVERSALLY KNOWN, WAS REALLY THE Convent of the Sacred Heart at Noroton, a small boarding school—only 70 students—located in a large Queen Anne mansion on a narrow spit of land that projected from the coast of Connecticut into Long Island Sound. My enrollment there was sudden. The family had spent the summer in California, and we learned when we got home that the car pool to my day school had collapsed. My parents were musicians; our home life was a frugal, Bohemian one in which spontaneous decisions were common.

It was, however, my orderly, upper-crust grandmother who made the call to Noroton. And it was Reverend Mother herself who said I could come, even though it was the last minute, and not to worry about the tuition, they would arrange for a scholarship—I could take the qualifying test later. This was because my mother and aunts had gone to Noroton, and my grandmother herself to a school run by the same order in Rome. So in one sense I belonged utterly at Noroton. On the other hand, at 13 I was a country girl from a household where there was a lot of chaos, and my primary identification at the time was with Huckleberry Finn.

We drove up to the front door, where ancient oak and beech trees shaded the grounds on either side and enclouded the house so that one saw only floating bits of façade—a swatch of brick, a snatch of ample white trim around a piece of ample window, a fragment of the big white pediment over the door. The house was four stories tall, and as we neared it the sky seemed filled with just trees and Noroton. At a glance we could see that every inch of the grounds was gardened, or in some way accounted for. On either side of the drive, however, we saw under spreading boughs clear through to a dazzling sea.

The next thing that I remember was finding myself alone in a white-curtained cubicle in a dormitory. There was a bed, and a crucifix, and a chair not for sitting but for putting your folded clothes on at night, I had been told. My cubicle was between the nun's cubicle, which had solid sides, not curtains, and the wall. This meant that I could not make contact with the other girls. Mine clearly was the most undesirable cubicle, a cubicle someone might be put in for punishment, though I knew that my placement probably reflected my last-minute acceptance—possibly also the fact that my parents weren't paying.

I remember nothing else of my arrival or first few weeks there: it is as if I went into a coma and then awoke as a full-fledged member of a world that I had always known. This reflects shock, no doubt, but it also makes sense in that the densely ornate, beautiful, and absurd life of Noroton was hermetically sealed off from the world in a way that defies the very concept of transition.

Though the real nature of Noroton arose out of intangibles—out of traditions and attitudes and even a mysticism of a sort—Noroton to me is the place: the grounds, the Sound, but primarily the house. It had homelike elements such as a big staircase that swept up from the front hall, an intimate wood-paneled library such as one would find in a home, a space we called the refectory that had once been a dining room, for Noroton had indeed housed a family originally, though on a scale too large-gauged for my imagination to connect with. The first floor especially seemed built for giants.

The structure was full of inferences of hierarchy and divisions. On the second floor, for example, the bedrooms were grand—four girls could sleep in each of them comfortably—with private bathrooms and big windows deeply set so that one could sit in them reading or looking out to the water. On the third floor the bedrooms had dormer windows and no bathrooms, and the ceilings were much lower; these were for lower classwomen. All the rooms that we were allowed into on the fourth floor—previously the floor for servants—were mingy. An exception was the squash court, a deep sky-lighted room of varnished wood in which we studied geometry and Thomas Aquinas.

Much of the fourth floor was out-of-bounds, however, because it was cloistered; only nuns could go there. Bits and pieces of the other floors were also cloistered. So while Noroton, in one sense, became as familiar to me as the house in which I grew up, a substantial portion of it was missing; as a result a coherent blueprint could never coalesce in my mind. It was a logical, highly architectonic structure containing abrupt interruptions of the unknown.

The nuns at Noroton belonged to an order, the Religious of the Sacred Heart, that had been founded in France in the early 19th century. Their habit was based on an 18th-century peasant costume: a fluted starched bonnet encircling the face closely, a black dress, and a shoulder cape with buttons down the front that were imported from France, as were the gold double wedding rings each had put on when taking her vows of poverty, chastity, and obedience in the ceremony of marriage to Christ. Their vows also included a dedication to the care and education of the "Children of the Sacred Heart," which was us. We were never students, we were children. We addressed the nuns as "Mother" and always signed notes and letters to them as "Your loving child." The nuns were cool, aloof, rarefied. Yet when we left on a holiday, which was not often, they would stand on the steps under the pediment and wave good-bye with the big white handkerchiefs that they always kept in their deep pockets.

Customs at Noroton reflected the world of European aristocracy to which earlier Children of the Sacred Heart had belonged, as had many of the earlier nuns, their peasant dress notwithstanding. The motto of the school, for example, was "Noblesse Oblige." A deep court curtsey, for another example, was a part of our daily routine. Whenever a girl met a high-ranking nun, she would curtsey before and after speaking to her. Even if one merely passed, say, the Reverend Mother in the hall, one would say "Good morning, Reverend Mother" and curtsey, though in that case one curtsey would do. We all developed the knack of curtseying without breaking stride for times when we were on the run. A few years ago I encountered a friend from Noroton who had moved to England, to a place near Prince Charles's country house. She had met Prince Charles, she said, and consequently had had an opportunity to use her court curtsey. This news of an interpenetration of the world of Noroton and the "real" world brought on a tiny unearthly thrill such as one would experience upon meeting up with something known only in dreams.

Although in my four years at Noroton there was only one French girl in the student body and no nun of French origin, many of the terms of daily life were French. Our afternoon snack was *goûter*, for example, our holidays were *congés*, and every Sunday night we had *Primes. Primes,* which we pronounced preems, was a ritual that took place in the front hall of the school, a long room with a high coffered ceiling, tapestries on the walls, wooden medieval furniture, and a vast Oriental carpet on the floor. The whole school would be present, seated according to height along the walls, with the nuns in three rows at one end. Each class would, in turn, march up to Reverend Mother, who sat front and center, peeling off in front of her and then circling around to form a small horseshoe directly before her. Fancy parade formations were another tradition inherited from the 18th century

Sitting at Reverend Mother's side, the Mistress General, a kind of dean of students, would say "First Academic Class all very good"—she would pause here while the class curtseyed in unison—and then continue "except for Suzannah Lessard, who loses her notes for . . ." "Losing your notes" was a punishment for anything from a minor infraction such as speaking after lights out to the grave violation once perpetrated by myself and my best friend when we took a tour of the cloistered parts of the house.

Those who didn't lose their notes would get a little blue card from Reverend Mother on which was printed *"Très Bien"* (very good). Those who lost their notes, and they were very few, often just me, would get a card that said *"Bien"* (good), and Reverend Mother would cast her eyes down and frown or look sad as one curtseyed and said, "I'm sorry, Reverend Mother." After *Primes*, the cards would be collected.

I lost my notes at nearly every *Primes*, but as I look back it seems to me that the pattern had nothing to do with the nuns, or the Noroton way of life, but rather with areas of unresolved pain that resulted from my growing up the oldest in a large family with parents who were very young and overwhelmed. For me, this predictable, unemotional punishment—unlike the thrashings at home—meant rules were rules, and adults were adults, and children were really children. It was a kind of luxury I couldn't get enough of. The nuns knew girls, the message was, including misbehaving girls like me. Almost with satisfaction—certainly without alarm—they openly attributed my waywardness to my "artistic temperament." I came to fully belong at Noroton, forming friendships that endured, and learning to trust the nuns implicitly, even as I disobeyed them. Certainly there was never any suggestion that my welcome at Noroton was wearing thin.

There was only one occasion on which the nuns' cool, unflappable love wavered. It had to do with my hair. My hair, when it grew beyond a certain length became a kind of uncontrollable Afro, defying the strict grooming standards at Noroton. I liked this. The rambunctiousness expressed in this way was a kind of safety valve, and though I suppose the nuns made comments and somehow encouraged me to have it cut or find a style that would contain it, I wasn't aware of a lot of pressure in this regard. I was, consequently, taken by surprise completely when one day as I walked by Reverend Mother's parlor she pulled me in, pushed me into a chair, and cut my hair. This violent and invasive action stands alone in all my experience at Noroton, a shocking aberration that reflects, perhaps, how frustrating my incorrigibility must have been.

The heart of Noroton, the place that was at once most formal and most intimate, was the chapel, situated behind the front hall in what had once been the drawing room of the house. A panelled room, with a parquet floor and large windows that directly faced the sea, our chapel had a private, privileged feeling that a church does not have. It was like a room in a home—it was personal—and yet there was the tabernacle, and inside was the host.

We went to mass each morning. In the winter months it would be dark outside and the chapel would be lit by low lights and a few candles on the altar. When we entered, most of the nuns would already be there in their stalls, personal kneeling places set apart along walls. Sometimes they would be finishing up the Office, a ritual of early morning prayers practiced by contemplative orders. In Lent they would have gotten up even earlier to say Matins. The mass was said in Latin then, and all of us, nuns and girls, would say the responses in Latin as well. We girls wore mantillas, the black lace veils that European women wore in church, but that were virtually unknown in America at that time. The kneelers were bare wood, and we all developed calluses called "chapel knees" that would get thicker as the years passed. One fasted before Communion in those days; occasionally a girl would faint.

The ceremony of our daily mass was austere. Kyrie Eleison, Agnus Dei, Sanctus, Sanctus, Sanctus. Over time that early morning hour became, for me, a space within which the tension inside me abated. That space contained the beginning of time and the end of time, and my birth and my death. Before dawn broke, the black sky would acquire depth, an irk blueness that seemed to be a physical manifestation of that space. It was a wild, boundless space, yet one made accessible by elaborate artifices: by the rituals, manners, and systems of symbols that made up our life there. Within its stillness, and its vastness, I experienced myself in a way that was supernally calm and pleasurable, yet also passionate. In that space I felt profoundly free.

Twice a year we had a three-day retreat, in which we observed a rule of silence from beginning to end. Our time was meant to be spent in prayer and recollection, we were allowed to take contemplative walks alone (something that I would have liked to have been able to do at all times), were served especially good food, and listened several times a day to a priest who would talk to us in the chapel. The priest was usually a Jesuit, but one year it was a Dominican who led the spring retreat, and I requested a private session with him. I wanted to tell him about an impasse that I had come to in that free calm space I had discovered at daily mass. As I told the Dominican, I had arrived at a point at which it seemed to me that I had to make a decision either to mindlessly do what the church taught, or to think for myself. The priest hesitated for a long time, and then he said, "You must think." The answer said to me, *Your existence is serious.*

Another set of structures containing the inner space I had discovered at mass was music. We sang a great deal at Noroton. Every day, for half an hour before lunch, the whole school would stand in the study hall learning and rehearsing sacred music, usually Gregorian chant, or the polyphonic music of the Middle Ages, and then we would sing it at Benediction or at Sunday Mass, or as part of the special liturgies of Advent, or Lent, or the processions around the grounds in May. This is music that was written not to impress or edify or give aesthetic pleasure, but to give glory to God. It's a kind of art in which ancientness is palpable and also in which there is a very clear underlying assumption of humility, of human tinyness, of awe. Gregorian chant sung on a dark morning in Lent especially creates an attitude quite at odds with modern conceptions of the nature of the world and man's place in it. The lusty and unreserved joyful worship of a Magnificat and the stately prayerfulness of an Ave Maria also opened up dimensions from another time.

It all fell away.

With the modernization of the church in the late sixties (I had graduated in 1962), the nuns left the cloister and went into the world in regular clothes, in many cases to serve in the inner cities. In a secular world, my ties to a changing Catholicism also fell away.

Noroton closed and the property was sold to a developer who, I heard, tore down the middle section of the house, the section that contained the chapel. This left two freestanding wings facing each other, which he renovated into condominiums.

One spring, long after all this happened, I was driving through Connecticut on the thruway when the exit for Noroton came up. On a whim I took it, and a little while later I was driving down the road that leads toward the end of the point. I parked outside the entrance and walked up the drive.

Where before there had been a facade enclouded in trees, there was nothing. In place of the middle section of the house there was just sky. You could walk right through to the sea on the far side. But I stood there on the site of the chapel, aware, first, of my feet on the ground, then of my weight, of my eyes, of my breath, of the interior of me, of my heart. Of my soul.

The Children's War

ANTONIA STEARNS

IN THE SUMMER OF 1942, WASHINGTON, D.C., WAS HOT AND overcrowded but brimming with patriotic spirit and communal purpose. At nine and six years of age, my older brother and I threw ourselves mightily into the war effort, hauling newspapers and scrap metal in our Radio Flyer wagons, planting a Victory garden, and feverishly knitting afghan squares that rarely came out symmetrical. Even our three-year-old brother was enlisted, to flatten tin cans with his toy hammer.

But the sleep of the just eluded us. At night, in a stifling attic, we lay panting and spread-eagled on sheets dipped in a bucket of ice water and wrung out, while a fan behind the bucket blew ostensibly cooled air in our direction. The attic was the boys' bedroom. Mine was on the second floor, but I was frequently relegated upstairs when transient Foreign Service colleagues—evacuated, like ourselves, from the war in Europe—camped out for indefinite periods among my dolls and teacups.

The fan over the bucket was a form of primitive air conditioning our Dutch mother had devised to counter the failure of American settlers to build with the subtropical Washington climate in mind—so unsensible, so unlike the well-ventilated colonial villas she had known as a child in the East Indies.

Mother's European prejudices caused us acute embarrassment when she trundled them out before our friends. That she was much admired for her style and sophistication, her fluency in languages, her exotic looks, and unusual background escaped our notice entirely. To us she was the mother who brought steamed vegetables to the school bake sale, where they lay like green valleys between Alpine peaks of angel food cake.

Our family had been displaced from enemy Berlin—our father to the American embassy in London and our mother to wait out the war with us in her adopted but still alien country. My recollection of our extended and somewhat harrowing repatriation, which took over a year, is only of strange beds, midnight trains, and chaotic border crossings, highlighted by the company of a downed British pilot who hid under our overcoats at the checkpoint between Norway and Sweden. As for our father, I took his absence and eventual return for granted, and followed his encounters with blackouts and bombs through cheerful but erratically delivered picture postcards.

Settled on a neighborly street, we were busily discovering American childhood rituals: peanut butter sandwiches and Saturday matinees, the freedom of wandering into brownie-scented kitchens and playing sidewalk games with a pack of streetwise little friends. The war and a foreign mother notwithstanding, 1942 seemed a pretty good year until the heat deprived us of companions as well as sleep.

Suddenly our new friends were dispatched to camps with Indian names or to resorts with pools and tennis courts in a holiday ritual our mother had failed to anticipate and, in any event, could not afford. But by August she had saved up enough cash and gas coupons for a week in the Blue Ridge Mountains, at a hotel offering rates too good to be true. After a day's drive, we pulled up before a decrepit wooden lodge, used occasionally for Bible retreats, and found that the recreational facilities consisted of a rickety veranda and a lounge with a broken Victrola.

Was there anything in the area with activities for children? Mother asked the kitchen staff dozing on the empty veranda. The cook scratched his head. "Hold on a sec," he remembered, "there's Maisie and Staylor's farm." A farm? We were all ears. "Maisie's boarding a city kid for the summer. I hear she's looking for more." As a last hope, Mother took directions and carted children and luggage back to the car.

We bounced over dirt roads through dense and untidy woods, which gradually gave way to fields and farms, each with a barn and a low line of chicken coops. Many of the spare frame houses and outbuildings were unpainted; this was depressed Appalachia, where bankruptcy hinged on a penny's rise in chicken mash or a nickel's drop in poultry prices.

We knocked a long time at Maisie's door, peering through yellowed lace curtains into a stiff front parlor before realizing that the back porch was the customary entrance. There tools and wood shavings were strewn among half-finished rocking chairs; a circuit board lay in a tangle of copper wire. Staylor was both a farmer and carpenter-electrician, scraping together odd jobs for cash to buy what the farm could not provide. Chicken prices were down that year, and Maisie, a practical soul, was looking for boarders to tide her family over during the summer.

All this my mother learned sitting at a long, linoleum-covered table in the summer kitchen while the diminutive Maisie set out supper for the men threshing that day in Staylor's field. It was a communal effort—a dozen or more farmers pooling their resources to rent a single combine. With the men out cutting and bundling hay, Maisie was left with the milking, the pigs and chickens, the vegetable garden and dairy house, canning, cooking, laundry, and tending her midlife baby.

Maisie scrutinized my older brother for his potential. He looked awfully puny beside the other "city boy," a strapping teenager from the nearest town, 20 miles away. The boarder took us on a tour of the farm while the two women discussed the situation and came to a perfect understanding. They immediately liked and trusted each other and found similar values across the gulf of their dissimilar lives. Both knew what it was to raise a family in hard times; both shared a strong work ethic and an uncomplicated belief that children adapted easily to whatever was expected of them. Of course allowance had to be made for age: they agreed that a nine-year-old could handle the rigors of farm life, a three-year-old could not, and I, sandwiched in between, was a question mark.

But not for long. As the boy took us on his rounds he gave us buckets to help milk the cows and slop the pigs. Twisting tails and thumping rumps, he maneuvered the cows into their stalls, where we followed him timidly for our first lesson in milking. We moved on to the sty. A sow had rolled on her piglets. He handed us pitchforks and told us to poke her hard while he waded in the muck to search for survivors.

By the time we returned to the summer kitchen we had tasted blood and would never be innocent again. A rat, which we had helped to corner, lay clubbed to death in the corn crib, and three decapitated hens swung by their claws from our triumphant hands. Maisie dropped the hens in boiling water before tossing them to us to pluck. We were hard at it when our mother kissed us good-bye and drove away in the dust, her youngest howling beside her, still clutching his trophy of feathers. Maisie rolled up four $5 bills and put them in an empty canning jar behind many rows of preserves. "All right, children," she said quickly, before our lips could quiver in the realization that we were in her care for two weeks, "Who's going to dig potatoes with me before we put the pie in the oven?" She took us by the hand and showed us the miracle of where potatoes come from.

It is on record that I spent the first night sobbing on Staylor's lap while he rocked me gently in one of his chairs, although I have no memory of it. I do remember the satisfaction and drudgery of bringing in the crops, churning butter until my arms ached, and guiding Peggy, the old workhorse, while Elwood, a muscular grown son, rode the tiller behind, shouting "Gee!" and "Haw!" as we ploughed new rows. I remember Peggy stepping on my brown bare foot, which sank into the warm soil, fortunately lessening the impact of her enormous weight. Even so, it hurt. I beat on Peggy's sweating flanks, but she refused to budge until an exasperated Elwood jumped off the tiller, and whomped her one. I waited for sympathy, but Elwood only scowled when he saw I had been leading Peggy in a crooked line. "Dad blame it all!" (the strongest language we ever heard), "Back her up, girl, and keep your foot out the way this time."

My brother pitched hay, fell out of the loft twice, and learned to drive a tractor. He dug fresh holes for the outhouse, located on top of the hill behind the chicken coops, a scary walk at night by flashlight.

He helped Staylor install a party-line telephone—three long rings, one short, he still reminds me. The first outgoing call was to Mother, begging her to let us stay longer.

In 1943 Maisie filled a second, then a third jar with board money. We arrived the day after school ended and stayed until Labor Day. Furthermore, we brought two friends, and in midsummer Mother brought two more. Everyone she knew was intrigued by the unusual and incredibly inexpensive camp she had turned up. The more our exploits gained attention, the more mother rose in our estimation.

"It's called the farm," I told Washington neighbors proudly. How nice. Were there horses? "Just Peggy," I said, "But we have 10,000 baby chickens." I explained how they came in boxes like furry Ping-Pong balls. "Some of them get squashed and die," I added knowingly. The mothers on the block were wide-eyed. Did these two quasi-European children with their laced Oxford shoes and satchels on their backs, with their music and dance lessons, and a mother whose idea of rural life was a stroll in the Tuileries, really spend their summers running barefoot through pigsties and cow dung?

With adults we toned down the gory side of farm life, but over marbles and jacks with the gang we spared no details: hogs squealing at the slaughter, skunks blasted to smithereens with shotguns, and chickens flopping about with their heads chopped off. "No kidding, for how long?" "Hours," I lied.

The next year there were 12 boarders. Staylor turned the attic into a dormitory and strung sheets across the middle: girls on one side, boys on the other. The summer kitchen was extended. Two of Maisie and Staylor's daughters left their five-and-ten-cent store jobs to run the kitchen and run us. We worked in squads and lined up by size for Saturday night baths in a galvanized tub on the grass. My little brother now led the procession. Beatrice scrubbed our heads with lye soap and Marjorie handed out clean sheets made of flour sacking to change our beds. Marjorie was a solemn young war bride; Beatrice was single but knew a thing or two. From her we learned about hanky-panky at the square dances down by the sawmill, and even worse goings-on at a moonshine still hidden in the woods. Before the weekly purification, we liked to get as filthy as possible playing War in the cornfield, where we slithered between the rows and lobbed rotten tomatoes at one another.

Sundays were strictly observed: no games, no books, and no radio for news of the real war, whose tide was now turning, as we knew it would, in our favor. We donned dresses, long pants, and shoes for Sunday school, and kept them on until after midday dinner. While Staylor led us to church, Maisie stayed behind to churn peach ice cream for dessert, and to replenish her spirits in solitary reflection. When we returned, there was usually an open Bible or Montgomery Ward's catalog on the porch swing.

Prosperity was bringing change and even public attention to the farm. A county health inspector appeared without warning and we kept him busy studying our tetanus shot records while Maisie rushed to put 20 jelly glasses out by the drinking pump. After he left we put them away and went back to using the communal tin cup. That year we pulled down the split rails around the pasture and replaced them with electrified barbed wire. The dairy house languished when a refrigerator was installed in the kitchen and a pickup truck began to make runs into town.

Victory over the Axis brought our father safely and joyfully home to be reintroduced to his long-legged offspring, who greeted him with trumpet solos, neatly executed pirouettes, and a mean curveball that made him duck. He had brought us Scottish woolens that were too small, and books we had outgrown. And with our family reunited, we began to outgrow the farm.

There was one last summer when Staylor built an indoor bathroom, which was much admired but never used, and when Elwood, to my annoyance, went courting at the next farm. I studied myself in his shaving mirror, tossing my pigtails and wondering what he would think of me in a Veronica Lake peekaboo hairdo. August passed slowly that year, and when our old Chevrolet swung into view on the newly paved road, I ran down from the outhouse for the last time, and, for the first time, ready to go home.

The Washington house was a jumble of packing crates. We were returning to Berlin, where our wartime saga had begun under giant swastikas and megaphones blaring *Sieg Heil* over the roar of the crowds.

It was not easy for my parents to shake the memory of those years, and they approached their assignment to occupied Germany with mixed emotions. We children were simply curious, and excited by the prospect of change.

No newsreel had prepared me for the devastation of the ruined city, for the lingering odor of war, the sheared-off buildings with plumbing fixtures still clinging to their inner walls, and women and children picking through rubble as high as slag heaps. We drove slowly along streets littered with burnt vehicles, past convoys of American soldiers directing civilian work brigades, to a bullet-pocked, requisitioned house in a once prosperous residential neighborhood.

Stepping into its ornately furnished rooms, I had a flash of myself in prewar Berlin sitting at a heavy claw-footed table laden with aromatic breads and hot chocolate and gazing at umbrella pines against a pale northern sky. But these rooms smelled only of abandonment. We stopped before the photographs, still on the piano, of the family that had been on the losing side. The children were our age, and could have been ourselves, smiling at the camera and unaware of what was to befall them. I studied their faces and understood for the first time what our father had survived, what our mother had accomplished, leading us out of Europe one step ahead of the German armies, and what we had been spared.

Upstairs in a strange bedroom, I unpacked my dolls and teacups, but soon put them away for good. My childhood was coming to an end, and I would never again be so cavalier about life and death as when War was just a game we played through all those violent, happy summers on the farm.

Things That Count

TERESA WENDEL

MRS. NESBITT LIVED ON THE CORNER NEXT TO OUR HOUSE. THE only time we ever saw her was in the summertime during raspberry season, and we never once saw her face, just the tip of her black hat over the raspberry bushes in the lot between our houses—20 rows or more. A name without a face and a black pointed hat. So if we children thought she was a witch, what else could we imagine?

All those raspberries. You'd think we'd be in heaven, sneaking into the back of the lot, stuffing our mouths until the juice dribbled down our chins. But we never touched a berry. We figured she had put a spell on them.

One day Mrs. Nesbitt was killed by a hit-and-run driver when she was crossing the road. It was dark and she was dressed in black, so the driver probably didn't see her.

Grandma and Grandpa came to visit us the weekend after Mrs. Nesbitt died. My father's parents lived on a run-down ranch out in the country and didn't have an indoor toilet, even though it was 1961. Grandma and I were playing rummy on a tattered quilt in our backyard. I laid down a run of hearts—4 through 7. Grandma thought a moment and looked at me the way she did when she was getting ready to lay down her whole hand. She let out a laugh.

"That's just what I needed, girl. Easier'n shootin' fish in a rain barrel." She laid her cards on the blanket. "Rummy!"

I hated when she did that. I was a good card player, but Grandma wasn't like a lot of grown-ups who let you win.

"It's too bad you and Grandpa can't buy Mrs. Nesbitt's house even though it's probably haunted," I told her after that hand.

"Maybe Grandpa and I will walk over later and take a gander through the windows," she mused as she dealt again.

I must say that the idea of having Grandma right next door was appealing. My dad was an engineer on the Great Northern Railroad, running freight trains back and forth over the mountains between Seattle and Wenatchee. He spent a good part of his time on the road, and the rest of it trying to catch up on his sleep. It was all he could do to fix everything that had fallen to pieces in our old house since the last time he had been home, let alone find the time to play catch with his kids. And Mom was just plain overwhelmed, trying to keep up with all the washing, ironing, and mending that her growing family generated. She was still using a wringer washer in the sixties and drying all the laundry outside on a line. My mom had my brother and me before the age of 20, and she had just given birth to my baby sister, number five, with no hope of a reprieve. It was plain to see why she couldn't waste her time passing out hugs and kisses. We learned early on that when Mom told us to go outside to get some fresh air, she was really telling us to get lost for the rest of the day. I swear we got more fresh air than any other kids in the town.

It was our good luck that our rural neighborhood north of Seattle was spilling over with large families like ours. We kids never lacked for something to do. We knew every stream, pond, field, and climbing tree. We roamed the countryside as long as there was daylight.

When we skinned a knee, we knew not to bother our mom for a squirt of Bactine or a Band-Aid. We tried to fend for ourselves, and when Grandma did move next door she filled the void. If my mom didn't have time for us, Grandma did. Nothing she was doing was so grand that it couldn't be put aside to deal out a game of rummy. And we could be sure that Gram's green cookie bowl would be full after we depleted the jar Mom struggled to keep filled. Having Grandma for a next-door neighbor was the best thing that ever happened to us kids.

I always thought that I was the one who gave Grandma and Grandpa the idea to move next door, but I found out later that Grandpa was just starting to get sick and the ranch was too much for them to keep up. After she and Grandpa settled in, Gram said the house was not haunted after all, but the first thing she did was plow under almost all Mrs. Nesbitt's berries, saving only one row along the wire fence between our houses. We kids would fill cracked crockery bowls with the plump red berries and Gram would sprinkle them with plenty of sugar. There was always enough left for her to make pint after pint of raspberry jam.

Grandma planted her vegetables where the raspberry patch used to be. The weeds always had the upper hand, but she never once asked us to help out with the hoeing. There was a big harvest even after the slugs had their fill. Grandma came from Missouri, and she was a born cook. Green beans with bacon. Corn on the cob. Creamed peas. Potatoes and carrots cooked in the juices of a huge pot roast. Bread-and-butter pickles, dill pickles lined up on the kitchen counter in Mason jars. We scrambled for our places around the kitchen table for Sunday dinners with our aunties and cousins.

In her yard the overgrown beds were tangled and unkempt with so many flowers she couldn't keep up. Forget-me-nots. Grape hyacinths. Purple crocus. Money plants. Foxgloves. Peonies. Poppies. Iris. Lavender. Larkspur. Snapdragons. Hollyhocks. Pansies.

In no time at all we wore a path between our houses. When Grandma walked over she leaned on a pointed wooden stick. "Got 27 slugs on my way," she'd announce, resting her pole against the back of the house. My stomach turned over at the sight of those slugs shish-kebabed on the end of her walking stick, pale yellow guts spilling out. "That makes 167 this week, and I haven't even walked home yet."

Grandma counted everything. How many trick-or-treaters came to her door. How many Christmas cards she received. How many pairs of mittens she had knitted. The number of blooms on her prize dahlia. The number of phone calls a day. She kept a green stenographer's notebook where all her lists were tallied by date and year. I wish I had that notebook now, because I still wonder how many slugs departed this life on the tip of Grandma's walking stick.

Grandpa was thin and handsome and had dark hair even though he was old. He smiled a lot and wore a tan felt hat. He could sign his name real fancy and draw very good eagles. He read the dictionary and memorized five new words every day. If we coughed long enough and hard enough, he'd reach in his pocket and give us each a pink peppermint lozenge.

"It just amazes me how you kids have lived so long with such severe cases of whooping cough," he'd remark between our fits of coughing.

The night Grandpa died was the saddest of my life. They made me go to school the next day anyhow. I stood behind the school building in a mud puddle and cried the whole recess, no matter that I was in the fifth grade. When all the friends and relatives left after the service, I watched Grandma write down in her green stenographer's notebook how many people had come to the funeral and how many folks put flowers on his grave.

After that, we kids would take turns spending the night with Grandma. We played rummy if nothing good was on TV. She usually fell asleep before bedtime, snoring in her overstuffed rocking chair. The first thing everyone would ask when you came home the next morning was, "What did Gram fix you for a snack?" The other kids got pie with ice cream, angel food cake with seven-minute frosting, banana splits, gooey cinnamon buns, or rice pudding with a thick custard on top. All I ever got was Jell-O. Somehow Grandma got it in her mind that I preferred that over any other treat, and she always aimed to please. She was nice and fat, and I always felt sorry for my friend Sherry—she had a skinny grandmother with pointy glasses. It was my opinion that women should let themselves get fat after their grandchildren are born.

Grandma wasn't much of a housekeeper, but she taught all the neighborhood girls how to knit and embroider, helping us fill our hope chests. She would listen to our problems; pull our loose teeth with her pointed pliers; cut and curl our hair; rub Mentholatum on anything that was hurt, bruised, or broken; and threaten to sell us to the gypsies if we misbehaved. She sang songs I never heard before, whistled when she did the dishes, and recited old-fashioned poems. She taught me to believe in fairies and showed me where they lived. We girls spent sultry afternoons trying to tame her cats. We didn't have to worry about what to call them or how to tell them apart. They were all calicoes, and Grandma named every one of them Minnie.

I left home to go to college in 1971. My folks are still convinced that sending their young daughter to Spokane, 300 miles away from home, was a big mistake. Grandma bought me two pairs of blue jeans before I left, the first I ever owned.

When I came home for summer break I was a different person, and those changes went far deeper than my newly pierced ears and blond-streaked hair. My father plied me with questions. Had I drunk beer? Yes. Smoked marijuana? Yes. He inquired about my virginity. None of his business.

It's no wonder they were disturbed.

I met Kurt at a college dance during those first few months away from home. Innocent and lonely, I was attracted right away by his worldliness, his long wavy hair, his dark Eurasian handsomeness. By the time I had sewn patches all over his jeans and embroidered flowers on mine, we had fallen in love. We were married two years later.

Grandma came with us to get our marriage license, and she was the only grown-up in my family who knew that the young man behind the thick black beard was good enough for me. My father was fit to be tied. He had always worked hard to give his family a better life, and he certainly had higher aspirations for his oldest daughter. My scholarship money got me into college where I was supposed to snag myself a clean-cut doctor or lawyer for a husband. You can imagine that Kurt, an anthropology major, was a real disappointment. Never mind that he was half-Japanese and any children he spawned would surely be born polka-dotted. I think the only redeeming feature my father could see was that Kurt was neither a Jew nor a Catholic.

I was happy to be the one to give birth to Grandma's first great-grandchild. Kurt would drop me and baby Jacob off at Grandma's house every Wednesday morning on his way to work. The sourdough pancakes were always sizzling on the stove when we arrived. My mother, still living next door, was now coping with three teenagers. After seven kids, grandchildren were no temptation to her. Grandma, on the other hand, was ready to start all over again.

I still feel bad when I picture Grandma leaning over the kitchen sink, exhausted after frying up the pancakes. I knew she was sick, but I let her insist on making my Wednesday breakfasts anyhow. She died when Jacob was about ten months old. I stayed with her in the hospital all the last week, listening to her rattly breathing. My sister, a nurse, kept a vigil, making sure Grandma was comfortable. Brothers, sisters, aunts, cousins, and friends came and went and came again. Her room was filled with the flowers she loved, all homegrown.

Kurt and I had been eager for his parents, 3,000 miles away in Hawaii, to see their first grandchild. Living on a shoestring, we saved for a visit for over a year. Grandma died the night before we were to leave. My great-aunt convinced us that Grandma wouldn't want us to cancel our plans. I regret to this day that I missed the funeral, because it was a whole year before I finally cried.

Mom, Dad, and the aunts squabbled over anything they thought might be valuable when they cleaned out Grandma's house while I was away. Things that really meant something to each of us kids ended up at the county dump. Decks of cards. Chipped flower vases. The green cookie bowl. Her button box. Crocheted doilies. Embroidered dresser scarves. Her knitting bag. All gone. Although Mom gave me the old iron bed that Grandma had promised me, and her chipped dishes were distributed among the cousins, nobody stopped to think that maybe we needed something personal to remember her by.

The house I live in now looks like Grandma's house, only not as messy. My garden is brimming with her favorite flowers. I don't have as much time for my kids as she had for us, but I leave a deck of cards on the table to remind me. I never married a doctor or a lawyer and we're always on a budget, but being married to a transit bus driver for more than 20 years suits me just fine. Whenever I see a Grandma kind of thing in a secondhand store, Kurt pulls out his wallet and hands me his lunch money without so much as a blink, convincing me to buy it. He loved Grandma too, and honors her for being a bright spot in my childhood. My keepsakes may not have belonged to Grandma, but whenever I salt the soup with the green Depression glass shaker that sits on my stove, or put a bouquet in a chipped plaster vase, I remember her.

And even though Grandma's green stenographer's notebook may lie buried in the dump, I'm glad I remembered one thing. I asked Auntie to show me the guest book from the funeral reception when I got back from Hawaii. I made sure to count how many people came to the service. I wrote down how many people sent flowers in my own green stenographer's notebook. I know if I ever see Gram again, that will be the first thing she wants to know.

If These Walls Could Talk

JUDITH BELL UNGAR

Says the Living Room

I'll go first, not just because I'm biggest, but because I am the front room. Open the door and *presto*! Here I am. To one side of the door stands a table with a mirror above it. There used to be a big music-box vase on the table that played the wedding song "Because you come to me with naught save love . . ." But the older girl, Judy, performing magnificent soaring *tours jetés* diagonally across the room, knocked it down and broke it. Her daddy's desk, which he built in his garage workshop, is on the other side of the door. It has a glass top, and on the side, a clever second drawer with his tiny black Corona typewriter in it.

The couch is for more than sitting. When Judy comes home from Girl Scout camp, all hoarse from shouting and singing and laughing, and dead-tired, she flops on it and catches up on her sleep. Her mama lies on her back on the couch with her head in her husband's lap while he plucks her eyebrows. On this couch Judy's mama gives her a booklet, *You're a Young Lady Now*, explaining changes—coming soon to a body near you—and Judy is furious. Furious with Mama for handing her the booklet instead of talking to her about it, furious with God for inventing such messy activities for our bodies. She's furious, furious.

Then not furious. She's thinking that having one of those periods will be a good thing. It will belong to her alone, it will be her secret from the rest of the world. She pulls up the wool afghan and smiles, thinking of all the periods she will have.

When Grandpa Weiner comes to visit after his surgery, he groans when he sits down in one of the two upholstered chairs, and again when he raises himself out of it. But when he is just plain sitting in it he feels fine. Judy considers this and then shows off:

"Oh, the transitions bother you," she says.

The wooden corner bookcase is the place for the annual Rosh Hashanah cards.

The Dining Room

I am the most unusual room in the house. Mama painted each wall a different shade of purple. The wall with the windows has dots painted on it in turquoise. The drapes are in the purple family with a turquoise paisley print swirling all over. None of Judy's friends has a dining room like this. None of them has a mama like hers, so creative, so original, so changeable from one mood to another.

The dining table, in fact all the dining room furniture, was an engagement present to Daddy and Mama from her parents in 1939. Eating in the dining room means using the sterling silver. Mama's set even has iced tea spoons. Mama's youngest brother, Solly-boy, drinks his iced tea with the spoon still in the glass, sticking up at the top. Judy, who is not allowed to leave her spoon in her glass, watches carefully to see Uncle Sol poke himself in the eye, but it never happens.

The table is good to hide under. "Stop giggling," Beverly from next door tells Judy when they play hide-and-seek there. "They'll find us."

"I know how to stop laughing: I'll pretend I have to stop taking ballet and then I'll feel like crying." This is even before Judy reads Anna Pavlova's life story and yearns to dance until her toes bleed.

The Kitchen

I'm the busiest room—let me speak, please. You wouldn't have fancy meals in the dining room if not for me. Here Mama bakes lemon meringue pie that makes the whole room smell yellow, and Daddy's favorite cake, devil's food, covered with seven-minute frosting, then coated with unsweetened chocolate. The brittle chocolate sounds a quiet pop of resistance when his fork breaks through it into the soft, creamy frosting. Most meals are eaten on my white table where Harriet and Judy learn the don'ts of dining-room and eating-out manners: don't chew with your mouth open, don't talk with food in your mouth, don't reach across for a serving dish. Especially don't play with your food by using mashed potatoes as pea-magnets or building vegetable dams to hold gravy.

The round-shouldered icebox (rarely opened between meals), skinny-legged stove, and white-tiled counter (where Daddy develops film at night with only a red lightbulb burning) leave little space in the middle of the room. But there's enough for the maid to set up the ironing board, and enough for Judy to lie at her feet and look up her dress and think that she is so cool, so casual, that no one can figure out what she is doing down there. One day, Judy sits at the kitchen table drawing. Daddy walks in from work at Sinclair Refinery, looks at her drawing, and says, "We do not make pictures of people's private parts."

After Judy and Beverly fight, Judy stands inside the screen at the kitchen back door and says, "You can't come in and help me shell peas, Beverly Montgomery." And Judy has not yet read about punishing somebody by not letting him help you whitewash the fence.

The Bathroom

I'm small, I'm important, I know a lot. When the girls were babies the bassinet was set up here for their baths. Then the water drained out the tube into the big tub. Only I hear Judy's dialogues, which she composes while she sits on the toilet.

"Travis says he'll nominate me for safety patrol—to be whistle captain. I think he has a crush on me."

"Eugene has a crush on me. He wrote me a poem."

In this room Daddy sterilizes a sewing needle in a match flame and gently works splinters out of soles and palms. He hangs strips of film from the shower curtain rod to dry. The girls love Mama to shampoo them and pull their sudsy hair up, up into pointy soft cones.

In the middle of the night, Judy wakes and goes into the bathroom. Mama hears, comes in to check, and finds Judy in the dark room. She smiles and pats Judy on the cheek.

"Ouch," cries Judy.

Mama turns on the light. Judy's cheeks are puffy with mumps.

When she's a little older, Judy spends time in this bathroom leaning over, coaxing her modest peaks into her double-A bra. Looking into the mirror over the basin, she prays, "Please help me fill this out."

My tile floor is known to be the best place indoors to play jacks. On my floor Harriet and Judy can use a golf ball, which bounces much higher than a rubber ball. Also, their hands don't get scraped like they do on the sidewalk.

The Hall

I'm even smaller than the bathroom, but I connect everything. And the telephone is here. Judy likes to sit on my floor, stretch out while she's talking to Patsy or Meredith, and consider what her legs will look like when she's allowed to shave them. The phone, KEystone 5-1-3-1, is a party line, so she sometimes hears voices she doesn't recognize. She follows the party liners' Golden Rule: Do not listen into others' calls, as you would not have them listen into yours.

The Parents' Room

Mama and Daddy have a big bed with a peach satin comforter that tries to slip out of the diamond-shaped opening in its embroidered white cotton coverlet. Wisps of feathers escape and settle lazily onto Judy's hair when she gets on the big bed.

Harriet and Judy look in Mama's jewelry box, brush their hair in front of her vanity mirror, and pat their cheeks with the powder puff in her compact. Before Daddy and Mama go out in the evening, she puts on perfume and then dabs a hint of it behind the girls' ears, barely touching them with the glass wand.

When Daddy works the night shift at the refinery and sleeps in the daytime, the kids have to be quiet outside the bedroom windows. Mama sets up her sewing machine in here. Once a lady comes with a folding table that turns out to be a skinny bed, and she gives Mama a massage right here in the bedroom. Judy thinks this is better, certainly less embarrassing, than going to the health club, where Mama takes her once for a massage. So many ladies under sheets but not under them enough. Inside Mama's closet are her size nine AAAA shoes. The closet is more special in the girls' room.

The Girls' Room

Three sliding closet doors run on tracks; don't step on them barefoot. The girls' shoes are lined up on the floor. They used to keep them in a hanging shoebag, but after they discover the forgotten Easter egg in it, they have to throw the smelly bag away. On the top shelf, pink polka-dotted boxes are stacked up, each with a different storybook doll in it. School clothes and good clothes are hanging on a rod. Mama has sewed matching organdy pinafores and sundresses for the girls and for herself.

You could say this room is custom-built. In his shop Daddy makes the girls' twin headboards, their matching desks with drawer pulls jig-sawed into wooden initials, the windowseat, and the toy shelf. He does working drawings of what he is going to build, then he takes photographs and they are published in *Popular Mechanics.* In the shallow top drawer of her desk Judy keeps Woody Tompkins's ID bracelet, even when he stops being her boyfriend. In the second drawer she saves letters from her pen pal who lives in Hattiesburg, Mississippi, and writes looking into a mirror. Judy has to read the letters the same way. The bottom drawer contains James Dean pictures Judy is pasting into a spiral notebook just about him.

The girls are close enough in age—three years apart—to share this room and the books and toys and games in it. *Mother Goose, Munro Leaf, A Child's Garden of Verses*, and *The Golden Egg Book* have gravitated to the bottom of their bookshelf; Nancy Drew mysteries and the 35-cent volumes they order weekly at school from the paperback book club are taking over the upper shelves. Monopoly and Clue have replaced big-piece puzzles.

Both girls have bead collections. They augment the beads they buy in glass vials from Woolworth's and the Hobby Shop by taking apart the broken or unwanted necklaces that Aunt Zelda, Aunt Annette, and Aunt Sandra give them. Special buttons qualify, too. Judy's prize acquisition is unlike anything else she has seen: four inches of sparkling glass with a hole at one end and a sharp point at the other. Her friend Adele Branson gave it to her, but refuses to say where she got it. When the two girls' families next get together at the Bransons' house, Judy hears Adele's mother talking to Mama in the dining room.

"I cannot imagine what could have happened to the central piece." Mrs. Branson gestures toward the crystal chandelier above her dining table.

Every night Mama and Daddy kiss the girls goodnight and tuck them in. "Sleep tight and don't let your big toes fight," Mama says.

When the family comes home late from an outing, Harriet and Judy fall asleep in the back seat of the Oldsmobile. Daddy carries them one at a time into the house and puts them in their beds. Sometimes the girls are not really asleep, but being carried is so pleasant that they pretend. The hard part is keeping their eyelashes from fluttering, but Daddy never catches on.

Staying home sick in bed feels good. If Judy's nose is stopped up, Mama puts a card table on the bed, a sheet over it, and the vaporizer under it. It is like playing house in a tropical jungle. For lunch Mama invents iceberg soup: a bowl of Campbell's vegetable soup with a scoop of mashed potatoes. Mama brings in the portable radio from the kitchen and Judy listens to Don McNeil on "The Breakfast Club" from Chicago, and to "Queen for a Day." She hears the three women's problems and roots for the one with the worst set—really the luckiest, because she will win the refrigerator. Judy's job is to drink liquids and have her temperature go down and to do the homework her friends call in.

So what if parties are in the living room and cake eaten in the dining room? I'm the room where the girls' birthdays begin. Early in the morning while the birthday girl sleeps, everyone else puts gifts on the end of her bed. Judy loves waking up to a skyline silhouette of presents just beyond her toes, and her family standing there waiting.

Things happen in bed that no one can see. The fairy takes away a tooth and leaves a nickel under the pillow. Dreams sneak in even with the hall light shining. In Judy's recurring bad dream Porky Pig clings to the metal bars on the inside of the garage door. He is not pink and funny like he is in the comics. He is too large and he won't go away.

So. That's the house. 2344 North Boulevard, Houston, Texas. Bought in 1939 for $4,000. Lived in by these folks for 14 years.

The Screened Porch

Wait! You forgot me.

I'm in front, white wood inside and out. A slatted swing hangs from my ceiling. Mama, a book in her lap, moves to and fro. Judy brings her doll dishes out, arranges them, and photographs them with her Brownie camera. She smells the grass clippings after Daddy mows, and hears bees in the hollyhocks. At night she watches lightning bugs glow and turn off, glow and turn off. June bugs cling to the outside of the screen. I am like a real room but with walls that breathe. Please do not think of me as anything like the back steps.

Back Steps

I'm happy with who I am. Nobody can come in the kitchen door without me. I could be in *National Geographic*—look at the banana trees growing around me (but watch out for the tarantulas in them). Mama even poses Judy here in a sarong. Without me how would you be able to pluck fresh mint right before supper to put in the iced tea? Where would you put the kitties' water bowl? Wipe off your muddy shoes? Chew ice on hot days? And sit and wonder?

Waiting for the War to End

PERDITA BUCHAN

DURING THE WAR WE LIVED, MY MOTHER AND I, IN TWO households, two houses, and two countries. Culham Home Farm, amid river meadows and sleepy villages in the heart of England, was the domain of my maternal grandparents; Ogalfaechwyn, at the edge of a moor and the foot of a mountain in North Wales, was my mother's escape house. Ogalfaechwyn in Welsh means "view of a departure point," and for both of us that was what it would be.

By the 1940s Culham Home Farm was no longer strictly speaking a farm. Standing on the outskirts of the village, it had lost its fields, and one of the barns had been annexed to the farmhouse itself. There was a jumble of other outbuildings, but except for my grandmother's two cairn terriers no animals were kept. Hurricanes and Spitfires may have cracked the skies above us, yet my earliest memories of Culham are of safety and calm, of the miniature yellow roses that climbed the walls outside my bedroom window, a Christmas tree in a clay pot with real candles like tiny stars in its branches, the sounds of my grandfather's violin from behind his study door. At teatime on winter afternoons I watched the blackout curtains being drawn. And once, very far away, I thought I heard a bomb, but it did not really frighten me. I remember my grandmother in her tin air raid warden's helmet far less well than I remember her on our trips to the cutting garden where she named for me each brilliant flower, or to the kitchen garden where we picked spinach or lettuce or broad beans.

My grandparents, who had lived through one war, did their best to preserve life in its peacetime patterns. There were afternoon walks and guests for tea, mealtime tables set with crystal and silver even if food was rationed. I knew the solemn ritual of the *BBC News At Six*, but only as another comfortable piece of routine.

Still, I can understand why my mother would have been restless, why she would have wanted to flee the world of her childhood. She had been married very young, on the cusp of war, and my father was thousands of miles away with the R.A.F. in Burma. I don't know how she found the cottage—Ogalfaechwyn was a good walk across the moor from the nearest village. It stood all by itself beside a grassy Roman road that was still used by the shepherds and cattlemen who grazed their herds on the moors. I can see the cottage clearly in my mind's eye, though the image is very small, as if it were a doll's house: whitewashed stone with a slate roof, doors and window sash painted red, a flint-walled scrap of lawn, and beyond that only moor and mountain, long harsh grass, and thickets of flowering gorse.

Across the Roman road, where the sheep grazed, there was a marshy patch of tall reeds where I loved to play. The reeds grew higher than my head, but they were easily trampled flat and I could make houses, like green cages, for myself, my stuffed animals, and my dolls. Looking through the reeds, I could see the blue slopes of the distant mountains. I would push my doll perambulator across the Roman road to the edge of the reeds, then I would lift its occupants out and disappear into my secret shelter. Sometimes, if I kept very still, the sheep would graze close by and the young bullocks come snuffling around the perambulator. Shy and slow-witted, with beautiful chestnut spotted coats, they blew constantly through their nostrils, huge eyes wide with fear or wonder. I was a little afraid of them, though in my reed cage I felt safe.

We had no electricity in the cottage, no running water, and, of course, no plumbing. The outhouse was built a distance away over the brook. I loved to go there. I could sit for hours on that comfortable seat, the stream rushing beneath me, the sheep calling to each other on the moor beyond, all the birds singing. After a while my mother installed a chemical toilet in the house but I refused to use it. The seat was too big, and I feared falling into that black ooze.

The center of the house was the kitchen, and the center of the kitchen was a coal stove with a heavy iron grating behind which the fire burned. On the apron, in front of the grating, I would soften the colored modeling waxes I kept in a chocolate box and form them into animals and people. There, too, I took my baths in a galvanized tin tub. There Bessie-by-the-Day, who came from the village to help us, heated flatirons, which she then wrapped in flannel to iron our clothes. She also spent a lot of time heating buckets of water to wash down the red tiles of the kitchen and the scullery.

For light we had kerosene lamps, mine a special child's size, painted purple. When we needed water we went out the back door and up the mountain to the waterfall. It was probably not a very big waterfall but to me it seemed huge—a steep white foaming cataract. We would stand at the edge and hold our buckets under the rushing water. Sometimes the strength of it would tear the bucket from my hands and it would have to be retrieved from the stream below. I thought it great sport. I thought every part of my life at Ogalfaechwyn great sport. I remember my mother, her dark hair streaming as she ran up the side of the mountain with me stumbling after. We were playing mountain goats on our way up to Mrs. Habberdaker-Eggs. Mrs. Habberdaker kept her ramshackle farm at the very top of the mountain behind the cottage, and she had a cow as well as the hens. Whatever the restrictions elsewhere, we always had new-laid eggs, brown and warm, and milk too.

There were no nearby children for me to play with, but I don't remember feeling the lack. In the village of Rhyd, however, on the other side of the moor, lived an English family, a mother with three girls called Gillian, Jennifer, and Rosemary. Often we would cross the moor to spend the afternoon with them. They were a lot older than I was; even Rosemary, the youngest, was at least five years older. They all had long thick plaits of dark hair, which I envied tremendously. Occasionally my mother would tie my hair up in curl rags, but it was always too fine to braid.

Because I was so much younger and a kind of novelty, Gillian, Jennifer, and Rosemary were very good to me. The older two were stolid and reliable. It was to one of them I ran if I skinned my knee or something frightened me. But Rosemary was different—smaller, thinner, with an impish little face. It was she who would take me running at a frantic pace over the fields or climbing on the rock walls of people's gardens. More than once I fell and she would be scolded by her sisters. It never bothered her one bit. She would give me a bright squirrel glance as if to say, "You'd rather come with me, wouldn't you, even if you do fall sometimes?" The answer was yes, of course. I worshipped her, with her long, skinny brown legs and her flying braids.

After our rambles round the village, we would go back to their house for tea and come blinking out of the sunlight into the cool dimness of the big stone-flagged kitchen. There was a long table covered with a white cloth, and we children would sit on the sides (me next to Rosemary) with my mother and Mrs. Morris at either end. I liked Mrs. Morris— she was small and round, not pretty like my mother, but very jolly. The kettle sang on the Aga cooker and the brown teapot waited under its flowered cozy. There were sandwiches of homemade jam and sometimes a cake. The girls were old enough to be allowed regular tea in the pink striped cups, but it was weak cambric tea in a Peter Rabbit mug for me.

The highlight of teatime in that house was King, the border collie, coal black with one discreet white patch on his chest, like a clean bib. He was totally unlike the border collies I watched the drovers working on the moors—anxious and businesslike animals, admirable but not friendly. King sat at the table with us, between Gillian and Jennifer. He had his tea in a bowl and lapped it with great delicacy.

Oh, how I wanted a dog like King, with his grave and perfect manners. What I got was Periwinkle. Evans-the-Post brought him one morning in his mail sack, a black border collie puppy who looked like King, except that his paws and nose were splashed with white. I saw that white nose peeping out of the mail sack and my breath stopped with joy.

"I've something for you," said Evans-the-Post. "Lift him out, then." And he knelt down so that I could get the fat, squirming, wriggling puppy out of his sack. Periwinkle licked my face and bit my hand with his needle-sharp teeth. That was only the beginning. He chewed everything: shoes, books, my dolls and teddy bears. He nipped me till I cried. But I loved him and I named him for the purple periwinkles that grew along the front wall of the house. He was quite unmanageable. He grew bigger but no easier to control. He chewed through every leash he was ever bought and even my mother could do nothing with him.

In the coldest months of winter we always went back to England, to Culham Home Farm, because the cottage was without heat and would be cut off when the snow came. We had to catch the train for the south at the station in Penrhyndendraeth. This necessitated getting up at 5 AM in the dark and crossing the moor on foot to the village, where the taxi would be waiting to take us to the train. The Morris girls would come with lanterns to wake us up and lead us over the moor. I was always awake before their coming and watched from my window their glow-worm progress. Then came the knocking on the door and their entrance in coats and hats and Wellington boots, Gillian putting the kettle on, and Jennifer coming up to help dress me in the warm clothes laid out on the chair by my bed.

Rosemary danced around, playing with Periwinkle. King had come with them, but he sat sedately outside on the doorstep. My mother slammed drawers and locked suitcases. We breakfasted, tea and a bun, and then we were off on that mysterious procession among the huge shapes of mountains and the smaller shapes of grazing animals. I had a flashlight and I raked its beams across the wet reeds.

"Oh, come along," my mother said to Periwinkle, who was fighting the leash.

There was one terrible thing about these morning journeys: it was the cow pats. They were everywhere in the tussocky grass. Inevitably, it seemed, I stumbled into one and had to be taken by my exasperated mother back to the house to be changed. This was a fearful event under the specter of the immutable schedule of the train. It was the only one, my mother told me sternly, that made the right connection. Aware of the danger, Rosemary held my hand tightly, and on this first trip with Periwinkle, my dog, I wavered but did not fall.

The car was parked on the road. When he saw us coming, Jones-the-Taxi started the motor and turned on the big, round head lamps. We clambered into the back seat, into the enveloping smell of leather and varnished wood, shoving Periwinkle with his wet feet down onto the floor, and the old car slowly set off down the road. I knelt on the back seat waving till the three lanterns and the ghost shapes of the village had vanished round a curve.

The train came steaming into the station, Periwinkle was handed over to the guard, and we got on board. In the compartment I knelt on the scratchy plush seat to stare out through clouds of white steam. It was a long trip with several changes, but at last the conductor called out:

"Culham Halt! Culham Halt!"

My grandfather and grandmother were waiting, my grandfather puffing on his pipe, my grandmother jumping up and down, crying, "Darlings! Darlings!"

"I have a dog," I shouted back over the train's explosive breath. Periwinkle was retrieved from the guard's van, where he was discovered to have chewed through another leash.

"Come along, sir," my grandfather said, taking him by the ragged stub and pulling him smartly to heel.

In the ensuing months, Periwinkle's lack of discipline was a menace to the well-ordered household at the Home Farm. My grandmother's cairns hated him and growled at his approach. He bumbled and bounced his way through everything, and when he began chewing carpets was banished to an outside pen. My grandfather made a tremendous effort to train him. He used petrol points on a special trip to Abingdon for a choke collar and a stout chain leash. But even he could do nothing and when we went back to Wales in the spring, Periwinkle was as wild as ever. That summer he began to chase sheep and had to be given away to someone who did not live in sheep country.

I loved Culham, but I also loved returning to the cottage. Ogalfae-chwyn was a place of unpredictable arrivals and excursions. People came to stay often. It was exciting to watch them approaching across the moor, or, occasionally, driving precariously up the Roman road. Leonard, the painter, and his family came on bicycles, a dead goose, limp and resplendently white, slung on the back of one of them. But mostly my mother's visitors were women, women now without men. They didn't seem to mind. They laughed a lot and did huge, complicated jigsaw puzzles on a table in the drawing room, a room we seldom used when it was just the two of us. My mother had all her own things in that room: a silvery Regency oyster chair, a Burne-Jones oil sketch of nymphs bathing, a pair of Baroque wooden cherubs. I would sit on the fur rug at their feet, watching and listening. Meals were informal. Bessie usually cooked a substantial lunch at midday; in the evening we would have a high tea, including eggs boiled in the teakettle. We played a card game we called Happy Families and curtsied to the new moon out on the Roman road.

Sometimes, when someone had come with a car and adequate petrol, we would go on a jaunt to the beach at Parthmadog or Portmeirion, but most often, on sunny afternoons, my mother and her friends sat outside in deck chairs on the grass slope beside the house, sunbathing in halter tops, skirts hiked up, murmuring in the peculiar code of adulthood. I would play nearby, using fallen roof slates to build barns and sheds and paddocks for the brightly painted wooden animals my father had sent me from India. Tigers and camels and elephants stood placidly in their stalls while the cows and sheep were scattered over the grass in imitation of the cows and sheep around us.

Some guests were constant and familiar, others occasional, like the tall American lieutenant, who came only once but nearly set all the gorse bushes by the house on fire with a careless cigarette. My mother sat in the deck chair, helpless with laughter as he and I ran back and forth with buckets to the waterfall. We put the fire out but I never forgot the orange flames among the yellow flowers.

There were people staying the day the war in Europe ended, a Hungarian friend of my mother's named Lys and her daughter, Caroline. The visit was practical since both Caroline and I had whooping cough and could keep each other company. Evans-the-Post came racing red-faced across the moor to tell us.

"The war is over!" he shouted.

Caroline and I were given hankies with Union Jacks printed on them. I wanted the white one but had to give it to her and take the yellow because she was the guest. I had a fit of coughing.

We left Wales early that year, as the bracken was just turning its red-fox color. When Gillian, Jennifer, and Rosemary came bobbing across the moor to fetch us, there was already light in the eastern sky. I fell in a cow pat that time, just across the Roman road. I was taken back to the cottage, cleaned off, re-clothed, and scolded, and we set out once more. My Wellingtons squeaked on the wet grass and mist lay pure white in every hollow. Sheep scattered as we passed them, disappearing in the mist. This time my mother took my hand while Rosemary chattered behind us.

"Do shut up, Rosemary," Gillian said amiably. And, in Rosemary's moments of silence, I could hear the lowing of the bullocks, the bleating of the sheep. Slowly we drew near the village, the last field, the stone wall, and Jones-the-Taxi waiting.

I didn't know that morning that a part of my childhood had ended with the war. I didn't know what was in the wind—that my mother would divorce my father and marry the tall American, or that I would grow up in another country across 3,000 miles of ocean. But this is childhood's gift: to be unaware of the future, as I was unaware the last morning in Wales.

My Grandmother's Table

A. M. HOMES

SHE RUBBED THE TABLE. HER HAND UNCONSCIOUSLY MOVED IN circles as if polishing the wood, stroking it like a talisman, for comfort, for the giving and getting of wisdom.

We were each in our familiar place: I was sitting on the outside corner and my grandmother was at the head. We were in her home in the Maryland suburbs. In her late 90s, she was older than the table—in my mind they are inexorably bound.

"We went to the farm," I said loudly.

"You did? And you were able to find it?"

"Yes."

The weekend before, my cousin and I drove up and down the hills of North Adams, Massachusetts, on a pilgrimage to find the farm where our grandmother grew up.

"Actually, there were two farms, the old farm and the new," my cousin said. "The new wasn't really new; they moved there in the 1920s. It was closer to town and had indoor plumbing—they thought it was very modern. The old farm was up there"—he pulled onto the shoulder and pointed. The dirt driveway had long ago dissolved, the only way to go was on foot. We climbed quickly, ascending into the mythology of the farm.

The original buildings remained, crumbling, collapsed, but still identifiable. I conjured images of my grandmother as a child, one of nine born to Lithuanian immigrants at the turn of the 20th century on this American dairy farm. I imagined her walking down the dirt road to a one-room schoolhouse, picking wild blueberries, helping my great-grandfather milk the cows and tend the chickens. I remembered her telling me the Mohawk Trail was just out the back door. In my mind, she was playing in a real-life version of *Little House on the Prairie*.

On an impromptu archeological dig, my cousin used a knife to poke in the dirt. "This must mean something," he said, pulling out an old bottle.

I nodded in agreement. We each took a couple of slate shingles from the crumbling roof, bits of our private history, and made our way back to the car.

Downhill at the new farm, we pulled into a cul-de-sac, and my cousin pointed to a brand-new house—part of a development in progress—freshly minted aluminum siding painted powder blue. "The farm was just about there," he said. "It's hard to see it now."

I returned to Washington and told my grandmother about the visit. "Tell me about the farm, how was it?" she asked, as if half-expecting there was still someone there leading the cows out to pasture and back home again at night.

"Interesting." I didn't tell her about the powder-blue house. I told her about the rolling hills, the tall trees, Mount Greylock in the distance. She closed her eyes. "Just as I remembered it," she said.

She looked at the table. I imagined this table echoed something in my great-grandmother's farmhouse kitchen. My grandmother rubbed her fingers along the grain of the wood. This was where we gathered, where my grandmother, our matriarch, held court, where her brothers and sisters and their children and their children's children came to celebrate, to discuss, to mourn.

My grandmother's table was made for her in the early 1960s by George Nakashima. She commissioned him to make the table along with a number of other pieces, including a buffet and a cabinet. Traveling to his world-famous workshop in New Hope, Pennsylvania, she picked out the wood for her table—her name is inked in black on the under-side. When I was born, an additional order was placed for a high chair.

Although my grandmother and George Nakashima met only briefly, the more I learn about each of them, the more of a connection I feel between them. They were both sources of great inspiration. They shared qualities of rootedness, stability, and grace. Nakashima was involved in Karma Yoga, the path of action; I believe my grandmother moved through life that way as well. She did everything with elegance, making the impossible seem effortless. She was at once grand and down-to-earth, a traveler, an adventurer, brave, and very proud.

The table is long and luxurious—French walnut, two book-matched planks with squared-off edges. It does not announce itself as something special until you spend time with it, and then its character becomes clear. Again, she stroked the wood. "Tell me about you," my grand-mother said.

"I'm fine; I've been working hard. I've been thinking about buying a little house out on Long Island, a cabin where I can go and write."

She nodded. "It's important to have a house of your own," she said.

"Tell me about you," I said back to her.

"I've got nothing to tell," she said. "I'm bored."

She had worked most of her life. In 1918, two years before women had the vote, she went to Washington by herself, got a job in the War Department, and soon brought her brothers and sisters down from the farm. She married my grandfather and together they started a wine-importing company, which is still in business—now run by my uncle. My grandmother worked full time until she was 86. When she was 78, in her spare time she became a founding member of the first bank in the United States organized and operated by women.

Whatever I know about how to live life, I learned from her. When I graduated from college and wanted to write, she loaned me the money to buy an IBM Selectric typewriter. I dutifully paid her back $50 a month, and when the debt was cleared she wrote me a check for the entire amount. "I wanted you to know what it means to work for something."

She sat at the table watching me—she could have passed for someone in her late 70s. She sighed. "I don't know what to do with myself. I don't feel useful anymore."

"Let's go for a ride," I said, getting up from the table. I drove her to a local Maryland farm, the place where my mother had taken me apple picking and pumpkin hunting as a child. We went up a rutted road toward the berry patch and parked beside a row of bushes.

She made her way to the blueberries and quickly started picking them and popping the fruit into her mouth—her 98-year-old fingers suddenly nimble. Sweeping her hair back, she looked up at the sky and moved down the row, picking rapidly. She was a girl again, filling a basket with ripe, warm blueberries. "This is exactly how it used to be," she told me.

In the car on the way home she squeezed my leg. "Buy your little house," she said, and I did.

I called her from Long Island. I stood in the small yard and told her I was planting rose bushes, seeds for carrots, beets, and squash. I turned over a square of land at the far end of the yard and began calling it "the field." I told her about tilling the field, tending my crop, the enormous satisfaction in this work, in being away from the city, deep in the dirt.

She turned 99. "When are you coming home?" she asked several times in each conversation. "Soon," I told her. "Soon, I am coming home."

And then she was gone, the only person I've known to die unexpectedly at 99. I hurried back to Washington. I went to her house, I moved from room to room. I sat at the table, waiting. She seemed still to be there, hovering, floating, packing.

At the end of the summer I pulled my carrots out of the ground, as proud of them as I was of any story or book I'd written. She was the person I would most want to share them with, the one who would understand when I held them up and proudly said, "Look what I made."

A couple of months later, my mother called and asked if I would like my grandmother's table. "I know it's big and your house is small, but I think it would be nice if you had it."

The table came in through the side door, carefully wrapped and shipped from Washington along with its chairs. "These are tables of great weight," one of the men said, and he was right. I had inherited more than an object—this was a mandate to live and work as hard and with as much grace and style as she had.

At first the table looked out of place, lost. I oiled it. I rubbed it with a soft cloth. Moving my hands over the surface, I noticed the richness of the tone, the marks of a lifetime.

The first time I used the table, I invited a friend over for lunch. I took my usual spot. Instead of looking at a painting on my grandmother's living room wall, I was now looking out a window at a bird feeder. I set two places at the table, my friend's and mine. She sat in my grandmother's place, closest to the window, and something felt strange. I sat for a minute and then said to my friend, "I need to change places with you."

The friend looked at me oddly.

"Could we switch?" I asked, and then I slid into my grandmother's seat. Now it is my place.

Montana December

RICK BASS

DRAMA! ON THE DAY OF THE SCHOOL CHRISTMAS PLAY, WENDY, the lead actress, is sick, throwing-up sick, fever sick. Her part in *Santa Claus and the Wicked Wazoo* is none other than the Wazoo herself, and as she is an eighth-grader, it's her last year to perform before she graduates and heads on to high school down in Troy. Her classmate Karen can't take her part because Karen is Mrs. Claus, often in the same scene as the Wicked Wazoo (whose goal is to spoil Christmas).

If Wendy doesn't rally, it will be up to my daughter Mary Katherine to learn the part—not just the 40 lines, but the timing, blocking, entrances, and exits—in addition to keeping her part as "Martha, a peasant girl." There are only five girls in the Yaak, Montana, elementary school this year—the eighth-graders, Wendy and Karen; Mary Katherine in the fourth grade; my other daughter Lowry in first grade; and Chiena in kindergarten.

Mary Katherine doesn't find out about Wendy's illness until mid-morning on the day of the play but gets right to work. She and Karen spend the day practicing, and when Mary Katherine comes home that afternoon, she's cool as a cucumber, casual and confident: not arrogant, just confident. She has neither stage fright nor overconfidence. Just another day in Paradise.

My wife, Elizabeth, and I would be jittery, and I can't help but think that this nonchalance on Mary Katherine's part is one of the products of place. She enjoys the myriad benefits of attending a two-room log school in which all the different grades sit together and interact every day, year in and year out, like family—learning lessons such as responsibility and loyalty in addition to the prescribed curricula.

It's a big deal, the Christmas play. Every year the whole town shows up, hermits and all. The plays are always delightful, and afterward there are cookies and cakes, and the kids and all our neighbors sing Christmas carols in our log cabin community center. Here we are, up near the Canadian line in the middle of the forest and over 40 miles from the nearest big town, and it's just nothing but sweet.

It is a revelation to see Mary Katharine come swashbuckling out from behind the curtains, booming that laugh of the great, villainous Wazoo. And a revelation again when Lowry, in her pink glittering ballerina outfit, comes twirling out to center stage, hands poised over her head in a graceful, elegant ballerina pose and cries out, "Help, help!" For me, with my recluse tendencies, it's a profound witnessing to learn that I don't necessarily have to pass on all of my less-than-wonderful attributes to my children. They will likely be better in the world than I am, and already have something to give to the world, and are giving it.

Outside, it's snowing hard. The pew benches in the community center are packed shoulder to shoulder and the woodstoves are popping. The beauty and purity of the children fill the center with a love so dense that after the play is over we linger, not wanting to part; and when we open the door finally and step outside into the falling snow, that love is adhering to us. Peace on earth and goodwill to men.

Such are the rhythmic cycles of our lives, here in this place-that-is-still-a-place, that the end of one thing can feel like the beginning of another. December is that way, as the last of the deer or elk is cut, wrapped, and frozen, the coming year's meat stored away by the hunter. The snow is always down to the valley floor by December—another beginning—and while the rest of the world, including our relatives in the more civilized places, enter into the full frenzy of the Christmas season, things are much quieter up here, amidst a complete absence of shopping malls. Yet the seasons are no less deeply felt. It's just hushed and slow—like walking in soft new snow at dusk.

It's the beginning of sleeping late, of play, of being able to spend even more time with family. We begin wrapping jars of huckleberry jam for gifts and take the girls out into the snow for the annual Christmas card picture. Elizabeth gathers boughs of cedar and pine with which to make beautiful, fresh-scented wreaths to mail to friends and family in the outside world.

Mary Katherine is dubious about Santa while Lowry is still a true believer, though as the days progress I notice that Mary Katherine comes back across the line, if only for one more year. Their Christmas lists are posted on the refrigerator. I suspect that my girls are as cutthroat and mercenary as any children anywhere, but I have to laugh at Lowry's list—a pencil and pencil sharpener, a Barbie (I know, I know), and, most curiously, a bottle of Wite-Out. Even Mary Katherine's list is modest: books and CDs, a new pair of snow boots, and a pair of ski goggles.

The holiday season begins for us, I think, on the day that we get the Christmas tree. For as long as the girls have been able to walk, they have gone into the woods with me each year to find a tree—always a young Douglas fir. Finding the perfect one is never easy. Any tree is beautiful in the forest, but we only had to bring one home one year that impressed Elizabeth far less than it did us that we vowed to never again settle for anything less than perfect.

I prepare the girls for the cutting as if we were going on a real hunt. On Sunday night, before they go to bed, I tell them that when I pick them up after school on Monday, I'll bring their cross-country skis and we'll look for the tree. That they're as thrilled with this news as if it were Christmas itself pleases me greatly.

It's bitterly cold when I pick them up, about 15 degrees, but with a rare breeze that makes it feel closer to zero, and more snow coming any minute. I've brought a thermos of hot chocolate, and on the way home we share a cup, drinking it out of the screw-on top like duck hunters, and then turn on the little road where we always turn and get out where we always get out. The girls are bundled up with as many clothes and coats as they can wear, and I have more of my own larger coats in my backpack, along with the thermos. The sky is the color of plums, the color of a seagull's back, the color of sharks, the color of oystershell. We take turns breaking trail through the new snow like explorers.

I'm glad the girls remember where we are going from all the other years. I'm glad to see what natural backcountry skiers they are, having grown up on skis—such a difference from my own south Texas upbringing. As we move through the woods, seemingly the only living creatures out and about in this vast snowscape and sleeping forest, there is a spirit that emanates from the three of us—a happiness that braids together to form a larger whole. I believe it's rare for an adult to experience, ever again, the happiness of a child. There are a million different sorts of adult happiness—satisfaction, pride, relief, euphoria—but what I feel, moving up that hill with my daughters in the approaching winter dusk, self-sufficient on our skis and snowshoes, is a child's happiness, and I cannot remember having felt that in a long, long time.

Once we reach the ridge, we begin to encounter the young Douglas firs growing in between older pines and larch. The girls are old enough this year to be good judges of physical character, bypassing weaker or asymmetrical trees, and judging also which trees are too large and which are too small. We look for a long time. The wind blurs our eyes and sometimes far-off trees look much better than they really are. We'll ski and snowshoe down into a bowl or ravine and up the other side to some such tree only to discover upon reaching it that it's not even remotely like what we're after.

For a long time, we have been bringing back a Christmas tree that even Elizabeth admits is perfect, with every branch, every needle, balanced and symmetrical. Although the girls are not aware of any sort of pressure, I'm less secure. As the dusk deepens, we travel farther, looking hard.

We pass over the stippled, methodical trails of deer and the seemingly aimless tracks of snowshoe hares. We cross the tracks of a mountain lion, one that I suspect has probably not eaten in a while and is hungry because we do not hear any ravens squabbling over the remains of a nearby kill, and so I keep the girls close to me.

We're all three beginning to grow chilled, so we huddle in a ravine beneath the shelter of a big spruce tree as if in a little fort or clubhouse and share another cup of hot chocolate. I bundle them further, putting my heavy overcoats on over their own, and making sure their mufflers are snug. Warmed, they're ready to play again and climb back up out of the ravine, herringboning on their skis, only to ski right back down, again and again.

They're laughing, shrieking, and I do not want to caution them to conserve their energy; I do not want to counsel moderation in their joy, though I am concerned that we're so far from the truck, and it's so late and so cold.

We find the perfect tree right at dark. I spy it first, and hardly daring to believe our luck, I snowshoe over to it without saying anything, wanting to be sure. I call the girls over, ask them to check it out, and they're very excited by its beauty. I take my saw out of the pack, tell the tree and the forest thank you, out loud, like a pagan, and then saw through the sweet green bark and sap, and the tree leans over slowly, softly, lightly, and settles into the snow.

We head back to the truck, taking turns pulling it. It's surprisingly hard work, and the tree's needles leave a beautiful, wandering, feathery trail behind us, completely erasing our tracks.

By the time we reach the truck we're all three cold again, and after loading the tree into the back I warm up the truck and we sit there in the cab, drinking more hot chocolate before I drive the short distance home. Elizabeth comes out onto the porch to inspect what we have brought to her.

She looks it over carefully.

"It's perfect," she says, finally.

Long after the tree is gone, and the year, I will remember that afternoon.

Runaways

MARYBETH LAMBE

FIVE-YEAR-OLD BRENDAN IS VIBRATING, IN THE WAY ONLY SMALL boys can, with absolute fury. In the spring he had made a dirt-and-grass kingdom under the apple trees for his garter snakes. Tonight, however, rain threatens and Brendan feels the snakes should come indoors like all civilized beings. It is futile to point out the obvious: snakes do not mind rain, I do mind snakes, snakes should be free, he has nowhere to put them in his room, snakes need live things to eat, I hate snakes, and so on. And the rain does begin, softly, almost invisible in the deepening twilight. Brendan is wearing a long tattered red plaid robe, the belt tied tightly around his tiny waist and dangling into the box of wriggling snakes. He is scuffing the grass with his enormous red rubber boots, now angrily kicking against the trunk of the tallest Macintosh tree; fragrant white blossoms are drifting down onto Brendan's shoulders.

"Stop," I tell him, in my sternest parent voice. "Stop hurting the tree."

These words are enough to knock him off his quivering axis. Spinning, he rushes by me. "That's it!" Unshed tears, or raindrops, make his blue eyes seem dark with sorrow and desperation. "I'm leaving!"

I am torn between laughter and love. Stupidly I repeat his words. "You're leaving?"

He reaches down, snags one of the snakes, and stuffs it into his bathrobe pocket. With all the small-boy dignity he can muster, he pulls himself tall. "Yes, you don't love my snakes. I'm running away to Grandma's."

Wise parenting books tackle this very subject. Good parents assure their children that running away solves nothing . . . Have a good talk, exchange opinions, be in charge, blah, blah, blah.

I simply stand there, my mouth hanging open, watching his rapidly departing back. Seconds later, I show a flicker of intelligence. I rush after Brendan, trailing him to my parents'.

Our farm rests at the end of a small dirt road. A hundred yards south, my parents' home is nestled behind a thicket of cedars and hemlocks. Brendan carefully clambers over their split-rail fence to take the supposed shortcut. Racing down their driveway, I actually beat Brendan to the house. My father greets me at the back door and I whisper to him about their visitor. Without batting an eye, he nods and heads to the front door. The doorbell chimes and I sneak back home. Halfway to the farm, I realize I forgot to tell my dad about the snake in the bathrobe pocket.

That was almost 20 years ago. My parents, amused and pleased to be a refuge for their young grandson, comforted Brendan and sent him home. They never knew about the snake.

I have given birth to five of our children, and my husband and I have adopted four. It seems we have always had a house full. Running away became a strange rite of passage for them. Brendan, the eldest, who started the practice, is now a grown man. Emma Rose, 12, and John Patrick, 11, each had their turn to flee. Three of our children came to us from China. Yuanjun and MeiMei, both nine, arrived here from Shanghai the same year, both aged six. Shen Bo, our youngest, now seven, is from Ningbo, China. Each of them fell into the pattern as well. Only Austin, too dreamy, and Sara, too determined to stand fast and scold us, never made the trip down the lane.

This is the story of those small journeys—not so much a tale of how and why they ran, but of whom they ran to in their haste to be done with strict parents, sanctimonious siblings, and sharing, always sharing.

Emma Rose has forever been melodramatic, so it was no surprise when, at five, she was carried away by her passion and fury over a slight.

Older siblings Brendan and Sara had not allowed Emma to be the banker when they included her in a game of Monopoly. Absurd! After all, she could almost count to 100 and was a full year older than baby John. When Emma ran away, she carried it too far. She loaded her bike with grocery bags on each handlebar, an enormous backpack over her shoulders, and cruised right past my parents' house toward the wide world beyond. She almost made it to the big road, but my father and a galloping Brendan caught her at the mailboxes. Trailing, I found all three of them panting. As we confiscated Emma's bike and pulled her out of the hot sun, she kicked and struggled. She was appeased only when Grandpa promised her she could spend the night with them. She turned from anger to delight in one breath.

When robust John Patrick was born, he was in the habit of howling from dinnertime to late evening. No amount of nursing, swaddling, unswaddling, carrying, burping, or jollying would soothe him. To relieve my husband and the other children, I developed the practice of walking down to my folks' each night. John Patrick's bellowing, like a siren on a highway, announced our coming. My mother would plant him on my father's lap, where John Patrick would eventually calm down, regard us with a Buddhalike mien, and finally fall asleep.

My dad would carry his namesake to the dining table where I would sit for hours with my parents, sharing their dinner and trading ideas about politics, religion, and family. Those were some of the best hours of my life. At last, I would come home with the sleeping John Patrick, my parents' magic still strong. My husband would think me brave for dealing with John's colic each night; the other kids were relieved not to hear such roaring. I was actually sad when John's colic abated after six weeks.

When we lost our son Danny to crib death at five months, it was I who ran away. Tormented by grief, I paced constantly. As my feet carried me along the lane and down hours of unknown roads, my father invariably joined me, without question or complaint. Mile after mile, day after day I walked, half-hoping I would be struck by a fast car and end the agony. My father made sure I lived. It was weeks before I could stay planted at home.

Yuanjun ran away the second week after we brought him here from China. He was, he announced, going to find a plane and head back to Shanghai. His grandparents in China let him eat sweets whenever he chose. He had lived in the city—not this horrid country life—and he had simply had enough of it. I stayed close on that journey, truly frightened Yuanjun might run away into danger. My heart ached for him and his loss. Strange then that it was his American grandparents, speaking no Mandarin, who pulled him off the road and into their hearts. They plied him with sweet mints and gingerbread cookies, thus proving his point: grandparents give sweets. Half a world away it was still true on this dusty country lane.

When John Patrick was old enough to have his feelings hurt, it was his turn. Convinced I was giving his siblings more attention than he got, he simply vanished one morning. He made no announcements, as the others had. We were frantic because John, slow to rile, could, when finally pushed, become more wounded and bitter than his older brothers and sisters ever did. Who knew to what length he would go to prove his grievance? We called my parents to alert them.

"Which one now?" inquired my mother, a woman experienced with missing persons.

I felt like I was filing a police report.

"Yes, it's John this time, Mom. We have been looking everywhere for him and—"

"Marybeth, what would you do if we didn't live here? I mean, have you noticed this seems to be a custom?"

What could I say?

My father found John in the woods across from their home. Poor John was not afforded much dignity. Our dairy cows had followed him across the pastures, over the stream, around the fallen trees, and into the deep woods. My father found them all, the Jersey cows patiently scrubbing John's bare legs with their rough tongues, John trying to be invisible among the shadows. After John washed at my parents, he joined them for lunch and a root beer float. As in his colicky baby days, he came home much later, sleepy and content.

Out of jealousy more than anything, MeiMei ran away too. It was a rainy fall day as she stood on the porch to telephone my mother with the news.

"I'm running away to you right now!" MeiMei sounded pleased.

My mother must have protested, but MeiMei was firm. "No, no. It is my turn and I am coming. Better start looking for me."

She came in, handed me the phone, gave me a big kiss and hug, and sauntered off through the cool drizzle.

My mother called back in an hour. "Next time," her voice sounded pained, "don't let them come sopping wet."

Another hour passed and she called again. "MeiMei has to go home now. She has talked our ears off for two hours."

Brendan went to retrieve MeiMei. It seemed fair since he had started the whole thing.

Finally, there was only one more child to make that indignant journey from home. Shen Bo had just turned seven when he became aware of the burdens of being in a large family. Everything was a hand-me-down, always first to bed, never allowed to "have fun."

Shen Bo felt tormented by his older brothers in particular. They could run faster; they were immeasurably stronger, and therefore complete bullies. Shen Bo was through with us all. Normally impulsive and madcap, Shen Bo planned his escape meticulously—only the best for his flight from home. He carted several laundry baskets upstairs and began filling them with his things. Unlike the other kids, Shen Bo would stay away a week, a month, a year! Yet how to get five baskets of belongings to the grandparents'?

My parents still laugh about Shen Bo's arrival. All the brothers he had complained about agreed to form a long line of litter carriers. Each bearer hefted a heavy basket to the door and silently departed. Shen Bo enjoyed an evening of being an "only," the center of my parents' undivided attention. First, he played chess with my father, changing the rules constantly to ensure his own victory. Then supper and then a second supper. Perhaps, yes, he could stand a bite of ice cream and cookies. And oh, had he told them he liked two pieces of toast before bed? Shen Bo had brought all the accoutrements of comfort:

a nightlight, his favorite lamp, a radio lifted from his older brothers' room, two pillows, and a menagerie of stuffed animals.

How sad he felt when his visit was over in a day. And the bearers were not too pleased to have to bring his things home the next morning.

And here is where it gets hard. For while my children grew up, my parents grew old. Young and active when Brendan and his snake first ran to them for comfort, they are now in their late 70s. My mother has had a tidal wave of health problems: breathing troubles, heart palpitations, painful arthritis, and so on. Still sturdy and fit, my father has had attacks of vertigo, weakness, and fatigue.

Sometimes, when I am in a verbal battle with one of the children, or bemoaning some mundane task, I forget how precious, how brief, our time really is. As the children have grown up and my parents grown old—with such breathtaking speed—I have been struck by the poignancy of this fact over and over again. A moment ago, Brendan was a small boy running away, and now he is a man embracing his future. A mere day ago, it seems, my parents held my own hand, shielded my child self with their love and strength. Their love remains, but their strength fades. Where was I when this happened? In the space of a sigh, everything changes.

The Blackfoot warrior Crowfoot said, "What is life? It is the flash of a firefly in the night. It is the breath of a buffalo in the wintertime. It is the little shadow which runs across the grass and loses itself in the sunset."

I want to run to my parents and hold them here forever. I cannot envision someone else living in the home my father built, cannot imagine no longer making the sweet walk down the road to greet them. Parents, like best friends, have known you forever. There is no need for pretense, no words that must be left unsaid. For my children, my parents have always been a sanctuary.

My parents scoff at such a description. "Stop trying to butter us up," my mother says. "You're probably just trying to get us to babysit more."

Even the children worry about a future without their grandparents. Yuanjun quizzes my father as they pick raspberries.

"What does it feel like to be old?" Yuanjun pauses to ask. "Does it hurt?"

Shen Bo peeks up from emptying his bucket of berries into his mouth. "You aren't going to die yet, are you?"

And John Patrick's eyes are suddenly watering. "I don't want you to die!"

My mother sits nearby in the wicker chair Brendan has carried over for her. She gives a loud laugh. "I think we're good till 80 at least. But eventually"—she glances over at me—"eventually, it will be our turn to run away."

Sara and MeiMei give her a puzzled stare. "I mean," she continues, "we're not going to live forever. Who'd want to?"

I open my mouth to speak but she forestalls me with a raised hand. "It will be Marybeth and Mark's turn to handle the runaways, their chance to be the grandparents."

She starts to chuckle. MeiMei drifts into Grandma's arms and begins to imitate my mother's laugh. They sound like the only two who have understood a secret joke. Finally my mother continues. "Oh, Marybeth, I hope they send you lots of grandchildren. Just wait. You'll see what it's like to be the place they all run to. My only advice is, be sure to always, always, keep the jar full of gingerbread."

Only in America

819 Gaffield Place

MICHELE BENDER

A RUN-DOWN, OFF-CAMPUS STUDENT HOUSE IN A FAMILY neighborhood, 819 Gaffield Place was where Zoe, Judy, Lisa, and I lived during our senior year at Northwestern University. The shingles and trim were covered with yellow and brown chipped paint and the roof was the pale, cloudy color of chocolate milk. Tiny splotches from the night we painted the living room marred the seven front steps. A worn white sofa sat on the porch among piles of mail and coupons delivered to anyone who had ever lived there. Our neighbors made fun of the sofa, our over-grown lawn, the bicycles chained to the stair rail. To them it must have looked like a perpetual garage sale, but to us it was a true home.

Whether it was framed by autumn's yellow and orange leaves, deep in the drifts of a Chicago snowstorm, or speckled with springtime sun and shadows, it was a soothing sight to me. One night I walked home from my boyfriend's apartment after our usual fight about what would happen to us after graduation. It was 2 AM, silent and dark, but as I turned the corner past Philbrick Park the lone street lamp illuminated Gaffield in the distance. I started to run, wanting to be there, to feel safe instead of empty. The curly numbers 819 came into view. When I opened the glass door and saw the first-floor light, tears welled in my eyes. I burst into the living room.

"Uh-oh," said Zoe. Grabbing her car keys, Judy said, "Slurpees." The others put on their sneakers. We always dealt this way with breakups, failed exams, and bad news from home. There was something reassuring about a Slurpee always tasting the same no matter what time it was or which 7-Eleven we went to. We walked to the back of the house, where the smell of Tide from the nearby Laundromat hung permanently in the air, and piled into Judy's old black Thunderbird.

After driving to the all-night 7-Eleven, we headed for Lake Shore Drive, our favorite ride. Lake Michigan was calm outside the car window; inside I was comforted within the cocoon of my friends by a blueberry Slurpee.

I would be OK.

I had not always felt OK. As a child growing up in New York City, I was often lonely. On Sunday mornings, I would sit in our sleek, white Formica kitchen hoping my mother would wake up and make waffles with raspberry jam and maple syrup. But my parents, tired from late Saturday nights, stayed in their room with the door shut until noon. Finally, I would pour myself a bowl of Cap'n Crunch.

My parents divorced when I was 12 and my mother moved out. Months passed between her visits and calls. I lived in my father's and brother's world of football games and boxer shorts. Although I needed someone to do my nails with, and talk girl-talk and cry to, all I had of my mother was our Art Deco apartment, which she had designed. The navy velvet and Lucite furniture gave us a place elegant enough to appear in several design books, but that didn't make me feel at home there.

There was no such thing as being late for dinner because most nights I ordered from a pile of takeout menus. A "family dinner" meant we all ordered from the same restaurant, but we still ate separately, each one of us watching television in our own bedrooms. I knew the string of delivery men who brought our dinners better than any neighbor.

So I was ready for Gaffield.

I first saw the house in my junior year when I visited a friend who was living there. The street was lined with trees, their limbs forming an arch of green above me. The rooms were spacious and drenched with sunlight from the many windows. Two six-year-old girls biked up and down the street screaming "Hi Sam!" to a white-haired man sitting on his porch. He teased them with funny faces as they passed and the girls laughed so hard their small bodies shook. I wanted to be part of that world.

When the resident seniors would pass the house on to their successors, everyone considered it an enormous favor. I was the one to arrange to live there next, and Zoe and Lisa were interested. To afford this house we needed a fourth. The current Gaffield girls suggested Judy, who they knew was eager to move in. Judy and I didn't like each other even though we had many mutual friends and were often at the same parties. How could we? A year before, she dated a guy named Josh for a few months. Then I did. It turned out he cheated on each of us with the other. Josh was out of our lives, but the jealousy and resentment lingered.

"You're a lot alike," said the mutual friends. "It's a big place, you'll hardly see her," said Zoe. I wanted the house and warily agreed. We took over on a June day after the resident seniors graduated. The price for all their furniture and dishes was $50—exactly what they had paid the girls before them and the price as long as anyone could remember.

For the first few weeks, Judy and I made stilted small talk when the four of us were together and avoided being left alone. One night I was boiling water for tea when Judy came into the kitchen to make popcorn. We proceeded in silence for several minutes. Finally, she spoke, "This is ridiculous." Startled, I burned my hand on the teapot. "I don't care about Josh anymore."

"Me neither," I said.

"But," she paused. "There are a few things I want to know." We talked for hours sitting on the wooden countertop with a bowl of popcorn between us. My other friends had always dismissed Josh as a jerk or a phony, but Judy understood his allure and the pain he could cause.

It wasn't until we talked that I realized how much Josh had hurt me and how I had buried this hurt inside, a strategy I had learned after my parents' divorce. Neither of them ever discussed it with my brother and me. My father acted as if my mother was just away on a business trip. On our occasional visits together, my mother never mentioned her absence or asked how I felt about the way my life had changed. I simply wasn't used to talking about what bothered me.

I was expecting just to live with my uneasiness about Judy, until she spoke up that night in the kitchen. It felt so good to say what I wanted and stop pretending things were fine. When Zoe and Lisa came home and found us together, they began talking quickly, trying to break through an awkwardness that was no longer there.

"It's okay," Judy interrupted. "We talked about everything." The four of us had already lived in the same house for almost a month but that night marked the real beginning of our life together. We started to develop routines and rituals. We had bagel breakfasts, walked to class together, grocery shopped on Wednesday nights. On rainy days, the house had a woody, earthy smell; returning from school, I would count the slickers on the porch railing to see who was home. In the fall and winter, Sunday dinner was Carmen's pizza, and in the spring we barbecued on the porch. But the best time was meeting at home at the end of each day.

One night I was late for dinner because I had a meeting with my American Literature professor. On my way home, I imagined Lisa, who loved to cook, at the stove in our huge square kitchen and Judy, who preferred to watch, asking, "Isn't Michele's class over at five?" I walked faster. The second porch step made its familiar comforting sigh as my foot landed on it.

"We were worried," said Judy when I walked in. Everyone was in her seat at the table beside the large bay window. The fourth chair was empty with a place set. My shoulders relaxed. I was back in my spot.

We weren't just a foursome. We had a neighbor, Jane, who came over on our first day there with her two young daughters. "When you're going to have a party," she said, "just leave notes on everyone's porch so no one calls the police." Then she wrote down her name and number. "I know you're far from home so if you need anything let me know."

In New York, contact with my neighbors consisted of a nod or guarded smile in the elevator, but Jane talked to me. "Did you finish that paper on Hemingway?" or "How was Lisa's date?" she would ask, remembering what I had told her the week before. Most afternoons her daughters were playing outside when I got home. They would yell my name when I passed, racing over to show me a new dress or an art project.

Russell, our landlord, who lived nearby, still wore the tie-dyed clothes popular in the sixties when he was a student at Northwestern. He was always the first person to arrive at our parties and the last to show up when the heating broke down or a fuse blew.

As seniors with most of our credits complete, we didn't feel guilty about cutting our afternoon classes. We would walk down the alley to buy tomato soup and Twizzlers at the deli and rent movies from the video store. We would spend the afternoon in the living room by the brick fireplace on the plump sofa covered in blue velour worn to the color of a spring sky. We talked about everything, from what we were learning from our majors to what we were learning about sex. I knew whose boyfriend liked red lingerie and whose preferred none. When my boyfriend said, "Don't tell anyone," the Gaffield girls didn't count. I saw them as an extension of myself; nothing I told them would go beyond our circle.

The morning I turned 22, I heard them coming up to my room at 6 AM. The walls of my third-floor bedroom were thin enough to hear the squirrel that lived in our attic, Lisa laughing on the second floor, and my roommates returning from classes or a night out. That day they sang "Happy Birthday" as they climbed the stairs. They decorated the door of my tiny closet with pink balloons and gave me a new journal, a box of my favorite Bic pens, and a key chain with an engraved charm dangling from it with my initials on one side and "Gaffield" on the other. The sun barely glowed in the sky, but we were up, gathered around the wooden table eating bagels and chocolate cupcakes.

The bookends of my days were the hours sitting around that table. At times like that I would feel that we had become a kind of family. I realized family doesn't have to be your relatives—family means that your life is part of someone else's, like sections of hair that need each other to form a braid. Often I would race upstairs to my journal to record these scenes. When I did, I would hear Zoe say "Another chapter," referring to the book on Gaffield that they always said I would write. Most of the entries ended with "This won't last forever."

But in some ways it has—just a different kind of forever. Seven years later, we all live in New York and try to see each other every few weeks. Recently, two nights before her wedding, I handed Lisa the blue satin garter I had worn at mine. On it I had sewn a piece of pink ribbon on which I wrote "The Gaffield Garter" in indelible ink. As the first of us to marry, I decided to pass my garter along. I know sisters who have such wedding traditions. My old roommates are my sisters.

"One more wedding and we can open that envelope," I said. During finals in college, punchy from too many hours of studying, we had made predictions. We wrote a list of questions: who will be the first to get married, the last, how many children will we each have, who will wed their college boyfriend. We put the answers in an envelope that we could not open until we were all married. In the meantime, I kept it in my fireproof box with my passport and birth certificate. And later my marriage license.

"I said Michele's would be the first wedding," said Judy.

"Let's just open it," said Zoe, who was still single. "Did you write that mine would be the last?" She paused. "'Cause I think I did." So did I. So much has stayed the same since we wrote our questions and answers, yet so much has changed. In college I would often wake to see Judy's boyfriend eating Frosted Flakes on the sofa and run into Zoe's in the bathroom in the middle of the night. Today I don't know their men as much as I know about them. Huddled over coffee and Sunday brunch, I hear details the men would not want me to know. Not everything, though. Now, I keep some things from my friends. We all do.

Occasionally we talk about visiting Gaffield, but we haven't. I don't want the house to be different from my memories. When I was 16, I visited the pool where I swam my first full lap at the age of four. The pool seemed small and dreary and all its magic drained out of my memory. I don't want this to happen to Gaffield, and I don't want to see other people's jackets hanging on the porch railing or another car parked in the alley.

We don't need to see that creaky house—it is inside each of us. One mention of Gaffield and all our faces relax with a softness usually reserved for remembering a first love. Recently, when I was giving blood, I felt faint and had to look away from the needle. "Think of something pleasant," said the nurse. "Like the Caribbean or ice cream." Like Gaffield's rainy-day smell or the softness of the blue sofa. Like seeing the curly numbers come into focus as I hurried down our street and ran up our porch steps. That's my something pleasant, now and always.

Foggy Bottom Blues

CHRISTOPHER BUCKLEY

WHEN I WAS 29 YEARS OLD, I WENT TO WORK AT THE WHITE House. Because the job entailed physical proximity to the vice president of the United States, the FBI expressed interest in my background. As part of this six-month-long "SPIN" (Special Investigation), I found myself filling out a form requiring me to list every address at which I had lived over the preceding 29 years. I phoned the FBI agent assigned to my case and said to him, "You're kidding, right?" He replied with the impeccable taciturnity of his ilk: "No."

I could count some 15 or so addresses that I had called home, including a pair of tramp steamers and a college secret society. To impress the FBI with my patriotism and lack of desire to assassinate the vice president, I asterisked the list and provided further details on a separate sheet. ("Ports Visited on Freighter Fernbrook: 24, mostly Far East; list on request.") I explained that no one associated with the secret society would speak to the FBI, but said that this should not necessarily alarm them. I was at this point a bit punchy and hoped that this footnote would cause them to dispatch their top investigators to the scene, along with a couple of bloodhounds.

The narrow three-story townhouse in which I filled out this interminable form was my first home in Washington, D.C. I am now on my fourth. I live there happily with my wife and two children and faithful hound. I plan to be buried there, or least to have my ashes used to fertilize the roses. But I often think back on the first place. It was where my adult life began. It was the last place where I was young and single and had not yet signed up for 30 years' servitude to the mortgage bank.

I arrived in Washington one hot summer night, having driven down from New York City with all my earthly possessions inside my Volkswagen Rabbit convertible. There was a telegram stuck in the door. Remember those white strips of teletype pasted onto yellow forms, how eventful they seemed, and so often were? It was from my father. It said: "the father of our country is as proud of you as your own." And with that lovely paternal benison I crossed over the threshold into a new life.

And into my first Washington July. The neighborhood, Foggy Bottom, is well-named; it used to be a swamp. What time I spent at home that first summer was in my boxer shorts. Not a pretty sight.

It was a sublet at first, from peripatetic friends in the diplomatic corps. I inherited temporary possession of a malevolent blue Persian cat named Chinchon, who despised me at first sight. Each morning she would leave mementos eloquent of her contempt in my shoes. Returning in the evening, exhausted from another 16-hour day at the White House, I became a version of Peter Sellers' Inspector Clouseau, tiptoeing into each room in anticipation of sabotage. It crossed my mind to arrange to have Chinchon accidentally "escape." Finally, our three-month sentence of cohabitation mercifully came to an end. Her parting billet-doux was a blue hairball inside my typewriter.

There was a little patio out back, perhaps 15 feet by 10 feet. I fecklessly attempted to kibbutzify with plantings, but the only thing that would grow was mint, which I determined would probably grow in soil irradiated by atomic bombs.

I loved my little patio garden. It was my own Eden, even with the overhead roar of planes taking off from and landing at National Airport. I would take out the typewriter and set it on the heavy Mexican tiled table and bang away at my first novel. First Washington house, first novel. Everything was so new. In those days I still smoked cigarettes and remember the smoke swirling upward.

The house had a fireplace, and I had romantic notions of writing by firelight. I moved my desk down to the ground floor, positioning myself between the hearth and the patio. It was heavenly, cozy. All I needed was firewood, which I had never before bought. Up until then, firewood was something that had always somehow managed to materialize on its own.

That first October there came a knock on my door. "Y'all need any far-wood?" Thus began my initiation, which 20 years later is still ongoing, into the vicissitudes of purchasing firewood. Here is what I have learned over two decades: there is no such thing as "dry firewood," no matter how long it is avouched to have been "cured."

My learning curve was steep. My first batch of "dry" firewood sent billows of steam up the chimney. Bubbles formed at the ends of logs. I burned enough back issues of the *Washington Post* and the *New York Times* to consume Joan of Arc at the stake. At a hardware store, I made the delighted discovery of a device consisting of a cast-iron dish with a porous brick inside. You saturated the brick with kerosene, which provided a 20-minute kindling flame. Kerosene is not an especially pleasant bouquet, but it did remind me of my year aboard freighters. At any rate, I was determined to write my great American novel by the fire.

The first time I tried my new device, the reservoir of kerosene burned itself out, leaving the "dry" firewood blackened with soot, the log-ends sullenly hissing and foaming. With tongs I extracted the red-hot iron dish from beneath the andirons and poured fresh kerosene into the brick. This was ill-advised.

The explosion sent me reeling backward and cinematically blackened my face. For a month at the White House people would ask, "What happened to your eyebrows?" When I think that the manuscript of my novel could have been immolated, I tremble for American literature.

As part of my futile but dogged effort at self-improvement, I spent a few days at a Catholic retreat house on the Potomac, led by a remarkable English Benedictine monk, a world-famous St. Thomas More scholar. In one of his talks, he mentioned the fact that More prayed face-down on the floor. I was struck by this and thought if this posture was good enough for the man who stood up to King Henry VIII, it was certainly good enough for a wretch like myself. I mention this only for the following reason: every night I would lie face-down on the floor of my bedroom and offer up my prayers. After a few months, I noticed that the spot on the blond wood where I was laying my forehead had darkened. Two years later, doing the end-of-lease walk-through with the real estate agent, she noticed the spot on the bare floor and said, "What's that?" I was too embarrassed to say, and mumbled that I would of course pay to have it cleaned up.

That was 19 years ago now. A few months ago, I found myself walking along 23rd Street in the direction of the Lincoln Memorial. There were construction vehicles. I heard the harsh sound of pile-driving. My nostrils caught the tang of wet cement. I stood on the sidewalk in front of what had once been Number 608. The wrecker's ball had been and gone. The space before me was empty, as if someone had hit a giant "Delete" button. All gone. I could see in the distance the Watergate.

I stood amidst the noise of building and tried to reconstruct it in my mind: where my bedroom had been, where the fireplace was, the refrigerator full of my bachelor's fare of frozen dinners. Now, a huge steel beam, the spine of some future George Washington University dormitory or office, was embedded in the earth where the patio had been. I comforted myself with the knowledge that the mint had surely survived.

Father's Treehouse

DAVID LANSING

I BELIEVE THIS: WHEN WE BEGIN TO LOSE THOSE CLOSEST TO us, we receive an aura, like the forewarning of an illness, just before it happens. One day my father started building a treehouse—an elaborate Disney-inspired fantasy—in our backyard. That was the day I knew our family would eventually shatter like a hot marble dropped in ice water.

A third-generation Californian, something rare in a state swollen with refugees from harsh economies and harsh winters, I come from a peripatetic family of movie people, most of whom never owned a home, preferring—or perhaps forced—to live in a series of rented bunga-lows, apartments, duplexes, and trailers. For 70 years, since Nana Trudy worked as an extra in silent two-reelers with Will Rogers, my relatives skirted the fringes of showbiz as bit players, stagehands, and costume designers.

My mother, a former Miss Hollywood, was a 19-year-old dancer when she met my father, a studio carpenter whose own father was a gaffer and whose stepmother was, among other things, Mary Pickford's seamstress. My father was a peculiar man—moody, indecipherable, a loner. Almost 30 when he met and married my mother, he had lived alone in a two-bedroom Mediterranean bungalow in Toluca Lake, midway between the Universal and Warner Brothers studios where he divided his time.

He hated Los Angeles and spent days camping by himself in the vast Mojave Desert, even after he was married and my sister and I were born. Since his work was never steady and depended on the vagaries of the motion-picture business, it was nothing for my father to suddenly pack the car and disappear into the wilderness without even saying good-bye. We seldom knew where he was or when he would be back. The three of us were nervous whenever we heard the engine of the family Pontiac racing as Father backed uphill out of our driveway, possibly leaving us behind again.

Early in 1955 my father went to see about a job down in Orange County, a place that, although only an hour south of Los Angeles, was still checkered with fields of lima beans and strawberries, citrus groves, and cattle ranches, and not many people. When he came back that night, he announced that he had gotten a construction job at the site of a new amusement park to be called Disneyland. We were all going to move. Furthermore, we were going to buy a new house—our first!— just blocks away from the theme park.

"You kids can go there anytime you want," he said.

It is difficult to say with any certainty how valid our first memories are. After years of hearing other people's versions of our childhood, we find that some stories take on a dreamlike quality, making it almost impossible to know what really happened.

Nevertheless, I think one of my earliest memories must be real, partly because no one else ever talked about it. It is a memory of seeing Disneyland for the first time, in its construction stage, when it looked more than anything like a desert oasis. There were acres of white sand, pockets of palm trees, and in the middle, like an apparition, the partially complete facade of Sleeping Beauty Castle.

Sometimes my mother made my father a hot lunch, and one day she took me with her to drop it off. I was standing next to my father, tightly gripping his hand, confused and probably a little scared by the frantic activity as men hammered away at what would be train depots and turn-of-the-century stores and a fort. I remember my father's smell of sweat and dust, and the clank of tools in his heavy leather carpenter's belt, which sat low on his hips like a gunfighter's holster, as we walked up a chalky road toward a castle that looked magnificent to me.

But most vividly I remember seeing Walt Disney, who I recognized from his Sunday TV show, *Walt Disney's Wonderful World of Color*, standing before the castle, a child's dream of spires and towers and a moat. "Every kid in America will want to live in that castle," Walt said, admiring his half-finished creation. "Wouldn't you?" I thought he was talking to me. But maybe not. Maybe he was saying it to my father, or even just thinking out loud.

For years I assumed this was a memory shared by my father and me, but the only time I brought it up, a few years back when he was living alone in an old trailer in the Arizona desert town of Quartzsite, dying of cancer, my father assured me it never happened. "I never met Walt Disney personally," he rasped, pulling off his oxygen mask. "Neither did you."

But I believe I did, and I often thought of Walt during the years when Mother was in and out of hospitals and Father had finally gone on a trip to the desert from which he never returned home. It was Walt whose smile and reassuring voice I could count on at least once a week. Though he never knew it, it was his approval I sought, his guidance I looked for. "What would Walt do?" I would often ask myself when confronted with such moral quandaries as whether or not to steal strawberries from the Japanese farmer's fields behind my house, or what to tell my teachers, stern Catholic nuns, when they demanded to know why my school uniform was unwashed or why I had no lunch. "Give this note to your mother and have her sign it before you come back to school," they would say, and I would forge her signature as easily as I wrote my own. Although I knew Walt wouldn't always approve of my transgressions, I believed he would forgive them.

In 1975, when I had just graduated from college and had not heard from my father in a number of years, he called unexpectedly. He was passing through and would like to see me. We met at a steakhouse close to my apartment. I chose someplace neutral. Someplace I could leave in a hurry.

Our conversation was strained. He wanted to talk about my future, which I could not see and did not care about at the time, and I wanted to talk about his past—our past—something he tried to wave away along with the smoke from his Camels. I was persistent. There were questions I needed answers to, I told him, the most important being this: When did he know Mother would never get well?

He put down his fork and knife, looked down at his nicotine-stained fingernails, examining knuckles that were twisted and swollen with arthritis. He answered my question with a question of his own: "Do you remember the treehouse I built?"

The treehouse was Father's version of a project he had worked on, the Swiss Family Robinson attraction, inspired by the Disney film. The Disneyland treehouse stood 80 feet high and was made out of concrete, steel, and vinyl leaves. Our treehouse was about half that height and sat not in a tree but atop two telephone poles acquired from a neighbor who worked for the phone company.

Construction began the weekend of Mother's first incident. Mother had stolen (Nana always said "borrowed") a neighbor's car early one morning, after my father had gone to work, and driven to Disneyland where she pulled up and replanted the marigolds on the sloped flower beds just inside the park. She spelled out her name in golden petals: JOAN.

Maybe someone recognized her or maybe she told the security guards that her husband worked there, but my father was called. He came and took her home.

After that weekend he worked on the treehouse day and night, flooding our backyard with construction lights, filling the air with the whine of his circular saw. Crossbeams halfway up the poles supported heavy sheets of plywood for a floor. Then walls went up with bamboo siding and a pitched thatched roof. My father worked tirelessly on this structure, which seemed to spring to life almost overnight with no prodding from my sister and me. In fact, we were a little stunned by the whole thing. It didn't dawn on me right away that he wasn't building the treehouse for *us*.

A few months later, Mother had to be hospitalized. By that time, the treehouse had grown considerably. There were now four bunk beds, a deck with railings, a larder for food, a trapdoor with a rope ladder, and the beginnings of a library against one wall.

Father started sleeping up there. Uneasy to be in the house without grown-ups, I sometimes joined him. It probably sounds like an adventure, something most kids would think was great, sleeping in a treehouse, but I didn't really like it—it seemed so unstable, the whole structure swaying when you shifted around in the dark. I slept there in the mistaken belief that Father wouldn't go away as long as I was with him.

Disneyland was visible from our perch. You could watch the fireworks at night in the summer, hear the plaintive blasts from the smokestacks of the stern-wheeler. "You can see the Matterhorn," he would say, smoking a Camel, legs hanging over the deck. "And there's Sleeping Beauty Castle." Then, almost to himself, he would whisper, "I helped build that, you know."

Over the years, Mother was in and out of hospitals. When she was home, heavily medicated with tranquilizers and antidepressants, roaming the house at night and sleeping during the day, my father couldn't stand to be in the same room with her or, it seemed, with us. He stopped having meals with the family; the extended silences at the table echoed his growing isolation. None of us talked about why Father slept in the treehouse or why Mom had to be hospitalized.

Father came inside in the morning only to shower, change his clothes, and rush off to work, dropping my sister and me at Disneyland's front gate in the summertime. As the children of an employee we were given free passes and spent so many days at the park that it functioned as our day-care center, the place where my father thought we were safer than being at home with my mother.

In his free time, my father continued making small improvements on the treehouse. He added electricity, he moved in a portable black-and-white TV from the family room. He replaced the rope ladder with a wooden staircase. We became a neighborhood attraction. People cruised by like gawkers at an accident scene, pausing to get a good look at the treehouse and to stare at its owner, who could often be seen sitting on the edge, smoking his cigarettes, looking toward Disneyland.

Then a strange thing happened. Mother got well. Not overnight but over a year or two she began slowly reclaiming her life and reestablishing some sort of tenuous relationship with my father. They were painful to watch together—Mother nervous but happy, Father observing her carefully, saying little. For a while, the treehouse was all but forgotten. The Santa Ana winds blew pieces of the roof off during one storm. Father didn't repair it. He was back in the house but we all held our breath, knowing, I suppose, that it couldn't last.

It didn't. It ended shortly after Mother was briefly hospitalized again, this time after trying to climb the fence into Disneyland one night where she told the security guards she had a very important meeting with Walt Disney himself. "It's extremely urgent," she told them, "Mr. Disney just called me"—a pathetic fantasy because Walt had died the previous December.

Father abandoned us, and for the next few years, as I floundered through high school, the three of us lived together as strangers. It was the late sixties, a difficult time for everyone. I was unsympathetic to my mother, who embarrassed me. I never invited friends over, afraid they would catch a glimpse of the ghost that she had become, wandering around the darkened house in her nightgown. My sister fled home for college. I mended the roof of my father's treehouse and moved in, decorating the walls with Day-Glo posters and replacing the TV with an old record player with detachable speakers that had been the last gift from my father. A week after my high school graduation, I left the treehouse and home for a summer job, knowing—though I didn't tell Mother—that it was for good.

Some years later, I gravitated back to Orange County with my wife after living in Oregon for a while. We bought a ranch-style house built in the 1950s not far from Disneyland. When my son was about eight, he begged me to build him a treehouse in our backyard. I wasn't crazy about the plan, listing all the reasons why it was a bad idea—dangerous, probably against building codes, the neighbors might complain.

But my son and his younger sister had recently seen an old Disney movie, *Swiss Family Robinson,* and loved the idea of building their own little castle in the sky, a treehouse with trapdoors and rope ladders and maybe even a couple of bunk beds so they could sleep in it.

I tried to put them off, telling them I would think about it, but they immediately began scrounging scrap wood and hammering two-by-fours in the crook of an old pepper tree in our backyard.

"You can't just hammer some boards onto the limbs," I shouted at them, annoyed. "You've got to build a proper foundation. And draw up plans. Particularly if you want it to last. Otherwise everything will just fall apart."

"But you won't help us, " they said.

So we went inside and I sketched plans for a treehouse. Nothing too elaborate. Plywood siding, a couple of windows, two bunk beds, an outside deck with a simple railing. A place where on a clear summer's night you can sit and watch the fireworks over Disneyland. You can't see the castle or even the Matterhorn roller coaster from our house, but if the breeze is blowing from the northeast, I hear the familiar cry of the Mark Twain as it begins another voyage around the Rivers of America. The sound of the whistle carries me back to when I was a child, living within the shadow of the happiest place on earth.

Sometimes after the fireworks the children ask me if they can sleep in the treehouse.

"I suppose so," I tell them.

Usually they ask me if I'll stay up there with them for a while and tell them stories about how their grandpa, who they never knew, helped build Disneyland.

"Absolutely," I tell them, unrolling their sleeping bags. "I'll leave when you're asleep."

But I don't. I tell them stories and then I stay the night.

Furnishing School

PATRICK DUNNE

AT 24, ONE REALLY SHOULD KNOW EVERYTHING. SOMEHOW most of my friends did, but then they were from the Northeast and were born with infused knowledge, all of it practical. I, on the other hand, knew almost nothing. These deficits were clearly the result of genetic flaws and my upbringing in that odd warp of South Texas coastal plain along the Gulf of Mexico just beyond the Nueces River. My ability to spot the juiciest prickly pear from yards away or knowing how to pat out a mean tortilla hardly compensates for gross ineptitude at self-serve gasoline stations. Still, I experienced a grave revelation when I got my first real apartment in the French Quarter: not only was it vastly empty, but even worse, I had no notion of how to furnish it.

This seems odd because my childhood is littered with memories of furniture. There was a tiny rosewood rocking chair and a pair of wonderful benches, which, in a given day, I might transform into theater stalls, stagecoach seats, or church pews. Castles came and went, and when my parents conveniently took off on trips, my inventive grandmother collaborated in the most thrilling redecoration schemes. Suppers were conjured by candlelight and costume in forbidden rooms; Turkish tents were created out of doors for nocturnal events under the cottonwoods. There was no dearth of props for these escapades. Tattered cushions were as plentiful as tumbleweed, and the yard could be carpeted at whim with vivid lap rugs smelling of that peculiar sweetness only damply stored old wool can emit.

While furniture filled the spaces of my youth, the notion of actually furnishing rooms was altogether foreign. Little seemed to change at home or in any other familiar house, all of them appearing eternally full of things. Stuff was occasionally given away or broken or consigned to sheds, but rarely did anything new appear except when some inheritance caused rearrangements. My father, being popular among his relations, often had first pick from these eccentric estates. We would wait breathlessly to see what he would choose. Once he came back from a familiar rambling house with only a box wadded with old newspapers. Even my mother could not conceal her disappointment when he produced a footed, cut-glass cake stand. "Just that?" we whined in unison, remembering a stereopticon and a stuffed coyote we used to see there. "Well, it always held my birthday cake," he rasped defensively, "and those cakes were always good!" We went silent as he clapped it on the sideboard. It held many a good cake afterward and no day was ever special without it. Now I bring it out whispering apologetic incantations lest the present confection offend against those collective memories.

At other times Papa's choices were triumphal. A cousin, who had been the state's poet laureate when those things seemed to matter, left us her books and a huge brooding sculpture of a raven, Edgar Allan Poe being her favorite writer. Executed in the 1920s by a famous Italian artist, it was made more menacing after Cousin Lillith had it fitted with green eyes that shone when a concealed electric cord was plugged in. It sat atop a bookcase in our library and was one of the creepy marvels of the world. As its fame spread, our house became first choice for every adolescent gathering. The raven presided over some raucous times and a few serious séances. The blinking eyes foretold romance, betrayal, travel, and alas, undulating current. It gradually acquired a hoary look because my mother's housekeeper would never touch it, certain that it bore ill omens.

Only once, during a very brief stint as a Cub Scout, did I glimpse other worlds that made me first ponder the mystery of furnishing. The den gathered at a house long and low and very modern. My fellow Cub had his own suite, unheard of in those days, when a child's privacy was somehow akin to heresy and certainly a threat to moral health. His room had everything built in. Frankly, I was electrified. The Scout's mother, probably delighted by my morbid interest, gave me a detailed tour, lingering on each modern touch. At the afternoon's end, sitting at the foot of my grandmother's bed whence she ruled, I gave a full report while she rearranged her pillows, sipped from her water glass, played with her dented sapphire bracelet. The eyebrows began to raise ominously. I knew that look. Determined to convince her, I delivered what I imagined would be the coup de grâce: "And the furniture in the house was specially ordered by a decorator and it all matches!" She smoothed an imaginary hair from her forehead and looked out the windows past me to an ancient, gnarled sweetheart rose. "Poor things," she finally pronounced with indisputable charity. "Let's never mention it again; it really isn't nice to gloat."

Later, after an interval decent enough to raise no specter of comparison, she reminisced about a decorating success or two that she herself had achieved. With riveting satisfaction my grandmother described the kitchen at the farm she once had painted Chinese red. I've longed to copy that in every place I've ever lived but always feared failure. A color richly mixed with words is the hardest one to match.

Almost nothing more disturbed my innocence of active decorating. College digs were always fitted out, sometimes badly enough to be poetical. One basement apartment in Washington actually had tattered rags for curtains, so perfect they could have been used as a prop for La Bohème. It wasn't until a few years later, having signed for that immense apartment of four rooms in the French Quarter, that the confrontation came. All I had were some books and a box of flatware, the same box my grandmother had packed so many years ago into my freshman trunk. At that time, in an emotional leave-taking, she extracted a solemn oath that I would always use her silver at mealtimes as "any other metal ruins teeth." This vow proved an enduring source of embarrassment; I became adept at sneaking out my fork at cafeteria tables under the critical eyes of egalitarian classmates, but promises were kept and my teeth stayed strong.

Even I knew these minimal possessions hardly constituted a household. Fortunately I had made a great new friend, Paul, whose French ancestors were hanging chandeliers when New Orleans consisted of not much more than shanties and a few delusions. Paul thought paying $100 a month for any apartment to be a senseless extravagance, but rose to the challenge of helping me to domesticate it. "It will take time, of course," he cautioned, his Creole charm taking a sharp turn. "Impatience will lead to vulgarity or the department store; I'll do my very best to keep you safe from both!" And so he did. Paul ruled the nighttime marine desk of a huge shipping line. In those pre-Internet days he was always first to know the path of hurricanes and every impending foreign crisis; because a telex sat on his desk, he was viewed by his friends as an oracle. Best of all were his eccentric hours and great taste.

He would call at dawn, his shift nearly complete: "Meet me at Morning Call; we'll have beignets, then hoof it to Christie's South," a code for the main warehouse of Volunteers of America. It was a period when the great old houses uptown were being emptied, and in the rush for resale, much was sent to charities. We arrived well before most slothful junk dealers were awake, so pickings could be very good. Paul went nearly every day, had a photographic memory, and spotted the "newly arrived merchandise" in a flash. He once confided his secret—that he only saw the misplaced thing: in ugly surroundings he instantly noticed the beautiful, among the trash the jewel. He was uncanny as we tripped through the gloomy recesses of those foul storerooms. "Over there!" he whispered, digging beneath disgusting heaps of gray-stained carpet to uncover a pile of Persian rugs, some of which I still have. "Look here!" Among the rusted metal a fine old silver tray. And so it went. In a gentlemanly way we divvied up, he reserving final call. "That painting's really not for you, I need it for Lothar!" Without arguing, I let it go, jealous that other rooms played upon his mind. Even then I knew this experience was an apprenticeship of sorts. In places such as these my skills were honed, judgments suspended until the search was done, my eye trained to sometimes forget the brain. With no time for second

Street, I got to know almost every dealer. They were a breed apart—suspicious, fabulous, full of secrets, and patient with a neophyte. They also seemed to have a hound-dog sense for likely buyers and would lean out their doors and call me in to see something irresistible inside. My rooms filled up.

Paul called. He had found a grand sofa in a shop, exactly right for me. I balked because there seemed no space. He countered, "The Swedish thing can go!" I felt a searing pang. "Nonsense! It belongs elsewhere now; you can't be selfish, these things are just for us to use a while!" As always, he was right. The costly replacement arrived—too wide for bringing up the narrow stairs. I was jubilant, but Paul, undeterred, discerningly recruited a crew of brawny passersby, promising jazz and rum punches for hoisting the heavy sofa over my high balcony. While he was placing it I was busy mixing punches and had no time to mourn the painful process of redecoration.

Seeking Our Fortunes

BETSY BROWN

"WHY DON'T YOU GIRLS PAINT THIS PLACE?" ASKED A FRIEND — married, of course.

It hadn't occurred to us. Why would it? Four young women, "girls," as we were called back in the late 1940s, sharing the second floor of a brownstone on West 74th Street a few doors from Central Park didn't think of it as home. Our plan, never voiced but understood, was to live there until we got married.

We considered ourselves lucky. The apartment was shabby but elegant. In the morning when I walked down the wide steps, with their heavy rounded stone sides, I felt like a character from Henry James, only lacking a long skirt and muff. Our neighborhood was full of music students, and on summer days the street rang with arias and pianos, violins and flutes.

Inside, the hallway was dark, the carpeting on the stairs was worn, and the only telephone in the building hung on the wall in the stairwell. We didn't care. It was Manhattan. We were all from out of town and we said laughingly that we had come to New York to seek our fortunes. I arrived from California with my friend Bonnie, each of us carrying $100 cash and a roundtrip train ticket. When we got jobs, we sold the return tickets and bought winter coats.

Bonnie went to live with friends in Greenwich Village, and I moved in with Idella, Bebe, and Eleanor. Our apartment had enormous 12-foot-high rooms. This was the parlor floor with the fanciest details. The living room fireplace didn't work anymore but it was as tall as we were, with a wide mantel. A crystal chandelier hung from a rococo plaster medallion, and a deep bay window looked out on the street. The room was furnished with a maroon day bed, a collection of unrelated upholstered chairs, a piano, and a small dining table with four chairs.

The kitchen was minimal but the bathroom was gigantic and drafty, owing to a window that wouldn't close tight, nor would the door lock. In a bedroom as big as the living room, we four shared two double beds. It never occurred to us to spend our own money on single beds—after all, we wouldn't be there forever. We didn't aspire to apartments of our own—there was still a postwar shortage, and anyway, people who made the kind of salaries we did never thought of living alone.

Idella and I had known each other in Berkeley—we were cooking partners in the eighth grade—and we bumped into each other in the reception room of *Newsweek*, where I was a researcher and she was applying for a job.

Idella didn't get the *Newsweek* job and instead became a writer on a children's magazine, where she claimed she had to describe everything as "fun," even "Coal mining is fun." Idella was so nearsighted she couldn't get out of bed without putting on her glasses. She took them off for dates and then she had a romantic, misty-eyed look, especially when she undid the prim braids she wore around her head and let the hair fall to her waist. She was in love with a man named Albert who had given up a solid career as a physicist to come to New York and write a play. Idella was waiting patiently for his future to become predictable.

Bebe was a pretty girl from Biloxi, a secretary, who told us uneasily that until she met us she had never known anyone who wasn't a Roman Catholic. She made her own clothes, even suits, and on weekends the dining table was often draped with her fabrics and patterns.

Eleanor came from New Jersey and was six feet tall, every inch gorgeous. She was studying voice and worked off and on in temporary office jobs. Once in a while she was hired as a church soloist.

Our rent was $120 a month, $30 each, and we put an additional $7 a week into the food kitty, except for Eleanor, who was taken out to dinner so often she didn't consider it worthwhile to chip in. She bought her own breakfast makings and had a designated shelf in the refrigerator. If one of us had a guest we put in 70 cents to pay for the extra meal. Years later, when Albert visited me and my husband in New York, he exclaimed over my cooking. "I thought you'd give me that tuna-fish casserole," he said.

We shopped on Columbus Avenue, where the proprietors surprised us by remembering our names and what we bought. Idella and I liked eggs for breakfast but they were expensive, so we bought two a week and each had one for Sunday breakfast. After a while we both got raises. That week, we asked the grocer for six eggs. She smiled and said, "Having a party?"

Together we had everything we needed. Idella and I owned typewriters, Bebe a sewing machine, and Eleanor a phonograph. We spent a lot of time and very little money on clothes and grooming. In the evenings we helped each other pin up hems and gave each other permanents, and it seemed one of us was always putting on nail polish.

I had Mondays and Tuesdays off and worked on weekends. While my roommates slept in and the neighborhood was still deserted, I would descend the front steps feeling enormously important, feeling that the world needed me. One winter Sunday I opened the door and found 18 inches of snow. As a Californian, I didn't know a big storm from a little one. "Boy, it sure snows a lot here," I said to myself, and when I got to the office I discovered that less than half the staff had made it.

At *Newsweek* a young mail clerk who sang while he sorted got a job as a spear carrier with the Metropolitan Opera, so a bunch of us bought seats in the top row for $2.40 and tried to spot him. I discovered theater too, and *Newsweek*'s drama critic sometimes took me with him. Often he invited me when he didn't expect a hit, and several times I saw plays that closed after one performance.

I belonged to the Newspaper Guild and picketed at lunchtime whenever the shop steward asked me to, wherever some outrage was supposed to be taking place. Once I went to a rally in Washington.

Idella thought I was brave, Bebe disapproved silently, and Eleanor laughed and shrugged when I told her what I was doing.

We visited back and forth with the four girls downstairs, out-of-towners like us. We were noisy—yelling to call each other to the phone—like players in a career-girl movie. Neither apartment had its own TV, but once in a while when there was something special on, such as a national political convention, we went to the corner bar to watch it.

We would have been embarrassed to say out loud that we were looking for husbands. We had blind dates, we went out with each other's brothers and cousins, friends of friends, men from home. There was a great churning of young people, everybody in motion, everybody looking for someone. We kept hearing about friends at home getting married, usually before they were 25, after which a woman might be labeled an old maid. That birthday was coming soon for all of us, but we weren't worried. We were career women and could take our time.

Idella was committed to Albert, but the rest of us didn't stick with anybody for long if it didn't look "serious." We always reviewed the parade of dates and told one another that so-and-so was too short (we were all tall), or not good-looking, or boring, or not to be trusted. We got jilted too sometimes, but we pretended we didn't care.

In the lulls when we had nobody go to out with, there was always Johnny. He was a showoff and a nonstop talker and dated each of us in turn until he caught on that none of us was interested. Unabashed, he took to phoning us as a group. "Anybody want to go to the Frick? Anybody want to go to Jones Beach?" Usually somebody did. When he became engaged, he brought his fiancée over in triumph.

Eleanor was a menace. She was beautiful and buxom with milky white skin and shining, wavy dark hair to her shoulders, a sexy laugh, and big eyes with long lashes, which she batted in mock flirtation, or not so mock. Eleanor liked to play the piano and sing Carmen's "Habañera" whenever there was a man around. We were nervous about her effect on our dates. I remember the time she played for Charlie, a *Newsweek* writer I really liked.

"Do you want to hear me sing?" Who could refuse? Charlie sat down reluctantly. And then she began *Si tu ne m'aime, prend garde à moi* (If you don't love me, watch out) in her throaty, suggestive soprano, somehow playing the piano while singing over her shoulder, holding Charlie with her eyes.

"That was beautiful, Eleanor, thanks very much," he said when she finished, and then to me, to my great relief, "Let's go."

The rest of us were secretive about what we did or did not do privately, but Eleanor slept with men on our daybed behind the heavy sliding door. One Saturday her date stayed all night. Because I worked on Sunday, that morning I was trapped. I couldn't leave the apartment without going through the living room. I banged around the kitchen to alert the pair and then negotiated the living room with my eyes averted. That night, after talking it over, Idella and Bebe and I asked Eleanor to move out.

She wasn't offended and cheerfully rented a single room on the top floor of our building. We let her use our piano and she often stuck her head in (we rarely locked the door) to tell us about a new job or some nightclub or restaurant she had been taken to. We decided we wouldn't get another roommate. By now we could afford $40 a month each and would take turns having one of the double beds all to ourselves.

When I had lived in the apartment six months and the others a year, we decided to paint it, even though I think we shared an unspoken superstition that if we made it too homelike we'd be stuck there. But our decorating instincts won and we set aside a weekend. We bought several gallons of Kemtone, a cheap water-based paint that was easy to apply and would last plenty long enough for us. We borrowed a ladder from the landlady and spent two hot, sticky days painting the wainscoting and the ceiling ivory and the upper walls sky blue. We collapsed at 12 both nights. The place looked clean and pretty, and the chandelier sparkled against the fresh paint.

Suddenly we felt proprietary. It was time for a party. We invited married couples we never thought to invite before, couples who had entertained us as if we were waifs. We basked in their compliments, amazed at our domesticity.

We decided to do more. Bebe made a swag of coppery satin for the bay window. I bought a reproduction of Franz Marc's *Red Horses* to go over the mantel. We put a lock on the bathroom door. We got our own telephone. Thanksgiving was coming and I assumed we would again scatter to the dining tables of friends and relatives as we had last year. But Idella said, "Let's face it, we're adults. Let's have Thanksgiving here."

What an idea! And I learned a lesson that stands me in good stead even today: if you are willing to cook, you never have to spend a holiday alone.

It was a coming of age. We invited our current boyfriends, friends from work who had nowhere to go, and one married couple. We borrowed an extra table from the landlady and ran the two tables the length of the living room. We didn't know much about cooking except for chops and spaghetti, but we roasted a turkey, which took an hour longer than we expected. While waiting, everyone got tight on Chianti from straw-covered bottles.

We were all given raises and we thought about going home, just to visit. Idella went first. There was a bargain airline that charged $99 to California, and an even greater bargain airline that charged $88. Idella took the $88 flight. Anxious, Bebe and I asked her to send us a telegram when she got there. We waited. Twenty-four hours went by. And then came the wire: "Next time take a broom. Idella."

I have always believed that romance and travel go hand in hand, or at least that travel hastens romantic decisions. This is the way it was during the war, when men who were about to go overseas rushed into marriage, and when young women rode buses and trains to see their husbands and sweethearts at camp.

This is the way it was with the three of us, too. Travel played a big part in all our romances.

Albert and Idella were not exactly engaged, but they seemed to have "an understanding." Then without consulting Idella, Albert announced that he was going to California and he would let her know when he wanted her to join him. Idella saw him off, brooded, then came to a boil. She wasn't going to be taken for granted or sit waiting at some man's beck and call. She sent him a scorching letter and in a couple of weeks was dating somebody else.

Albert flew back to New York in a panic. At first Idella wouldn't talk to him. He hung around the apartment raging to Bebe and me and telling us how much he loved Idella. Finally she forgave him, quit her job, and they went back to California and married.

Bebe and I didn't think we could manage the apartment alone. We checked with everyone we knew, but we couldn't find a roommate. We put an ad in the paper and got 85 answers. We screened them on the phone and invited three or four to be interviewed. Reluctantly, we picked a lonely young woman who was obviously pining for a boyfriend who had dropped her. She was no substitute for Idella.

Then Bebe went to Biloxi to see her family. She came back happy and daydreamy. Next to her on the plane was a man named Earle, a southerner who lived in New York, and he was wonderful. From then on, she was out half the time and the other half was putting 70 cents in the kitty for Earle's dinner. He took her home to meet his family. They disapproved. "You're the most wonderful girl, but why do you have to be a Catholic?" his Baptist father asked. "Talk to Earle," she said. "He brought me here. I didn't come on my own." The romance continued.

I decided to visit my parents but a friend at *Newsweek* pointed out that it was just as cheap to go to England, where I had relatives, and I could visit my parents the following year. I had enough saved for a few days in Paris too. And then suddenly *Newsweek* sent my friend Charlie to Germany as a foreign correspondent. I resolved not to pursue him in Europe. He didn't really care about me or he would have said something before he left, and I'd just get my heart broken and spoil my trip.

But the very moment I walked into my hotel in Paris, he was on the phone. Would I meet him to talk things over? I would. And then, when we met, would I marry him? I would. Our Paris wedding took place first, as legally required, in the *mairie* of St. Sulpice, in a room filled with gilded red velvet chairs. The ceremony was performed by the mayor, who urged us to settle in his arrondissement. And then we were married again in the American church before two pews of newspaper friends, with my great uncle Bernard from London to give me away.

Bebe shipped all my worldly goods—two suitcases of clothes and my typewriter. Then came her letter. She and Earle were getting married in Biloxi.

I never knew what happened to the new roommate, or to our apartment. Two years later when we got home from Europe, I wheeled my year-old son past it and there were milk bottles sitting in the bay window and poor families in the neighborhood. I suspected our apartment had been divided in two, like a lot of apartments in those years.

Decades later, the neighborhood turned upscale. The groceries and drugstores and Laundromat where people knew us have been replaced with chain stores like Gap and Starbucks and fancy specialty shops and noisy restaurants with outdoor tables.

The last time I passed our house, not long ago, the windows had fashionable wooden inside shutters, and big flower pots flanked the front door. I wonder whether our second-floor apartment is back in one piece, or whether the whole building has been made into a big beautiful one-family house, the way it started out a century ago.

Eleanor married and disappeared from our lives. Idella and Albert had two daughters and Albert went back to being a physicist. He became famous and his picture was on the cover of *Life* magazine. Idella died in her 40s, and Albert didn't answer when I wrote to ask what had happened. Bebe and Earle had six children and live in Virginia. I'm still in New York, a widow with two grown children and three grandsons.

Those were the fortunes we found.

Sabbatical Houses

LISA JENNIFER SELZMAN

I HAVE ALWAYS LOVED DRIVING AT NIGHT, MOVING THROUGH darkness with the drowsy satiation of a day coming to an end. Even as a small child I would peek into the glowing windows of other people's houses as we passed. I would imagine the layout of rooms beyond those I could see, how I would furnish them if they were mine. The windows gave me anonymous entree into the worlds of strangers, and ordinary houses became marvelous with all they held, all they concealed. I caught snapshots of life: a little boy reaches for a cat on the windowsill, a woman bends to look in the oven, an elderly couple sits side by side reading the newspaper. A mother opens a front door and a girl runs toward her across the lawn; I feel that quiet comfort of stepping into a lighted front hall, of coming home.

When I was 13, I had the chance to venture inside houses not my own in a way that went beyond glimpses through windows. At 65, my grandfather retired from the oil company where he had worked as a geophysicist for his entire adult life and began his second career. His alma mater invited him to join its faculty, and for the next 17 years he and my grandmother spent much of September through May in Ithaca, New York, returning to their home near us in Houston each summer. Eventually they tired of the biannual repacking of boxes and rented a modest place of their own in Ithaca, but for nine years they moved each fall into a different house vacated by a Cornell University professor on sabbatical. Sabbatical. Such a wondrous word, I thought—a word that suggested adventure, encounters with the unknown. One family vanishes and another—ours—inhabits their world, while someplace far away that family has stepped into other people's lives, and on and on.

I close my eyes and try to remember each of the sabbatical houses. I list them less confidently with every passing year, as if recalling fading details of long-ago sweethearts. Sometimes parts of these houses loom up in my dreams—a sunlit hallway, the dining room the year the Chinese professors came for dinner, a garage where my grandfather stacked firewood, a staircase carpeted in white.

How magical those houses were to me. Looking back on them I can trace my growing up more clearly than when I think about my own childhood home. My annual visits to those Ithaca houses marked my progress forward in life, winter by winter. Among the ghosts of the absent families I felt surrounded by possibility, by all I could learn.

The first house was the only one I ever saw in late summer. I made the long trip from Texas with my grandparents on their maiden journey. We were on the road each morning in darkness so that we could travel beside the sun as it rose. Somewhere in Tennessee or Kentucky we had a flat tire, and my grandfather maneuvered the car off the highway to a gas station. Watching him roll up his sleeves to help the mechanic, I thought of photographs I had seen of him as a young man exploring for oil, studying wide canyons, dust-blown plains, the terrain deep beneath the oceans. In those pictures he gazed directly into the camera with a considering gaze, as if he were about to answer a question.

Arriving at last in Ithaca, I was entranced by the hills, the rural spaciousness, the multistoried houses that resembled the oddly human ones children draw: windows for eyes, door for a mouth, chimney like a jaunty hat. It was all so different from my native city, with its downtown of glass high-rises, suburbs laid out in even grids of ranches or bungalows, and flat land as far as the eye could see. Here, the air felt silken. Even the light was different, paler and suffused with gold. Stepping out of the car into this place I had never been before, I felt I had come home.

The tall white house stood high on a hill with a view of the surrounding neighborhood sloping down to farmland. In the distance, Lake Cayuga blinked in the sun. Two stories in front and three in back, the house was built, as were so many structures there, into the incline. It had an enormous basement that ran the length of the building, fascinating to me as there were no basements where I came from, where the water table lies just below the earth's surface. We could walk to fields of corn for picking, and my grandmother and I would enter the rows with awe, as if coming upon a hidden country. The corn was the sweetest I had ever tasted.

When I returned at Christmas, this time with my parents and two brothers, I was visiting the house as well as my grandparents. In the books I loved to read, leaves changed colors, snow fell, women left for parts unknown to follow their dreams. I wanted to live in such a world. Perhaps my longing to go north was woven through my DNA, passed down by ancestors who had lived in the New York area. In this place that introduced me to the beauty of bare branches etched against the sky, and the wonder of a whole town burning a single white candle in each window during the holidays, I somehow felt freer to be myself than I ever had at home.

It was thrilling to use another family's Bugs Bunny tumblers and spoons, to eat Cap'n Crunch out of adopted bowls. To try on someone else's life. Each end table and kitchen chair, each closet lined with quilted hanging bags, each book title allowed a small guess about those people whose house we borrowed. The professor had four children, and we could tell from the decor which of the upstairs bedrooms belonged to each family member. I got to sleep in what was, in my eyes, the most beautiful of the bedrooms, that of the eldest daughter. As the oldest child and the only girl, I felt a kinship with this daughter, about whom I knew next to nothing beyond the fact that she was 17.

I opened the empty drawers of her bureau, felt along the bottoms for clues to her life. Her vanity table was empty but I sat before it and imagined an array of potions that made certain girls so dazzling. I wondered if she had a boyfriend she was sad to leave behind for a year, if in fact she had stood before her parents refusing to go, angry and hurt as I so often was with mine in those days. I wondered if a boy would ever love me.

Each day when my brothers and I came indoors, my grandfather built a fire. I had never been as cold as I was in Ithaca, where I touched snow for the first time. For someone from a place where you needed a coat for little more than a month a year, a fireplace was thrilling. We lounged in front of it, our feet stretched toward the blaze, eating our grandmother's fruit pie. My grandfather made fires calmly, precisely. He enjoyed each step of the process, explaining to my brothers and me as he went. "The key is patience," he'd say, rolling newspaper into tight cylinders and lining them in a row under the logs. "You can't rush a fire."

Throughout the evening, his steady tending at the hearth was the rhythm underneath whatever else went on in the room, as he rearranged the logs with an iron poker or carried in more wood, bringing with him a cloud of sharp fresh air. Although we kids often helped, the fire always seemed to be something my grandfather gave to us.

That year as we drove around campus, the college students seemed very old to me. I couldn't understand why my grandmother referred to them as "the kids." My grandfather pointed out landmarks of his school days, when according to my grandmother—who had met him on a blind date when she came up from New Jersey for a football weekend— he was quite a big man on campus. "Well," my grandfather said, "I don't know about that. But your grandmother, she was a good-looking girl." I loved the story of how, that first semester back as a professor, my grandfather sat at the counter of a luncheonette where he had eaten throughout graduate school. Not having seen him in 40 years, the owner took one look, instantly recognized him, and called out, "Sid!" Visiting my grandfather's office in the geological sciences building, I would marvel at the machine that registered and measured earthquakes as they occurred throughout the world. In the hallway, behind glass, hung a tremendous fossilized footprint of a dinosaur.

The first winter, my brothers and I stayed on in Ithaca for several days after my parents returned to Houston, and on the morning we were packing to leave, my grandmother suddenly sat halfway up the staircase, her arms filled with folded laundry. "I don't want them to go," I heard her sob to my grandfather, who took her in his arms and spoke softly to her. I stood on the landing, struck by the force of her love for us. "Shh," my grandfather said, stroking her hair as he often stroked mine. "They'll be back, they'll be back."

Other houses followed. There was the one with the icy driveway, where I watched horrified as my brother slipped backward and caught his entire body weight on his elbows. There was the house I left to go jogging, and when darkness fell quickly, I realized I was lost. I had no idea of my grandparents' address or phone number, nor would they be listed in the phone book. Theirs was just the house with the rooms of dark wood filled with books. I finally knocked on a door where inside I saw a couple preparing dinner. They welcomed me and as luck would have it, the man was a Cornell professor, so he looked up my grandfather in the faculty directory.

There was the house with the tasseled Oriental rug in the living room furnished in white. There was the house with big stepping stones leading up to the entrance. One winter when my grandmother and I drove through campus to the Ag school, where we bought ice cream made with milk from the school's own cows, I was almost the age of the students walking through the slush. Then I was their contemporary.

The year of the vast kitchen I was a college senior and visited for a weekend with my boyfriend. My grandmother was in Texas for a wedding, and I remember how odd it felt to see my grandfather in the house without her. He made his own lunches of sardines on toast, puttered with his stamp collection—all without my grandmother there rolling dough with the phone pressed between her shoulder and her ear, lying on her side on the bed playing solitaire. My grandfather built us wonderful fires and then retired, perhaps thinking we wanted to be alone. Watching him walk upstairs with a cheery goodnight, I felt time collapse for an instant: everything was the same, everything was different.

Later, after my grandparents were in their own place in Ithaca and I was working in Manhattan, I would visit several times a year. From the bus I would spot my grandfather before he saw me and know that as usual he had arrived at the station 15 or 20 minutes early. "To be on the safe side," he would say. I would ask him to light our fires earlier and earlier each day, and we would share a conspiratorial pleasure in the indulgence of a fire crackling at one in the afternoon. My grandmother and I would bake her mother's recipe for chocolate cake, filling the rooms with sweetness.

My grandfather's work had always allowed them to travel extensively. I loved going through the crystal bowl filled with the holiday cards they received each year, with exotic postage stamps and greetings in many languages. Every Thanksgiving my grandparents took in a few souls in need of a home-cooked meal: foreign graduate students, visiting scholars, faculty whose cultures didn't celebrate our holiday. A woman from West Germany was with us the year the Berlin Wall fell. Chinese or Australian or British geophysicists arrived with gifts for my grandmother, the den melodious with talk and laughter. An Arab couple close to my grandparents came often. The husband and wife were both professors, and I admired the decorative robes the woman wore, how the gold threads caught the candlelight and shimmered. We would talk about the work she did as an advocate for the rights of women in her homeland. The world opened up around me during the lively table conversations as we heaped our plates with my grandmother's fragrant food. My grandfather, who was so often quiet at home, spoke animatedly about politics and football, the shifting of the planet's surfaces, the subtle rising of oceans.

The last year my grandparents lived in Ithaca together, I came up to visit and spent much of each day writing my master's thesis. Late one afternoon I took a break and wandered out of the bedroom to find my grandmother sitting outside on the back porch, wrapped in a jacket, gazing at the woods behind the house. I felt my head clear in the crisp, cold air. My grandmother told me she was waiting to see if any deer would appear. They often did at twilight, stepping out from the cover of trees delicately, as if they were dancers en pointe. She asked me how my studying was going, was I working too hard, was I hungry—dinner would be ready soon. She looked out again at the darkness and pushed her hair behind her ear with the gesture of a young girl. "It's so beautiful here," she said. "I love Ithaca."

That summer, back in Texas, my grandmother got sick. It took her a year to die, a harrowing decline. My grandfather flew to Ithaca and spent a few days packing up the house and arranging for their belongings to be moved back to Houston. He then devoted himself to caring for my grandmother. He bathed her, walked her back and forth to the bathroom, fed her bags of nutrient fluids through a tube he inserted through a shunt in her chest when she was no longer able to digest food. He stroked her back as she vomited. He lost over 20 pounds, and I doubt he slept more than a few hours each night, awakening to check on my grandmother every time she shifted in her discomfort. He nurtured her task by task, just as he had built fires, patiently, tenderly. He took joy in any small sign that—for even a moment—my grandmother felt better. "Today your grandmother told me where to hang a picture," he would say. "Today she sat at the piano and played a whole song."

Seven years after my grandmother's death, my grandfather is still a professor at Cornell. He communicates by computer from Houston, and he drives to Ithaca several times each semester, the familiar journey along the East Coast that he so enjoys, up before the sun. When he is in Ithaca he now stays in a hotel, but I think he has become comfortable with this new routine. I imagine him checking in and quickly heading out to campus in time for lunch at the faculty club with his colleagues, a few of whom were once his students.

Recently, he showed me a photo album I had never seen before that had been his mother's. "You see these pictures?" he asked, pointing at long-ago gatherings of people dear to him, whom he has for the most part outlived. "I took them. I'd just gotten a camera for my bar mitzvah, so I must have been 13." He had learned to develop the film himself: "I sent away for a kit!" A series of brown, fading pictures of a family picnic showed a boy superimposed onto the branches of a tree, ghostlike, smiling mischievously. "See, I was experimenting with double exposure. I put myself in a tree." At 90, my grandfather is still so like that bright child, reveling in the singular moments of life.

I married a man much like my grandfather—someone I think my grandmother would have loved—who also graduated from Cornell. A few months ago, we were in central New York and took a day trip to Ithaca, where I had not been since my grandmother died. My husband showed me the places on campus that had once been important to him, and I too walked again through memories along the suspension bridge that hovers above a jagged ravine, through the lush quadrangles, past the stone buildings, the clock tower. The students we passed looked startlingly young, like children.

At the end of the day, we stopped our car at an intersection instantly familiar to me. Just down the road was the house I visited the year I got lost jogging. And, yes, just up the hill was the house where I ate a pear in the library after everyone else had gone to bed, the silence surrounding me like a blessing. Somewhere within those curving streets beyond the stoplight was the house where my grandmother showed me the book she was translating for the French class she was taking. The light changed and we drove on.

Once I thought of those sabbatical houses as filled with the spirits of their owners. Now I know they also hold a wisp of my life. Driving through Ithaca on our way home, I felt my grandparents to the right and left of me, above and below me, traveling alongside me. I couldn't help but dream that if I found my way to each of those nine houses and knocked on the doors, my grandmother would open them—arms outstretched, a dish towel in one hand—and inside, there would be my grandfather straightening up from the fireplace, smiling widely as he moved to embrace me, saying, "Look who's here, look who's here!"

Seeing It Through

SALLY RYDER BRADY

LAST WEEK I WATCHED A GIANT YELLOW BACKHOE DEMOLISH my house. Nothing was left but the frayed swing dangling from the Norway maple beside the shed, and the lilacs, still guarding what used to be our front door. My husband and each of our four children had already said their private farewells to the place, but I had come here, alone by choice, to see it through. At the end I stood quietly looking out across the lawn, the fields, the woods—exactly the same views I had cherished for 18 years. Except that my house was gone.

In the early 19th century, the building was a schoolhouse in the next town. At the turn of this century two teenage boys, the Berry brothers, who had probably outgrown their parents' nearby farmhouse, dragged it through the snowy woods on runners pulled by a team of oxen. They set it down over the cellar hole they had dug themselves and lined with stones before the ground had frozen. Everyone called it the Berry Cottage even though it eventually exceeded cottage size with each successive family adding a room or porch or shed. The local historical commission judged it to have no architectural value.

When my husband, Upton, and I moved in nearly two decades ago with four children under five years of age, we were amazed at our good luck in renting this slightly crooked, porch-studded farmhouse on a peaceful 1,000 acres 40 minutes from Boston. Last year the owners agreed to sell 300 acres, including our house, to a developer; only in this way could they afford to keep the rest of the property intact. We were not permitted to buy. The developer evidently agreed with the historical commission about the value of the Berry Cottage, and so Upton and I (only the two of us, now) moved out just ahead of the wreckers, and into another sweet farmhouse half a mile down the same narrow road. Our luck still holds. We are not homeless, not even geographically uprooted as so many are in this unstable world.

But when the backhoe advanced over the lawn like a single-minded prehistoric predator—through the garden, across the front porch, right up to the white clapboards of the house that had held us all so safely for so long—I did not feel lucky at all. I felt helpless and, worse, disloyal. I was powerless to stop the demolition machine. All I could do was stand and watch. The dark windows stared back.

The outside wall facing me came down, all of it quite neatly after only a few blows, and suddenly what had been our private refuge was as naked as the back of Sarah's dollhouse. I felt a little naked too, seeing my bathroom exposed for all to see, as if my personal hygiene were everybody's business, and our bedroom wide open as if our marriage were suddenly a public affair.

The arm with its clam-bucket claw reached up to the top of the house, and then suddenly the roof over the two already exposed attic bedrooms came off like a hat. When we were allowed to build these rooms for Andrew and Nathaniel, we never guessed that this would be the Berry Cottage's final addition. Andrew's Grateful Dead mural glowed and throbbed in the autumn sun. I gazed at the rows of shelves that had first held teddy bears and LEGOs, then electric trains and G.I. Joe, and finally, just last summer, Nathaniel's thick college textbooks and greasy Volkswagen parts.

I thought of the hidden part of the closet up there, the shadowy wedge of space where Andrew had stashed bottle rockets and bongs and probably other contraband that I really didn't want to know about. I thought of the costume box, which unfortunately became a nursery full of infant flying squirrels whose parents had moved into the fiberglass under the eaves. And what about the curious ham-mice, an interesting new species that evolved when Natty's hamsters escaped for a night on the town?

Now the brutal claw swung over the second floor as if deciding where to strike next, giving the sleeping porch a playful swat. The white railing dipped in a curtsy. Thank you, I wanted to call out, for all the moments I spent against your columns watching the older boys in pajamas galloping bareback on their ponies into the early slanting sun. I remembered Nathaniel standing motionless under the maple tree, wearing a sombrero he had filled with sunflower seeds, his head covered with chickadees. How ephemeral their childhoods had seemed even as I watched them unfurl. I realized that the house had kept the children as children for me. From now on I would have to trigger the memories myself.

Now the arm hovered over Sarah's room with its flowered wallpaper. The room had been her Christmas present from me the year she turned 11. Her own room, with the four-poster bed that was mine when I was her age, my old bureau, too, and a dressing table with a three-way mirror and a flouncy skirt. I had started stripping off the layers of old wallpaper Thanksgiving night, and by Christmas Eve, when Upton and I set up the bed, the room still held the sugary smell of damp wallpaper paste and latex paint.

Sarah turned from child to woman in this room, felt the first flood of passion and then the bitter wrench when she was spurned. Here she carefully and sorrowfully put away her bride doll to make room for her stereo and makeup. Standing outside looking in, I was proud to see how gamely the plaster wall I had patched withstood blow after blow, touched that the flowers on the wallpaper looked as graceful and full of summer when the wall finally cracked apart as they had that Christmas morning 16 years ago.

Alexander's room hung wide open long enough for me to see once more the graffiti that I couldn't bear to paint over, the lumpy self-portrait, the autographs of *not*-famous people, the penny forever stuck to the wall with superglue, the bullet hole in the window (a decal). Alex is our baby, the little fellow who used to clamber out his window onto the porch roof in his fuzzy blanket sleeping suit to wave at our surprised neighbors on their way to work (until they called and told me he was out there). He was the cheerful villain who day after day picked at a hole in the crumbling horsehair plaster behind his crib until it was big enough for him to drop in his brothers' Matchbox cars, his socks, and finally his tiny sneakers, several pairs. This particular wall was so crammed with treasures that I half expected to see them fly out when the wall itself shattered, but all I could see was dust.

Our bedroom went down fast while my brain teemed with all I had learned there. How I grew in courage and independence when I finally confronted my husband's alcoholism. How he grew even more when he confronted it himself and began to deal with it. In this room I met raw loneliness, felt its sharp edges even when—especially when—I lay beside the one I loved. Love had given way to anger in this room, then anger to sorrow, and sorrow back to love, but the fight was long and deep. I thought of how, night after night, we had lain together, each entrusting our vulnerable, unconscious selves to the other.

I thought of my desk in that room, whose drawers had gotten so crammed that I couldn't even open them. I simply stopped using the desk, but just before we moved I took a deep breath and yanked open every drawer. Inside were valentines painstakingly made and proudly offered; the letter that began "Dear Mom, I'm sorry I was bad. Here is a list of things I want to do to be better . . ."; a letter from my mother dated October 1962 urging me not to marry Upton; a letter from my father with the same date sending his blessing. I sighed to see the glamorous head shots of me, taken when I was 20, an ingenue surely headed for Broadway. What had happened? Love. Babies. Life. A new career as a writer. I studied the face, still familiar, still mine. She was a pretty little thing, Sally Ryder. But what caught me the most was how vulnerable and unformed she looked. What happened to this Sally? I looked in the mirror over my desk to see, and beneath the wrinkles and the half-glasses found a vulnerability still there, a new brand, that of the soon-to-be-old. Yet there was no trace of the unformed; I saw purpose, endurance.

I thought of nights full of thunder and lightning, when our bed burst with shivering children and dogs; nights when the high-pitched tattoo of spring peepers lulled us to steep; eerie winter dawns full of mystery and snowflakes and the possibility of no school. I closed my eyes for just a minute to hold all this in, and when I opened them, all that was left of the second floor was the back staircase, lurching crazily but still intact.

These perilous stairs twisted through the core of the house, every tread a different width and every riser a different height. Grown-ups had trouble here, but children's feet always fit. Even the wobbliest toddler could scramble up and down while we mothers held our breath.

The stairs flew like kindling. Now only the ground floor remained, slanted floors still perfect for marbles. All through the weeks of packing, I came across marbles by the dozens. Most of them I put into a tin for a future grandchild and brought with me to the new house (where the floors, I am happy to say, are just as slanted). But when the tin filled up, I did what my naughty children used to do—I dropped the marbles into the floor registers where they made a most satisfying thunk and lazily rolled through the heating ducts.

The backhoe found the kitchen, morning sun still streaming in through the tall bay windows. The table used to be there, with children and Play-Doh and bread dough all basking in the warm light. I said good-bye to the kitchen sink, perched on porcelain legs whose shape always reminded me of those of my college roommate. Good-bye to the row of waist-high brass hooks in the pantry, the string of clothespins for mittens and hats still dangling. Good-bye to the pantry doorway, where I could see the ladderlike 18-year record of everyone's height crack like my heart.

The rest was quick. The huge downstairs bathroom which, along with the usual bathroom fixtures, used to hold our restaurant-size freezer (my mother always thought that was very unsanitary), laundry machines, a Ping-Pong table, and the newest litter of kittens. The living room, its mantelpiece permanently studded with Christmas-stocking nails, its hardwood floor permanently stippled one New Year's

Eve by the spike heels of Andrew's high-school sweetheart. There had been a formal party, the first time Andrew ever wore a dinner jacket. Upton had taken great care to show him the intricacies of evening dress—silk socks, a cummerbund, gold cufflinks. It was a rite of passage marked by little heel pricks in the floor. A house needs good scars.

All of it was gone in a flash, but the chimney remained, rising straight up out of the wreckage. Again and again, the yellow claw would swing at it, and the column would curve like a snake, individual bricks separating so I could see air between them. Then, as if responding to some hidden force, they would reassemble back into their old chimney shape, standing straight as they always had. Finally the spaces were too great and the snaking column collapsed.

Only the ponies' shed was left. It used to share the kitchen wall, so we could watch each other, ponies and people, through the back door. Bucky and Snowball would thump their heavy heads on the glass and nicker for oats while I flipped pancakes. The shed just fluttered down like a house of cards.

The yellow machine turned off its noisy engine. I stood silently with the workmen in their hard hats around the rubble. And in this pause the house, what was left of it, let out a huge sigh. I looked at my watch. Forty-seven minutes was all it had taken.

A small army of dump trucks rumbled in to take away the big pieces of wood and the doors and windows still in their frames, and then a bulldozer buried the rest in the cellar, covering everything with soft brown earth.

I went home to my new house where Upton met me, his arms open wide, his shoulder the right height to cry on, a clean handkerchief waiting in the pocket of his shirt. It was his idea that I spend the rest of the afternoon planting daffodil bulbs in my new garden, thinking ahead to spring. I was on my knees, lost in my thoughts, when suddenly my trowel struck something hard, with the chink of metal. I dug deeper and pulled up a small toy tractor, crusted with rust. The wheels were metal, not plastic, with thin, hard spokes, and in the driver's seat a little metal farmer with a farmer's hat sat up tall. I brought the tractor in. I washed and dried it. And then I just held it in my hand. What had become of its original owner? My fingers curled around the farmer, still sturdy and upright after long years in the ground.

I set the tractor on the porch railing where I can see it from my kitchen window. When I look at it I will think of our old house, and of all the marbles waiting to be discovered somewhere in the loose earth between the front-door lilacs and the backdoor Norway maple. I imagine a car with parents and eager children driving past. The car slows down and the mother unrolls her window and leans out. "Look!" she says. "Oh look! What a perfect place for a house."

Author Biographies

EDNA O'BRIEN first made her name with the novel *The Country Girls* in 1960. She has written plays as well as numerous novels and contributes regularly to the *New Yorker*. *In the Forest* (Houghton Mifflin) is her most recent novel. An honorary member of the American Academy of Arts and Letters, Edna O'Brien divides her time between her native Ireland, London, and New York.

ELAINE GREENE is the originator of *House Beautiful's* "Thoughts of Home" feature and the editor of this book. She has worked in the shelter magazine field since 1965 and was also the editor of *Mark Hampton on Decorating* (1989).

STACY SCHIFF is the author of *Saint-Exupéry: A Biography*, and of *Véra (Mrs. Vladimir Nabokov)*, which won the Pulitzer Prize for biography. She is at work on a portrait of Benjamin Franklin in France during the American Revolution.

MICHAEL PYE is the author of eleven books, including *The Pieces from Berlin*, *The Drowning Room*, and *Taking Lives*, which has been made into a movie. He spends as much time in Portugal as possible.

FRANCES KOGEN calls herself "a sometime journalist" whose articles have appeared in the *New York Times* and the *Miami Herald,* and has two non-fiction books in the works. She and her husband live in Miami, Florida, not far from their ten grandchildren.

JOSEPH GIOVANNINI, architect, teacher, and author, is architecture critic at *New York* magazine. He lives in Manhattan with his wife, the writer Christine Pittel, and their nine-year-old daughter, Isabella.

HOPE COOKE, who lives and works in New York, writes for magazines and lectures throughout the country. *Seeing New York* (Temple University Press), her latest book, deals with the poetics and politics of space. She is currently researching a book about Asia.

CYNTHIA ANDERSON's work has appeared recently in the *North American Review*, *Tulane Review*, and *Iowa Review*. Her essays have twice been recognized as Notable in *Best American Essays* (Houghton Mifflin). She lives outside of Boston with her family.

ROBERTA BROWN ROOT lives with her husband, Randy Hoehn, in a cottage on Lake Washington in Seattle, where she raised three of her four now-grown children. She is in the second year of an MFA program with Bennington Writing Seminars and is working on a novel.

STARR COLLINS OSBORNE and her husband live in Philadelphia with their three children under seven. She is planning a book about their fixer-upper farmhouse, and writes when she can find the time.

SHARON WHITE lives in Philadelphia and teaches writing at Temple University. She has published a memoir, *Field Notes, A Geography of Mourning*; *Bone House*; a collection of poetry; and many pieces in magazines and anthologies. *Field Notes* was awarded Honorable Mention for the Julia Ward Howe Award from the Boston Authors Club. She has won numerous other awards and fellowships.

STEVE ELLIOTT has left the newspaper business, and in 2004 moved out of his trailer to remarry. He still writes (screenplays mostly), runs a bicycle touring company with his wife, Diane, and recently opened a small bookbindery. His family, including two step-children, live in Angels Camp, California.

ANN PRINGLE-HARRIS, an adjunct professor of English at the Fashion Institute of Technology in New York City, won a prize from The Newswomen's Club of New York for this essay. Her travel articles appear often in the *New York Sunday Times*.

KELLY CALDWELL is a writer living in New York City. She has written for many newspapers and magazines, including *New York Newsday*, *Men's Journal*, and *Time-Out New York*. *Best American Essays* (Houghton Mifflin) named "Garret Girl" a Notable Essay of 2000.

PHILOMENA C. FRIEDMAN has spent most of her adult life as a Foreign Service wife in Europe and Africa and now lives in New Hampshire, where she write occasional pieces on various subjects. *House Beautiful* has published five of her personal essays.

ALEIDA ALMENDARES DE VILLALBA now makes her permanent home in Havana, which she says gives her great joy despite the considerable difficulties of life there. Sans Souci is a place she visits as a sanctuary. She has two adopted sons and is writing a screenplay about Cuba today called *Prisionero en paraiso* (*Prisoner in Paradise*).

DALE MACKENZIE BROWN is a retired editor of Time-Life books and the author of five of his own including one about the Alaskan wilderness and another about the painter Diego Velázquez. He lives in Alexandria, Virginia, and publishes occasional magazine articles about travel and design.

LUCINDA PARIS divides her time between Durham, North Carolina, and York, England, depending on her husband's professorial assignments, but wherever she is, her book is in progress. Called *Learning the Language*, it will consist of short stories set in foreign places.

SUZANNAH LESSARD is the author of *The Architect of Desire: Beauty and Danger in the Stanford White Family* (The Dial Press). She is currently writing a book on the changes in the American landscape over the past 50 years, for which she won the 2003 Anthony Lukas Work-in-Progress Award. She lives in New York City.

ANTONIA STEARNS, a Foreign Service wife as well as daughter, now lives with her husband, a former Ambassador to Greece, in Cambridge, Massachusetts. Three of her essays about her family life in Europe, Africa, and Asia have appeared in *House Beautiful*.

TERESA WENDEL lives with her husband in Wenatchee, Washington. Her essays have appeared in such varied publications as *Country Living*, *Baby Talk*, and *True Story*. She is currently compiling a collection of short stories.

JUDITH BELL UNGAR is a staff attorney for the New Jersey Law Revision Commission and a professional book discussion leader. She and her husband, a rabbi, have four children and eleven grandchildren. Her writing has appeared in the *New York Times* and numerous literary magazines.

PERDITA BUCHAN has published short stories and articles in a number of national magazines, as well as a novel, *Called Away* (Atlantic Monthly Press). She lives on the New Jersey shore and teaches writing at Rutgers University. She is at work on another novel and a memoir.

A. M. HOMES, a New York resident, is the author of numerous books, most recently an award-winning collection of short stories, *Things You Should Know* (HarperCollins), and a travel memoir, *Los Angeles People, Place, and the Castle on the Hill* (National Geographic Directions). She is currently writing another novel.

RICK BASS has written twenty books of fiction and nonfiction, with a novel, *The Diezmo*, to be published in the spring of 2005. From northwest Montana's Yaak Valley, where he lives, he is active in a number of wilderness and conservation issues.

MARYBETH LAMBE is a family practice physician and a freelance writer. She lives with her husband and children on a farm near Seattle, Washington.

MICHELE BENDER is a freelance health, fitness, and beauty writer who has contributed to *Cosmopolitan*, *Real Simple*, *Seventeen*, and the *New York Times*, among others. She lives in New York City with her husband and their small daughter.

CHRISTOPHER BUCKLEY is the founding editor of *Forbes FYI* magazine and the author of ten books including *Thank You for Smoking*, *Little Green Men*, and *The White House Mess*. His essays and satire have appeared in the *New Yorker*, *Vanity Fair*, *Esquire*, and elsewhere. His next book will be *Florence of Arabia*, a novel.

DAVID LANSING is a prolific travel writer who is a regular contributor to *National Geographic Travel* and *Sunset* magazines. His essays appear frequently in the *Los Angeles Times* Sunday magazine. In his spare time he writes fiction and hopes some day to do a book about growing up in the shadow of Disneyland. He lives in Newport Beach, California, and San Miguel de Allende, Mexico.

PATRICK DUNNE is the proprietor of Lucullus, a shop in New Orleans that deals in antique culinary objects, art, and furnishings. He has written on the history of food and tableware for numerous magazines, and in 2002 Little Brown published his book *The Epicurean Collector.*

BETSY BROWN lives in Ossining, New York, and is now recording oral histories of older residents for the local historical society. Her essay led to a reunion after 50 years with her long-ago roommate Bebe. When Bebe's children read the piece, they invited the author to be a surprise guest at Bebe's Golden Anniversary party.

LISA JENNIFER SELZMAN has published fiction, essays, and book reviews in numerous publications including *North American Review* and the *New York Times Book Review.* Currently at work on a non-fiction book, Selzman lives in western Pennsylvania with her husband, daughter, and son.

SALLY RYDER BRADY is a writer who has published a novel *Instar* (Doubleday) and *A Yankee Christmas* Vols. I and II (Yankee/Rodale). She is also a literary agent and runs weekly writing workshops in Vermont, where she lives, and in Cambridge, Massachusetts.

Index